The Link

The Secret Relationship between Saddam and Al Qaida

Louis Fairmont

copyright © 2008 Louis Fairmont

*All rights reserved,
including the right of reproduction,
in whole or in part in any form.*

ISBN 978-0-578-00274-3

Contents

No Smoking Gun? 9

Origins of al Qaida 23

Influence of Sharia 37

History of Iraq 45

Rise of Saddam 65

Gulf War 89

State of Terror 133

The Missing Link 147

Never Forget 173

Master of Deception 193

Appendix 211

Cast of Characters

Name	Alias	Affiliations	Responsibilities
1993 World Trade Center Attack			
Mahmoud Abouhalima	Mahmoud Abu Halima, Mahmud Abouhalima	Al Qaida, Organized Islamic Group (OIG)	- Obtained smokeless powder for the explosives. - Mixed chemicals for bomb.
Ahmad Mohammad Ajaj	Azan Mohammad, Khurram Khan	Al Qaida, Organized Islamic Group (OIG)	-Trained in Afghanistan at al Qaida camp. - Brought terrorist kit used to build the bomb. - Arrested upon entering US for forged passport.
Nidal Ayyad		Al Qaida, Organized Islamic Group (OIG)	- Worked at chemical company which gave bombers access to bombing materials. - Opened joint bank account with Salameh and deposited funds to finance the bombing.
Eyad Ismoil	Eyad Ismail	Al Qaida, Organized Islamic Group (OIG)	- Drove bomb laden van to WTC
Usama bin Laden	Osama	Al Qaida	- Financier and leader of al Qaida - Provided financing to the Alkifah Refugee Center located in New York estimated at several million dollars a year.
Ali Mohamed	Abu Mohamed al-Amriki, Abu Mohamed the American, Bakhbola, Bili Bili, Haydara, Abu Omar	Al Qaida, Egyptian Islamic Jihad (EIJ)	- al Qaida trainer - US Army sergeant stationed at Fort Bragg.
Khalid Sheikh Mohammed	Khalid Al-Shaikh, "Uncle of Yousef," Khalid Shaykh Mohammad, Mukhtar,	Al Qaida	- Resided in Iraq and sent money to Yousef by depositing money into the joint bank account opened by Ayyad and Salameh.

Name	Alias	Affiliations	Responsibilities
Umar Abed al Rahman	"Blind cleric," Omar Abdul al-Rahman, "Blind Sheikh"	Al Qaida, Organized Islamic Group (OIG)	- Issued fatwa of 1993 and 2001 WTC attacks. - Arrested for conspiring to blow up the United Nations building and the Lincoln and Holland Tunnels in New York City.
Mohammed Salameh		Al Qaida, Organized Islamic Group (OIG)	-Yasin taught to drive in order to rent the Ryder van used to deliver the bomb. - Opened joint bank account with Ayyad and deposited funds to finance the bombing. - Rented New Jersey storage facility used to store the chemicals and bomb making materials. - Mixed chemicals for bomb.
Abdul Rahman Said Yasin	Abdul Rahman Said Yasin, Aboud Yasin, Abdul Rahman S. Taha, Abdul Rahman S. Taher, Aboud	Al Qaida, Organized Islamic Group (OIG), Iraqi Agent	- Mixed chemicals for bomb. -Taught Salameh how to drive so that he could rent the Ryder van. - dual citizenship US and Iraq
Ramzi Ahmed Yousef	Abdul Basit Karim, Abdul Basit Mahmoud, Azan Mohammad Rashed, Kamal Ibraham, Adam Ali Qasim, Naji Haddad, Dr. Paul Vijay, Dr. Adel Sabah, Amaldo Forlani, Muhammad Ali Baloch	Al Qaida, Organized Islamic Group (OIG), Iraqi Agent	- Operational commander of bombing team. - Expert in explosives - Trained in Afghanistan at al Qaida camp. - Iraq citizenship

Name	Alias	Affiliations	Responsibilities
2001 World Trade Center Attack			
Mohamed Atta		Al Qaida	Lead hijacker – pilot American Airlines flight 11
Tawfiq bin Attash	Kallad	Al Qaida	First group of trainees for 9/11 attacks
Fayez Banihammad		Al Qaida	muscle hijacker from United Arab Emirates for United Airlines Flight 175
Abu Bara		Al Qaida	First group of trainees
Ramzi Binalshibh		Al Qaida	Hamburg Group
Ahmed al Ghamdi		Al Qaida	muscle hijacker from Saudi Arabia on United Airlines flight 175
Hamza al Ghamdi		Al Qaida	muscle hijacker from Saudi Arabia on United Airlines flight 175
Saeed al Ghamdi		Al Qaida	muscle hijacker from Saudi Arabia on United Airlines flight 93
Nawaf al Hamzi		Al Qaida	Second-in-command hijacker – pilot, American Airlines 77
Hani Hanjour		Al Qaida	Pilot on American Airlines flight 77
Ahmad al Haznawi		Al Qaida	muscle hijacker from Saudi Arabia on United Airlines flight 93
Salem al Hazmi		Al Qaida	muscle hijacker from Saudi Arabia on American Airlines flight 77
Ziad Jarrah		Al Qaida	Pilot on United Airlines Flight 93, Hamburg Group
Usama bin Laden		Al Qaida	Leader of al Qaida

Name	Alias	Affiliations	Responsibilities
Khalid al Mihdhar		Al Qaida	American Airlines flight 77 hijacker
Majed Moqed		Al Qaida	muscle hijacker from Saudi Arabia on American Airlines flight 77
Zacarias Moussaoui		Al Qaida	9/11 hijacker that was arrested before attacks
Ahmed al Nami		Al Qaida	muscle hijacker from Saudi Arabia
Abdul Aziz al Omari		Al Qaida	muscle hijacker from Saudi Arabia, hijacker of American Airlines Flight 11
Ahmed Hikmat Shakir		Iraqi Intelligence Agent	Met with Khalid al Mihdhar, hijacker of American Airlines Flight 77
Marwan al Shehhi		Al Qaida	United Airlines Flight 175 hijacker
Mohand al Shehri		Al Qaida	muscle hijacker from Saudi Arabia on United Airlines Flight 175
Wail al Shehri		Al Qaida	muscle hijacker from Saudi Arabia, on American Airlines Flight 11
Waleed al Shehri		Al Qaida	muscle hijacker from Saudi Arabia on American Airlines Flight 11
Satam al Suqami		Al Qaida	muscle hijacker from Saudi Arabia on American Airlines Flight 11
Ayman al - Zawahiri	Ayman Mohammed Rabie al-Zawahiri	Egyptian Islamic Jihad (EIJ), Al Qaida	Founder of EIJ, Second in command of al Qaida

1

No Smoking Gun?

"If you tell a big enough lie and tell it frequently enough, it will be believed."

- Adolf Hitler

In March 2008, the Pentagon released Saddam Hussein's classified documents that were captured during Operation Iraqi Freedom. These documents called the Iraqi Perspectives Project Saddam and Terrorism: Emerging Insights from Captured Iraqi Documents Volumes 1-5 (Redacted) are a compilation of "more than 600,000 original captured documents and several thousand hours of audio and video footage archived in a US Department of Defense (DOD) database. As of August 2006, only 15 percent of the captured documents have English translations."[1] These documents provide insight into how Saddam operated his regime and his ties to al Qaida.

A few days before the report was to be released an "anonymous source" leaked to the media that there was no "direct operational link" between Saddam Hussein and al Qaida. Warren P. Strobel with

McClatchy Newspapers wrote an article that began with "An exhaustive review of more than 600,000 Iraqi documents that were captured after the 2003 U.S. invasion has found no evidence that Saddam Hussein's regime had any operational links with Osama Bin Laden's al Qaida terrorist network."[2] The article went on the say that "the new study of the Iraqi regime's archives found no documents indicating a 'direct operational link' between Hussein's Iraq and al Qaida before the invasion, according to a U.S. official familiar with the report. He and others spoke to McClatchy on condition of anonymity because the study isn't due to be shared with Congress and released before Wednesday."[3] McClatchy is a newspaper service that releases articles that are then reprinted in newspapers across the nation. Following the release of Strobel's article, other major news outlets followed suit with similar headlines:

ABC: Report Shows No Link Between Saddam and al Qaida

CNN: Hussein's Iraq and al Qaida not linked, Pentagon says

New York Times: Study Finds No Qaida-Hussein Tie

Washington Post: Study Discounts Hussein, Al-Qaida Link

AFP: No link between Saddam and Al-Qaida: Pentagon study

McClatchy: Exhaustive review finds no link between Saddam and al Qaida"[4]

To make matters worse, the first page of the Executive Summary of Volume 1 of the Pentagon report on Saddam says that this "**study found no 'smoking gun' (i.e., direct connection) between Saddam's Iraq and al Qaida.**"[5] This is a definitive statement to make when the forward specifically says that only fifteen percent of the documents have been translated as of August 2006. Most of the media pulled the no "smoking gun" remark from page one and ignored the actual report entirely stating simply that there is "no link". Some of the more sensitive documents were not even released with the initial report because they are still considered classified and are being used by various government agencies.[6]

Why would no "smoking gun" be added to page one? The Pentagon report on Saddam was due to be released during an election year (March 2008). Anti-Bush politicians did not want the truth **that Saddam had direct operational ties with al Qaida to be revealed** to the American public. As a result, no "smoking gun" was placed on page one of the report to give the media an out. Many in the media and in politics have been perpetuating a lie that there was no direct operational link between Saddam Hussein and al Qaida. Even impeachment allegations have been made stating that the Iraq War was based on faulty premises. If the truth that is in these memos, transcripts, and documents became public knowledge, the "Bush lied" mantra would be revealed for being totally false and completely misleading. This truth could influence the outcome of the 2008 presidential election. The truth that there was a direct operational link between Saddam and al Qaida is revealed in the Pentagon report on Saddam and will be demonstrated in this book.

What is al Qaida?

To fully understand the relationship Saddam had with al Qaida we have to explore what al Qaida is. Al Qaida has been described as an umbrella. At its core, it is a terrorist group, but it also functions through alliances with other terrorist organizations. Some leaders and members of these organizations have sworn an oath or "bayat" to al Qaida. Even non-al Qaida members operate under orders from al Qaida at times. This provides concealment of the higher echelons of al Qaida and causes confusion for law enforcement in trying to unravel the al Qaida terrorist network.

Usama Bin Laden's al Qaida was officially formed in 1989. Bin Laden and his chief deputy Abu Ayoub al-Iraqi called a formal meeting and invited all the terrorist organizations that would join his al Qaida. For clarification, "al-Iraqi" means that Abu Ayoub is from Iraq. At this meeting, Abu Ayoub was named the "emir" of al-Qaida. The emir was considered to be the general commander. Abu Ayoub reported directly to Bin Laden who was the president of al Qaida.[7] A citizen of Iraq was the first emir of al Qaida. At this meeting each leader of each terrorist organization attending signed a contract in triplicate and swore an oath or "bayat" to al Qaida.[8] Each of these terrorist organizations remained in tact while operating under allegiance to Bin Laden. Al Qaida's alliances span the globe:

- Al Qaida/Islamic Army
- Al-Jihad /Egyptian Islamic Jihad (EIJ)
- Gamaa al Islamiya/Islamic Group Organization (IG)

- Abu Sayyaf Group (Philippines)
- Armed Islamic Group (Algeria)
- Harkut ul-Mujahidin (Kashmir)
- Islamic Army of Aden
- Islamic Movement of Uzbekistan
- Al-Itihaad al-Islamiya
- Jamaat e Jihal al Suri
- Libyan Fighting Group
- Salafist Group for Call and Combat (Algeria)[9]

Of these, the two most important al Qaida subsidiaries are the **Egyptian Islamic Jihad (EIJ)** [Al-Jihad] and the **Islamic Group Organization (IG).** The leaders of the EIJ and IG became influential leaders in al Qaida. In 1989, Bin Laden admired Umar Abed al Rahman, the leader of the IG, greatly and "acknowledged him as the undisputed leader of the international *jihadists*".[10] Later on he was appointed as the spiritual leader of al Qaida. He issued the fatwah for the 1993 World Trade Center bombing. Although Rahman is not reported to have sworn an oath to Bin Laden at the 1989 founding of Bin Laden's al Qaida, he and his group, the IG, are reported to have been working with al Qaida since 1990. (see Appendix, section 10.3) In 1989, Dr. Ayman al-Zawahiri, the leader of the EIJ, was appointed to an advisory council called the Shura. Zawahiri would become a mentor and close confidant to Bin Laden. In 1998, Dr. Ayman al-Zawahiri with Usama Bin Laden issued a worldwide fatwah to all Muslims. The fatwah called for "the murder of any American, anywhere on earth." Three months later Bin Laden went on the say that "it was more important for Muslims to kill Americans than to kill other infidels." "We do not differentiate between military or civilian. As far as we are concerned they are all targets."[11]   Although the EIJ and IG are two separate terrorist organizations, they both operate under the al Qaida umbrella. As a result, they can be considered al Qaida. Some experts want to use semantics to say the EIJ and IG did not merge with al Qaida until 2001. When in reality these groups were operating with Usama Bin Laden and al Qaida from 1990 or earlier. The EIJ and IG were working with and carrying out orders of Usama Bin Laden and al Qaida from its founding.[12] (see Appendix, section 10.2)

Saddam's direct operational ties to al Qaida

In Volume 3 of the Saddam papers there is a memorandum number 110/2/43 dated January 25, 1993 (see Appendix, Figures 4-8). This memo is from the director of the Iraqi Intelligence Service (IIS) sent to the secretary of the President. There are some interesting facts contained in this memo that illustrate Saddam's alliance with terror and more importantly ties to al Qaida. The memo lists ten terrorist organizations that were affiliated with Iraq. These organizations were ready and willing to carry out Saddam's orders. Of the ten terrorist organizations listed, Iraq was regularly providing financial support to five of them. More interestingly, than this is that both the Egyptian Islamic Jihad (EIJ) and the Islamic Group Organization (IG) are listed in this memo. Let's take a closer look at what this memo says about these two al Qaida subsidiaries.

Regarding the EIJ also known as al-jihad, memo 110/2/43 dated January 25, 1993 says "**it believes in Jihad armament (Military Jihad) against American and Western interests.**" This memo is saying that the EIJ believes in terrorist attacks against the West. The memo continues "**It also believes that Saddam Hussein is the leader of the believer group against infidels**." This is saying that the EIJ, an al Qaida subsidiary, believes that Saddam Hussein is the leader of the radical Islamic terrorists who are fighting against the West. This begs the question was Saddam Hussein the leader who gave the order for the 1993 and 2001 World Trade Center attacks?

Another important aspect of this memo is that it says, "The Organization's chief, visited the region [Iraq] two month ago. The organization showed [a] willingness to carry out operations against American interests at any time." Essentially by Saddam meeting with the EIJ, he was meeting with al Qaida. The founder of the EIJ, Zawahiri, had sworn an oath of allegiance to al Qaida in 1989, four years prior to this meeting. Keep in mind, this meeting with al Qaida was four months prior to the 1993 World Trade Center bombing in November 1992.

Memo 110/2/43 (Appendix, Figure 6 2A) describes the IG as having been created in 1979 and its leader is Dr. Umar Abed al Rahman. Rahman, the blind cleric, issued the fatwah for the 1993 World Trade Center bombing. The memo goes on to describe the IG by saying "It is considered one of the most radical and violent Egyptian organizations." It was responsible for the execution of the Egyptian President Anwar Sadat in 1981. Most interestingly is that this memo says that Saddam Hussein met with Umar Abed al Rahman on December 14, 1990. At this meeting they **"agreed on a plan to move against the Egyptian regime through Fedayeen operations, provided that we guarantee them [financial] aid, training and whatever they need**." Since Rahman was the spiritual leader of al Qaida from 1989, Saddam was financing, training, and supporting al Qaida in whatever they needed. This memo also shows that Saddam's Fedayeen troops were carrying out his directives in cooperation with al Qaida. Most importantly, Saddam was working with Umar Abed al Rahman, the blind cleric, in 1990 three years prior to the 1993 World Trade Center bombing.

In this one memo, we have linked Saddam to the two most prominent al Qaida subsidiaries, the EIJ and IG. It establishes beyond any reasonable doubt that Saddam had direct operational ties to al Qaida. Saddam met with the IG's leader Umar Abed al Rahman three years prior to the 1993 WTC attack. In addition, Saddam met with a prominent leader of the EIJ in November 1992. The EIJ said it viewed Saddam as the **"leader of the believer group against infidels**." This is evidence that Saddam Hussein was considered to be the leader of the Islamic terrorists. Could Saddam have issued the orders for the 1993 and 2001 WTC attacks?

Iraqi directive to "hunt Americans"

At the beginning of Memo No: 110/2/43, where 10 terrorist organizations are listed, it says that the organizations are able to carry out the mission described in another memo 425/K dated 18 Jan 1993. What was the mission that these terrorist organizations were being considered for? Memo 425/K says the directive is to kill Americans on Arab soil. This is just one month prior to the 1993 WTC bombing (see Figure 1).

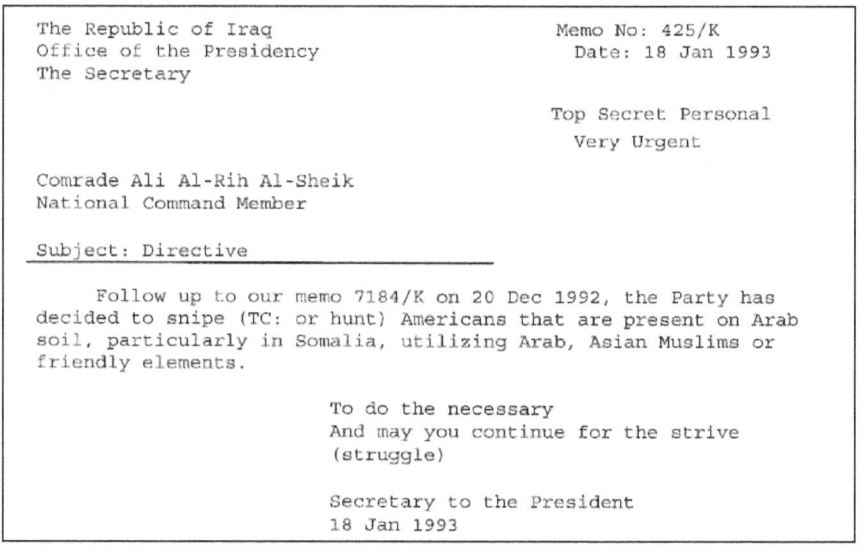

Figure 1 – 1/18/93 Directive 425/K to kill Americans on Arab soil[13]

Saddam meets with al Qaida

Memo 140/D'/4/533 is a memo dated March 11, 1993 from the director of the Iraqi Intelligence Service (IIS) to the Secretary of the President of Iraq which describes that one of the leaders of al Qaida wants to meet with Saddam on 13 March 1993 (see Figure 2). This is only two weeks after the 1993 World Trade Center bombing. The Sudanese leader of the National Islamic Front (NIF), Sheik Ali Uthman Taha, was acting as an intermediary between Iraq and al Qaida. Interestingly, in the early 1990's al Qaida partnered with the NIF to develop "chemical, biological, radiological, and nuclear (CBRN) weapons of mass destruction." Al Qaida and the NIF with the help of the Sudanese military had a laboratory in Khartoum that was used to design and develop explosives. "According to the CIA, Osama also purchased one kilogram of uranium from South Africa and hired an Egyptian nuclear scientist" to work at this lab.[14] This same organization, the NIF, was acting as a mediator between al Qaida and Saddam. This memo says that the EIJ leader was to be flown to Baghdad in a Sudanese meat cargo plane in order to avoid any records of his flight. Could this person being flown to Baghdad have been Zawahiri, the founder of the EIJ? It is very likely it was Zawahiri himself since he was meeting with Saddam Hussein and such care was being taken to hide it. What we do know from this memo is that eight years before the September 11, 2001 World Trade Center attacks, Saddam met with Zawahiri or another influential leader of the EIJ. Since the EIJ joined al Qaida in 1989, this meeting can be viewed as a meeting between Saddam and an al Qaida leader.

> Republic of Iraq   Memo No: 140/D'/4/533
> Office of the Presidency   Date: 11 Mar 1993
> Intelligence Service
>
> Top Secret Personal
> Very Urgent
>
> To: Mr. Secretary to the President
>
> Subject: Request for approval
>
> The President's "May God keep him" order that we were notified
> through according to the esteemed presidential memo Top Secret
> Personal and Very Urgent 282/K on 8 Feb 1993, we would like to
> point out the following:
>
>   2. We received a telegram on 9 Mar 1993 from Sheik Ali 'Uthman
>   Taha – Deputy to the Director of the Sudanese Islamic Front,
>   via our ambassador in Khartum, pointing out that he wishes to
>   send one of the leaders of the Egyptian Islamic Jihad (TC: in
>   Arabic it is literally "Tanzim AL-Jihad Al-Islami Al-Masri" or
>   "The Organized Egyptian Islamic Jihad"), which was previously
>   in Afghanistan and currently is in Khartum. He is on his way
>   to Baghdad to meet with us. Subsequently, on 10 Mar 1993, we
>   telegrammed Sheik Ali 'Uthman Taha to take their time
>
>   in sending the aforementioned, for the time being and We will
>   notify him of our decision at a later time.
>   2. On 11 Mar 1993, Sheik Ali 'Uthman Taha stressed on his request
>   and notified that the aforementioned person is ready and will
>   be sent to Baghdad on a Sudanese meat cargo plane on 13 Mar
>   1993 for an important matter.
>   3. We suggest notifying Sheikh Ali 'Uthman Taha of the approval
>   to send the aforementioned in a manner that insures that his
>   arrival to Baghdad is secret. So we know what he has to offer.
>
>   Please review - your instructions
>
> With respect, [signed] Director of IIS
> 11 Mar 1993

Figure 2 – Planned meeting with leader of EIJ, al Qaida affiliate
13 Mar 1993

al Qaida in Iraq

At least eleven years before the September 11, 2001 attacks, we know that Saddam was establishing relationships with all the key al Qaida leaders namely Umar Abed al Rahman and Ayman al-Zawahiri. What about al Qaida residing in Iraq and working directly for Saddam?

MV	فيهيك ظرف سيدي صعب ويقدمون للعراق هذا التقديم الكبير أنا شوف يساتهلون كل التقدير والاحترام من عندنا والامر متروك للقاعدة الله يحفظها. شكراً سيدي.	In this time it is difficult sir and they present Iraq with this big present I see they deserve all appreciation and respect from our part and the thing is left to al-Qaida God preserves it Thank you sir
Saddam	هم اقترحوا خارجية أنا ضاعفتلهم المقترح مالهم فرحانين و مكيفين إنه أني مطلع على جهودهم إلى حد التفاصيل و كل ما يرفعون مطالعة نقول لهم سوا لفلان شي الخ يعني وهم يبادرون يعني ما	They suggested an exterior I doubled the proposal that's why they are happy that I am aware of their efforts to the details and every time they present a finding we tell them to do to this person this thing etc I mean and they take the initiative

Figure 3 - Excerpt of Saddam and Command Members discussing al Qaida[15]

This excerpt is taken from transcript ISGQ-2003-M0006443 which is a conversation that took place in 1995 during a discussion about the United Nations (UN) weapons inspection after the Gulf War. Keep in mind, that this transcript is dated six years prior to the 2001 WTC bombing. One of Saddam's command members wants al Qaida to be recognized for their efforts. An unidentified person labeled as MV for male voice says, **"In this time it is difficult sir and they present Iraq with this big present I see they deserve all appreciation and respect from our part and the thing is left to al Qaida God preserves it."** Saddam replies, **"They [al Qaida] suggested an exterior [and] I doubled the proposal that's why they are happy that I am aware of their efforts to the *details* and every time they present a finding we tell them to do to this person this thing etc I mean and they take the initiative."** This conversation shows that al Qaida is sharing proposed operational plans with Saddam, **"they suggested an exterior."** Also, Saddam was supporting al Qaida's operations with funds, **"I doubled the proposal."** It is interesting that Saddam says **"I am aware of their**

[al Qaida's] efforts to the *details*." This tells us Saddam knew about al Qaida's operations in Iraq. We see that Saddam was issuing al Qaida directives, **"We tell them to do to this person this thing... and they take the *initiative*."**

Apparently some of the mujahideen forces from Afghanistan were relocated to Iraq to aid Saddam after the Gulf War. In memo 110/2/43 dated January 25, 1993 described previously, the relocation of al Qaida members who fought in Afghanistan is discussed, **"To make use of the Arab Islamic elements [al Qaida] that were fighting in Afghanistan and do not have current operating bases. They are dispersed in Sudan, Somalia and Egypt."** (Appendix, Figure 7, 2B) Part of the agreement that was made between Iraq and al Qaida was that some of the al Qaida forces would relocate from Afghanistan to Iraq. Keep in mind this is 1993, eight years prior to the 2001 World Trade Center attacks. These are the same al Qaida forces that Usama Bin Laden headed during the Soviet-Afghan War. This is an al Qaida camp located in northeastern Iraq.[16] Here we see Saddam was offering al Qaida a safe haven in Iraq. Can any rational American believe that al Qaida would not also support Saddam-backed terrorist operations against the West? The 9/11 attacks certainly appears to be one such operation! This book will establish Saddam's complicity beyond any reasonable doubt!

2

Origins of al Qaida

"To kill the Americans and their allies -- civilians and military -- is an individual duty for every Muslim…"

- Usama Bin Laden

Soviet-Afghanistan War

To fully understand the origins of al Qaida, one must understand the Soviet-Afghanistan War. Usama Bin Laden built an international recruitment, fund raising, and training organization to supply freedom fighters, arms, and funds for the fight against the Communist invaders of Afghanistan. This organization was called the "Services Office", which was the forerunner of al Qaida.[17]

Leonid Brezhnev was the Soviet leader from 1964-1982. He thought the Middle East was vital to the Soviet Union's global dominance. The start of his Middle Eastern Communist intervention began with Yemen. Leonid Brezhnev provided direct assistance to the

Communist rebels who overthrew the South Yemen government in 1969. This aided the Soviet Union by giving them an Indian Ocean port and a gateway to the Middle East. The West was concerned that this would give the Soviet Union access to the oil rich Gulf region of the Middle East. To further the Soviet's reach into the Middle East, Brezhnev gave support and weaponry to the Baathist regimes in Syria and Iraq.[18]

In 1979, Leonid Brezhnev set his sites on Afghanistan because of its proximity to the Soviet border, Persian Gulf, and India. Technically Afghanistan is not considered to be in the Middle East, but is actually located in Central Asia. Russia had ties to the region for many years prior to the Soviet-Afghan invasion in 1979. For nearly 200 years prior (1690-1858), Afghanistan had been locked in between Russian expansion to its North/Northwest and British Imperialism to its East/Southeast. In 1931 and 1951, nonaggression pacts were signed between the Soviet Union and Afghanistan. In return, the Soviets provided development loans for Afghanistan projects which included road construction. In 1965, the first Afghanistan Communist Party was created. It was called the "People's Democratic Party of Afghanistan (PDPA)"[19]

In the mid-1970's, the Afghanistan leader Muhammad Daoud saw the PDPA as a threat to his regime and began to repress them. The Soviet Union saw this as an opportunity to build a relationship with the PDPA and to turn Afghanistan into a client Communist country. In April 1978, with the backing of the Soviet Union, the PDPA overthrew the Afghanistan government. After the coup, the Democratic Republic of Afghanistan (DRA) was founded. The newly formed DRA created an alliance with the Soviet Union. Immediately the new Marxist government enacted sweeping reforms that were contrary to deeply seated Muslim traditions. As a result, a resistance formed against the new government. The country was fractured into a three way civil war. The PDPA was split in two, along ideological lines, and the third faction was the mujahideen. The mujahideen were Muslim fundamentalist freedom fighters who were against the anti-Islamic reforms that were being mandated by the new Marxist government.

The Soviet Union provided military assistance to the DRA including advisors, troops, and equipment. As the insurgency grew, the Afghanistan military was weakened and increasingly became dependent on the Soviet military. As the situation deteriorated, the Soviet Union seized the opportunity to overthrow the current leader and put in another one that was more compliant with their goals and objectives. Although the Soviet Union had invaded Afghanistan and propped up their own head of state, they could not maintain control outside of Kabul. The majority of people that resided outside the cities in the countryside were opposed to the Communist government. The Afghanistan freedom fighters known as the mujahideen made it virtually impossible for the Soviets to hold any area outside of urban localities.[20]

The Afghans began to protest the Soviet troops being in their country. The Soviets brutally put down the protests which ended up killing many Afghan civilians. This spurred the mujahideen on to further fight against the Soviet occupying forces. The Soviets resorted to unconventional tactics in an attempt to put down the mujahideen such as "poison gas, napalm, and booby traps."[21] This caused the Soviet occupation to be viewed quite harshly by the rest of the world. The United Nations, NATO, Pakistan, and other countries in the region did not want the Soviet Union to succeed in making Afghanistan a client Communist country. Saudi Arabia concerned about the Soviet Union gaining a foothold in the Middle East, began to fund the Afghan mujahideen. Eventually the Saudi's support turned into recruiting Arabs to fight in an Arab mujahideen alongside the Afghan mujahideen. By 1984, the United States, Pakistan, and other countries started to provide arms to the Afghan mujahideen to thwart the Soviet efforts in Afghanistan. President Jimmy Carter was the first U.S. President to authorize funding to the Afghanistan mujahideen. The war continued on in guerilla warfare style until 1989. Once Mikhail Gorbachev took office he at first continued the policy in Afghanistan the same as his predecessors. As time went on, he came to the conclusion that the war was not winnable. In April 1988, Gorbachev signed the Geneva Accords that guaranteed the Soviet Union would withdraw its troops from Afghanistan by February 15, 1989.[22]

al Qaida Emerges

From the Arab mujahideen al Qaida emerged. There were three distinct groups: the Afghanistan mujahideen, the Arab mujahideen, and the Pakistan backed Taliban. Pakistan provided the Taliban with "training, logistical support, and equipment."[23] Pakistan's support was a major factor in the Taliban being successful in seizing the city of Kabul in 1996. The Taliban became the ruling force in Afghanistan and gave Usama Bin Laden and al Qaida sanctuary. This allowed Usama Bin Laden to freely build up his al Qaida forces and train them in terrorist training camps within Afghanistan. "In Afghanistan, the terrorist training camps were [operating] under the international organization of the Muslim Brothers in connection with Bin Laden. These camps [offered] training in bomb-making, car-bomb attacks, and other techniques of urban warfare; they [operated] with the approval of the Taliban leadership. In the area of Peshawar, the camp of Pabi (with approximately 200,000) [was] the command center of the organization of the secondary camps of Warsak, Saada, and Miram Shah. There [were] two other important camps in Quetta, in the tribal border near Afghanistan. Many other camps [lined] the road connecting Kandahar to Khost, where one of the headquarters of Saudi Usama Bin Laden [was] located."[24]

Usama Bin Laden was from a wealthy Saudi family. He was raised as a conservative Sunni Muslim. While attending the King Abdul Aziz University in Saudi Arabia, he adopted a more radical form of Islam. One of Usama Bin Laden's professors was Dr. Abdullah al-Azzam. Azzam was a radical leader in the "Jordanian branch of the Muslim Brotherhood."[25] The Muslim brotherhood is an Islamic organization that was started in 1928. The goal of the group is to "compel governments in Muslim countries to adhere to *sharia*, or

Islamic law."[26] Historically violence has been an acceptable means to the Muslim Brotherhood in furthering their goals. Dr. al-Azzam went to Afghanistan to fight with the Afghan mujahideen. He ended up becoming a leader of the Arab mujahideen during the Soviet-Afghan War. The Arab mujahideen fought alongside the Afghan mujahideen in order to defeat the Soviet Union. This is important because the United States sent aid to the Afghan mujahideen, not the Arab mujahideen. Azzam cast the Soviet Union as non-Muslim infidels who have invaded sacred Muslim territory. In 1979, Usama Bin Laden moved to Afghanistan to join his college professor in the fight against the infidels. This is how Usama Bin Laden ended up as a freedom fighter with the Arab mujahideen.

Umar Abed al Rahman, the blind cleric of the 1993 World Trade Center bombings, was also part of the Arab mujahideen. Umar Abed al Rahman was a professor at the University of Assiout in Egypt and was involved with the radical Islamic movement taking place at the Universities in the mid 1970's. He first met Usama Bin Laden in 1977 while visiting Saudi Arabia. Usama Bin Laden became a financial supporter to Rahman's new Islamic Group Organization (IG).[27]

Azzam, Bin Laden, and Rahman created a jihad recruitment and fundraising network that spanned the globe. There were offices located throughout the Middle East, Europe, and the United States. This recruitment organization was called the "*Maktab al-Khidamat* (Services Office), also known as *Al Khifah*; many experts consider the *Maktab* to be the organizational forerunner of al Qaeda."[28] The U.S. based

Services Offices were located in several U.S. cities including Tucson, Arizona, Boston, Massachusetts, and Brooklyn, New York. The Boston based Services Offices is also known as CAIR International.[29] The Services Office along with the Benevolence International Foundation (BIF) and the Saudi government became the financial and recruitment support system of the Arab mujahideen.

Once the Soviet-Afghan War was coming to an end, Azzam, Bin Laden, and Rahman began to plan how their Services Office could be used to further their radical Islamic ideals. Azzam and Bin Laden had different views. Azzam wanted al Qaida which in Arabic means "the base" to act like a special forces Islamic terrorist organization. Whenever an Islamic country or group was being attacked, then an al Qaida unit would be dispatched to aid them. Usama Bin Laden had a very different idea in mind entirely. Bin Laden wanted to make al Qaida an "unflinchingly hostile global terrorist force, established with the aim of destroying America and Israel and reestablishing the Caliphate by means of worldwide jihad."[30]

Out of the Services Office al Qaida was formed. A meeting was held in 1988 where Azzam, Bin Laden, and al-Zawahiri met with their fellow Arab mujahideen leaders. At this first meeting they decided to name their new organization al-Qaida. They formed an advisory council called a Shura. Usama Bin Laden and Dr. Ayman al-Zawahiri among others were assigned to the Shura council. Although Zawahiri was on the Shura council and swore an oath or "bayat" to al Qaida, he decided to keep the organizational structure of the Egyptian Islamic Jihad (EIJ) in tact while cooperating with Usama Bin Laden under al

Qaida's leadership. A bayat is an oath of allegiance to al Qaida's worldwide jihad. In addition, the individual is swearing to obey the emir and must carry out any order given whether individually or as a group. Essentially Zawahiri was the leader of the EIJ and a high level member of al Qaida. Al Qaida's structure is actually complex with operations divided "amongst various wings, including a military committee, a security committee, a financial committee, a religious legal committee, a political committee, and a media committee."[31]

Many experts think the differing opinions of Azzam and Bin Laden can be credited to Bin Laden's Egyptian terrorist connections. Abed al Rahman, leader of the IG, and Dr. Ayman al-Zawahiri, leader of the EIJ, became confidants of Bin Laden. Abed al Rahman is the blind cleric who issued the fatwah for the 1993 World Trade Center bombing. Dr. Ayman al-Zawahiri first met with Usama Bin Laden in 1986 in Peshawar when al-Zawahiri came there to treat injured mujahideen. In 1998, Dr. Ayman al-Zawahiri with Usama Bin Laden issued a worldwide fatwah to all Muslims. The fatwah called for "the murder of any American, anywhere on earth." Three months later Bin Laden went on the say that "it was more important for Muslims to kill Americans than to kill other infidels." "We do not differentiate between military or civilian. As far as we are concerned they are all targets."[32]

The dispute between Bin Laden and Azzam about how al Qaida should operate became a chasm between them. Usama Bin Laden decided to side with the more radical idea of toppling secular, pro-

Western Arab leaders and the Western world. Usama's disagreement with Azzam was settled in violent jihad fashion. Azzam and both of his sons were killed by a car bomb on November 24, 1989. Once Azzam was dead, Usama Bin Laden gained full control over the Services Office network. Although Usama Bin Laden has not been formally tied to the execution of Azzam, it seems very likely he was behind it since he was then able to take control over al Qaida and turn it into the more radical terrorist organization it is today.

Now that Azzam was dead, Usama Bin Laden was able to turn al Qaida into a more radical group conducting a worldwide jihad. Usama held a second meeting with all the terrorist organizations in Khost, Afghanistan that would join al Qaida in his worldwide jihad. At the time Usama Bin Laden's chief deputy was an Iraqi named Abu Ayoub al-Iraqi. At this meeting, Abu Ayoub was named the "emir" of al-Qaida. The emir was considered to be the general commander. Abu Ayoub reported directly to Bin Laden who was the president of al Qaida.[33]

At this meeting, the leaders of all the terrorist organizations attending signed a contract in triplicate and swore an oath to al Qaida. The oath was made before the al Qaida leadership including Usama Bin Laden and the emir, Abu Ayoub al-Iraqi. The following Islamic terrorists were in attendance and swore the oath to al Qaida:
- Dr. Ayman al-Zawahiri, the leader of the EIJ,
- Dr. Fadhl el-Masry from Egypt,
- Abu Ubadiah al-Banshiri from Egypt,
- Muhammed Atef from Egypt,

- Jamal Ahmed al-Fadl (aka Abu Bakr Sudani) from Sudan,
- Abu Faraj al-Yemeni from Yemen,
- Abu Masab al-Saudi from Saudi Arabia.[34]

With the alliance of these terrorist organizations, Usama Bin Laden saw an opportunity to use this network to further his goal of "destroying America and Israel and reestablishing the Caliphate by means of worldwide jihad."[35]

With the death of Azzam, Bin Laden "acknowledged [Umar Abed al Rahman] as the undisputed leader of the international *jihadists*".[36] Later on he was appointed as the spiritual leader of al Qaida. Rahman took this opportunity to seize control of the U.S. based Alkifah Refugee Center. This allowed him to organize the bombing group that would carry out the 1993 World Trade Center bombing. Azzam had been Usama Bin Laden's mentor. With his death, there was a void for Usama that would be filled by Dr. Ayman al-Zawahiri. In Azzam's absence, Usama would mature as a radical jihadist under Zawahiri's influence. Zawahiri also became Usama's personal physician. Zawahiri would become Usama Bin Laden's chief deputy and his designated successor. Zawahiri would become al Qaida's principal strategist that would oversee al Qaida's terrorist operations worldwide.[37]

In memo 110/2/43, in Appendix A, Figure 10 D, the memo says that "The Organization's chief visited the region [Iraq] two [months] ago. The organization showed [a] willingness to carry out operations against American interests at any time." The Al-jihad discussed in the memo is just one cell of Zawahiri's international terrorist organization. Taking into account that Zawahiri had sworn an oath to al Qaida in 1989, Saddam met with al Qaida in November 1992. Also consider that this meeting was just four months prior to the 1993 World Trade Center bombing.

al Qaida's Move to Sudan

As previously discussed in memo 140/D'/4/533, Sheik Ali Uthman Taha, leader of the Sudanese National Islamic Front (NIF), was acting as an intermediary between Iraq and al Qaida as early as January 25, 1993. It turns out the NIF first approached Usama Bin Laden in 1989. The NIF sent a delegation to Peshawar, Afghanistan to tell Usama that America could be defeated like the Soviet Union. In 1989 the NIF had overthrown the Sudanese government. They put in place a figurehead president while the NIF was in control. The delegation made it clear that the new NIF backed government in Sudan wanted to form an alliance with al Qaida to attack America. Usama agreed to this alliance and offered to train the NIF members in guerilla warfare. The Sudanese delegation asked that al Qaida move to Sudan and help fight against their opposition, the predominately Christian Sudan People's Liberation Army (SPLA). Usama agreed to move al Qaida to Sudan. "From 1989 to late 1991, most of al Qaida's best trained and experienced fighters, numbering 1,000-1,500, moved to Sudan, although Usama retained an extensive training and operational infrastructure in Afghanistan and Pakistan."[38] Usama's right hand man, Ayman al Zawahiri oversaw al Qaida's relocation to Sudan. Al Qaida bought two large farms that would be used to house and train al Qaida members. Zawahiri lived on one of the farms. The farms were also used to grow and produce crops that were processed and sold through one of Usama Bin Laden's companies.

Usama invested his money in various businesses in order to support al Qaida which cost an estimated $30 million per year. Because Usama was financially supporting the Sudanese government's fight against its opposition, al Qaida was allocated land for training camps. Usama Bin Laden invested $50 million in a Sudanese bank which was linked to the Sudanese upper class.[39]

Surprisingly, al Qaida was supported almost entirely through donations received via charitable organizations. An international charitable organization which began in the 1980's to fund the Arab mujahideen was incorporated in 1992 in Chicago, Illinois as a non-profit organization. This organization named the Benevolence International Foundation (BIF) was a front for al Qaida. Many who donated to BIF thought the money was to be used for humanitarian purposes unknowing the money was going to al Qaida.[40] Surprisingly, since the BIF was incorporated as a U.S. non profit organization, Muslim Americans who worked at large U.S. corporations were able to get corporate matching of their donations.

Originally it was thought that since Usama's personal inheritance was worth nearly $300 million that he was able to sustain al Qaida from his personal wealth. Due to increased pressure internationally after the 1993 WTC bombing, Saudi Arabia forced the divestment of Usama's share of his father's fortune. Although Usama had investments in Sudan, these were not nearly profitable enough to sustain the ongoing costs of al Qaida. Once Usama was forced to leave Sudan, the Sudanese government seized his assets. Herein lays the reason Usama created a charitable network as a front to support al Qaida.

al Qaida's Move to Afghanistan

In June 1995, al Qaida attempted to assassinate the Egyptian President Hosni Mubarak. Hosni Mubarak is the one who stood up to Saddam Hussein and told him he was wrong in asking that Iraq's debts from the Iran-Iraq War be forgiven. Considering the rift between Mubarak and Saddam, it is very likely that Saddam ordered Mubarak's assassination. Mubarak was able to escape the assassination attempt. The international community had been pressuring Sudan to expel Usama Bin Laden. With pressure mounting, Usama decided to move al Qaida to Afghanistan. Within five months of Usama relocating al Qaida to Afghanistan, the Taliban took over the country. Usama quickly made an alliance with the Taliban. He supplied the Taliban with "weapons, funding, propaganda and other support."[41] Even a special guerilla warfare unit was created where Taliban and al Qaida members trained and operated together. The Taliban gave al Qaida sanctuary to operate freely in Afghanistan. Al Qaida set up training camps and was given weapons and equipment.[42]

In Afghanistan, Usama relied on the Taliban until he could reenergize his fundraising by tapping the wealthy Saudi donors known as the "Golden Chain" who had sent aid during the Soviet-Afghan War. "Charities were a source of money and also provided significant cover, which enabled operatives to travel undetected under the guise of working for a humanitarian organization."[43] Although the 9/11 Commission Report says that the Taliban was the only government that funded al Qaida, we know from memo 110/2/43 that Iraq was also financing al Qaida through his financial payments to the EIJ and IG. Memo 110/2/43 says **"We've previously met with the Organization's representative on December 14, 1990, and we agreed on a plan to move against the Egyptian regime through Fedayeen operations, provided that we guarantee them [financial] aid, training and whatever they need."** This clearly shows that Saddam was financing al Qaida because by the writing of this memo Umar Abed al Rahman was the spiritual leader of al Qaida.[44]

3

Influence of Sharia

"The basis of the message is that one should accept the sharia without any question and reject all other laws in any shape or form. This is Islam. There is no other meaning of Islam."

- Seyyid Qutb

Sharia law is a manifestation of Islamic Fundamentalism that provides the basis for Islamic Terrorism. Sharia law is more than just religious law. It is a socioeconomic, political, legal, and religious law that encompasses all aspects of life. When instated in a country, it provides the legal, social, economic, and religious laws for the society. There are five major interpretations of sharia that have developed over the centuries. Four of the interpretations are along Sunni traditions and one in the Shiite tradition.[45]

Economic laws based on sharia prohibit the charging of interest and excessive profits. Investing in projects that are contrary to Islamic law is forbidden. For example, investing in a brewery or casino is against the law. Sharia influences crminal law by mandating Islamic law in the legal system. "Because these offenses are mentioned in the Quran, committing them is considered an affront to God. They are:

- Wine-drinking and, by extension, alcohol-drinking, punishable by flogging
- Unlawful sexual intercourse, punishable by flogging for unmarried offenders and stoning to death for adulterers
- False accusation of unlawful sexual intercourse, punishable by flogging
- Theft, punishable by the amputation of a hand
- Highway robbery, punishable by amputation, or execution if the crime results in a homicide."[46]

Social laws, marriage, divorce, polygamy, custody, and inheritance are all defined within sharia. Socially men have more power than woman under sharia law. Regarding marriage, the husband is the head of the household, and the wife is subjugated to her husband. Husbands can use physical force against their disobedient wives according to the Quran. A Muslim man can marry a non-Muslim woman, but a Muslim woman cannot marry a non-Muslim man. In fact, Muslim men are encouraged to marry non-Muslim women in order to convert more non-believers into Islam. Of course any children born into the family would be raised Muslim. Western laws protect Western women from being subjugated to her Muslim husband as it would be in the Muslim world.

If a Western woman marries a Muslim man and they move to the Muslim world, she will be subjugated to Muslim law. Nonie Darwish warns in her book that every "Western woman needs to understand both the negatives and the positives of marrying into the Middle Eastern Muslim culture before taking a step that might change her life forever."[47]

Divorce is easy for a man. All a man has to do is say "I divorce you" three times to his wife, and they are considered divorced. A woman on the other hand has very few legitimate reasons to get a divorce. "Classical *sharia* lays out very limited conditions under which a woman can divorce a man - he must be infertile at the time of marriage, insane, or has leprosy or another contagious skin disease."[48]

Polygamy is allowed under sharia. The Quran allows a man the right to have up to four wives. A woman has the right to divorce her husband if he takes a second wife. In a divorce, custody of the children goes to the father. Polygamy negatively affects the family structure because it creates distrust between the husband and wife. As soon as a husband begins making more money, the first wife becomes suspicious of when the next wife will arrive. Young Muslim women many times prefer to marry a wealthy older man than a young poor man. The economic distress on young Muslim men who graduate with little to no job skills and then have to "compete with older, wealthier married men for single women" makes joining the jihad all the more favorable.[49]

The imposition of sharia law can be damaging to a society for many reasons. One is the economic depressing factors because it limits the free market. "There is ample evidence that Islamism, and its imposition of *Sharia* law, results in crippling limitations to economic development, and thus to the socioeconomic well-being of Muslims. Relevant cases are Pakistan, Iran, Sudan, and Nigeria."[50]

Sharia law has a negative effect on education. Education is primarily focused on studying the Quran. The problem is that no practical job skills are being taught. When a young person graduates they have few job skills, thus making them vulnerable to joining the jihad in acts of terrorism. Islamic schools like public schools in the United States are rising in functional illiteracy. Because some Islamic fundamentalist countries do not allow women to attend school, illiteracy rates among women are high. Education in science and technology is viewed unfavorably which negatively affects the economic development of these countries. "The 2004 UN Report on Arab Human Development shows that the Arab world has yet to join the Industrial Revolution - let alone the *Information* Revolution - and that it neither produces much scientific literature nor carries out real research."[51]

Human rights are an issue in countries that are ruled by sharia. Women are treated like second class citizens in these countries. "From uncivilized practices such as forced marriages to truly inhumane treatment such as genital mutilation and "honor" killings. Virtually all of these extreme Islamist tenets and practices stand in direct contradiction to the UN Universal Declaration of Human Rights - an international human rights standard to which all of the sharia-dominated countries nominally adhere."[52]

Muslim Religion

According to Bassam Tibi in the <u>The Challenge of Fundamentalism: Political Islam and the New World Disorder</u>, Islam is the religion of peace. The effort of spreading the true religion of Islam is called jihad. Like Christian Evangelism, the da'wa is the conversion of the world to Islam in peace. But if the people who hear the message of Islam and do not convert, force may be used. This struggle is called qital which means defense. The use of force to simply further a country's territory is forbidden under Islam. At the same time, the use of force is acceptable when trying to further the religion of Islam in a territory where the inhabitants are not willing to convert to Islam. This is seen as a defense to the Muslims bringing the true word of God to the unbelievers who are hindering the spread of Islam.

In modern day Islam, jihad has taken on a whole new meaning. Now jihad means holy war. This holy war is translated into terrorist aggression toward other non-Islamic nations and even Islamic nations that are perceived to be too secular or Western. The father of this new definition of jihad and Islamic Fundamentalism is Seyyid Qutb.

Seyyid Qutb was an Egyptian who came to the United States for academic training in 1948-1950. While in New York, he "read the book <u>L'homme cet inconnu</u>, the French Nobel Prize winner Alexis Carrel, in which the French scholar described in most pathetic terms, the alienation of man in modern industrial societies. Qutb felt lost in the West and projected onto New York City his vision of the decline of Western civilization and its replacement by Islam."[53] In Qutb's writings, he repeatedly emphasized the moral decline of the West, and how this will lead to its downfall. Qutb believed that Islam was the only religious, socioeconomic, and legal means that could fill the void that would exist when the West falls.[54]

When Qutb returned to Egypt, he was an ardent anti-American and anti-Western Muslim. He was determined to lay the foundation for the modern jihad that he hoped would lead to the overthrow of the West by Islam. Although Qutb had been a member of the Muslim Brotherhood prior to going to the United States, upon his return to Egypt, Qutb became a leader in the group. In 1952, he was employed by the Muslim Brotherhood. He was in charge of writing books and articles that were used to further the Muslim Brotherhood's Islamic views.[55]

Qutb viewed colonialism as a front to take back the Holy Land for Christianity. In Qutb's ground breaking book <u>Milestones,</u> he states the "truth of the matter is that the latter-day imperialism is but a mask for the crusading spirit, since it is not possible for it to appear in its true form, as it was possible in the Middle Ages."[56] By the mid-1960s, Qutb thought that because Egypt had not instituted sharia law, it was actually not Muslim at all. His only solution to this problem was to either force the government into instituting sharia or to overthrow the Egyptian government entirely and replace it with a fundamentalist sharia system.[57] Because of Qutb's involvement in the attempted assassination of Gamal Abd Al Nasser in 1954, he was arrested and sentenced to 15 years imprisonment. After 10 years of serving his sentence, he was released from prison. After less than a year, he was again arrested for his involvement in trying to "overthrow the Egyptian government by force."[58] In 1966, he was sentenced to death by a military tribunal.

Qutb's writings laid the ground work for the modern day jihad. The popularity of his works in Islamic circles can be compared to the "Communist Manifesto in the period of the early worker's movement in Europe and later under Communism. His basic missionary message was that world peace can be achieved only under the banner of Islam within the framework of *jihad* as an expression of 'world revolution'."[59] In Qutb's Milestones book, he specifically denounced the interpretation of jihad as being only a defensive war. "This group of thinkers, who are the sorry state of the present Muslim generation, have nothing but the label of Islam and have laid down their spiritual and rational arms in defeat. They say, 'Islam has prescribed only defensive war'!"[60] Qutb states that sharia is the Divine Law that needs to be established on the earth while abolishing all man-made laws. Individuals can only be truly Muslim by submitting themselves to sharia. "Sharia of God is meant everything legislated by God for ordering man's life; it includes the principles of belief, principles of administration and justice, principles of morality and human relationships, and principles of knowledge."[61] Qutb specifically chastises Muslim's who compromise and do not whole heartedly accept sharia in all forms: political, social, economic, religious, and legal.

The influence that sharia law has on a society is the driving force behind the modern jihad. Qutb demands that all Muslims submit themselves freely to sharia in order to truly walk the straight path. In

Qutb's jihadist manifesto, <u>Milestones</u>, he states that all Muslims **"should accept the Sharia without any question and reject all other laws in any shape or form. This is Islam. There is no other meaning of Islam."** Qutb is quite clear and definitive that sharia is a requirement for all Muslims. As a result, Muslims must wage war in order to overthrow all governments that do not allow sharia to operate as the governing law.

In reality, sharia law is what is keeping the Muslim world in the backward third world sector, which means a lack of economic development, widespread poverty, poor education, and intense human suffering and hopelessness. Prescribing to such archaic laws that discriminate against women, limit the free market, and view science and technology unfavorably is driving young men and women in the Arab world to hopelessness and despair. This leads them to become suicide bombers and join the jihad against the infidels. It is a vicious cycle. What the Muslim extremists are fighting for is leading to their own demise.

4

History of Iraq

"Those who cannot remember the past
are condemned to repeat it."

- George Santayana

To fully understand how a brutal dictator such as Saddam Hussein and the Baathist party were able to take control of Iraq, one must understand the history of Iraq. From the Ottoman Empire to British Imperialism, the political, social, legal, and economic changes imposed on Iraq affected the country and its people in many ways.

Ottoman Empire

In the mid-1800's, the ruler of the Ottoman Empire wanted to extend its authority into the countryside of Iraq. Tribes had ruled the countryside of Iraq since the Thirteenth century. The Ottoman Empire imposed Midhat Pasha as the Governor of Baghdad. Midhat Pasha enacted sweeping Westernized reform to Iraq. He set out "to reorganize the army, to create codes of criminal and commercial law, to secularize the school system, and to improve provincial administration. He created provincial representative assemblies to assist the governor, and he set up elected municipal councils in the major cities. Staffed largely by Iraqi notables with no strong ties to the masses, the new offices nonetheless helped a group of Iraqis gain administrative experience."[62] This reform led to a new system in the countryside. The 1858 TAPU land law enacted by Midhat allowed tribes to own the land they have settled. This led to tribes settling down and abandoning the ancient nomadic lifestyle of the desert. It also allowed property taxes to be levied on the new land-owners. The land was registered to the tribal shaykhs which ended up making them wealthy landowners, while their tribesmen ended up being no more than sharecroppers. The vast wealth enjoyed by the shaykhs drew them into politics to have some influence on government policy. Also the sharecropper status of the tribesmen led to a class envy situation where the tribal shaykhs lived in lavish estates and the tribesmen were mere peasants.[63]

British Imperialism

British ties to the region go back hundreds of years to trading routes within the Ottoman Empire. In the late nineteenth and early twentieth centuries, with Russian expansion and Germany establishing a foothold in the Middle East, Britain felt compelled to ensure its trading routes to India.[64] At the time India was a British colony. Germany had been granted the right by the Ottomans to build railroad lines from "Konya in southwest Turkey to Baghdad in 1899 and from Baghdad to Basra in 1902."[65] The British were concerned that their supply lines to India may be disrupted by the Germans.

During World War I, Turkey entered the War on the side of the Germans. Britain decided to protect its interests by sending troops from India to Basra, Iraq. "By March 1917 the British had captured Baghdad. Advancing northward in the spring of 1918, the British finally took Mosul in early November."[66] The Iraqi people wanted to be emancipated from Ottoman rule. Once the British took Baghdad, they assured the Iraqi people that they would relinquish some power to the Iraqis so they could rule themselves. In order to maintain immediate British rule of Iraq, a British High Commissioner named Sir Percy Cox was appointed. Sir Percy Cox delegated leadership of Iraq to his deputy Colonel Arnold Talbot Wilson.[67]

Concerned about the British takeover of Baghdad, three anti-colonial political organizations arose during 1918 and 1919. An interesting dichotomy of people came together in different areas of Iraq in order to fight against the British colonization of Iraq. The three groups were as follows:

- An Najaf, Jamiyat an Nahda al Islamiya (The League of the Islamic Awakening)
    - Its various members included religious leaders, journalists, landlords, and tribal leaders in the city of Najaf.
- Al Jamiya al Wataniya al Islamiya (The Muslim National League)
    - It was formed with the intent of mobilizing the people of Iraq for a major resistance against the British.
- Haras al Istiqlal (The Guardians of Independence)
    - It was a coalition of "Shia merchants, Sunni teachers and civil servants, Sunni and Shia ulama (religious leaders), and Iraqi officers."[68] It spanned several cities including Karbala, An Najaf, Al Kut, and Al Hillah.

Husayn ibn Ali was a formidable figure and considered the father of pan-Arabism. Ali's family descended from the Prophet Muhammad. Ali was born into the Hashimite family that inherited the Meccan emirate in the early 1800's. Ali was the emir of Mecca from 1908 to 1916. Prior to World War I, Ali had been loyal to the Ottoman Empire. During World War I, he saw an opportunity to establish a monarchy separate from the Ottoman Empire, an independent Arab nation. This was a sentiment that many nationalists in Iraq held also. The desire for an independent secular Arab nation is called pan-Arabism. The pan-Arabists believe that all Arab speaking nations should be united into one Arab nation. The division of the Ottoman Empire is seen as a purely Western sanctioning imposed on the Arab world. Pan-Arabists believe that all of the Arab nations joining together as one nation would benefit all of them economically. For example, instead of having multiple seaports in one area that span multiple Arab countries, they would have a few strategically placed seaports that would benefit all of the Arab nations. Secondly, the natural resources that span several Arab nations would be shared among the Arab provinces of one Arab nation.[69] Husayn ibn Ali was the originator of the pan-Arab movement because he was the first leader to suggest that the Arabs rise up against the Ottoman Empire to form an independent Arab nation. In 1915, Ali's son Prince Faisal Ibn al-Husayn I traveled to Damascus, Syria to meet with secret Arab nationalist societies in order to gain their confidence in joining him and his Father in opposing the Ottoman Empire.[70] This led Husayn ibn Ali to join with the British and fight against the Ottoman Empire.

After World War I, the Allied powers formed the League of Nations. It was the precursor to the United Nations.[71] Husayn's son, Prince Faisal Ibn al-Husayn I, represented Iraq at the 1919 Paris Peace Conference. Iraq was classified as a "Class A mandate entrusted to Britain."[72] Article 22 of the League of Nations covered countries that were no longer under the same rule as before World War I, but were seen as unable to "stand by themselves under the strenuous conditions of the modern world."[73] The independent Arab monarchy that Husayn ibn Ali and his family sought would have to wait.

The challenges to Britain in ruling Iraq were immense. The Northern Kurdish part of Iraq was still not occupied by the British. "The holy cities of An Najaf and Karbala and their satellite tribes were in a state of near anarchy."[74] The Iraqi nationalists were angry that

Iraq was given a class A mandate status. They wanted Iraq to be a sovereign nation. They were suspicious that the British just wanted to colonize Iraq like they had done with India. To add insult to injury, Colonel Arnold Talbot Wilson staffed his administration with professionals that he trusted and that had previous experience with him. Because he came from India, this meant that Indians, not Iraqis were staffing the post-war government. This added to the Iraqi's discontent with their current situation.

Iraqis began to protest the British rule of Iraq. "Religious leaders exhorted the people to throw off the bonds of imperialism. Violent demonstrations and strikes followed the British arrest of several leaders."[75] In May 1920, a group of Iraqi delegates decided to meet with the British High Commissioner of Iraq, Colonel Arnold Talbot Wilson. The delegates demanded the independence of Iraq from British rule. Wilson completely disregarded the demands of the delegates. This ignited the nationalist's fervor for independence. The religious leader of Karbala, "issued a *fatwah* (religious ruling), pointing out that it was against Islamic law for Muslims to countenance being ruled by non-Muslims, and he called for a jihad against the British."[76] This led to the Great Iraqi Revolution of 1920. For three months, Iraq was in a complete state of chaos. In order to regain control, the British ordered air bombings on the resistance areas.

The British knew they had to appease the Iraqis by giving them more control of their own country. As a result, Britain removed its imposed High Commissioner and instated a representative Iraqi government. The plan was to allow the Iraqis to govern themselves but to work closely with the British government. Britain wanted to protect its trading interests in the Middle East. Sir Percy Cox called a truce and announced Britain's intentions of creating an Iraqi government. Important Iraqi nationalists and leaders were brought together to decide how the Iraqi government would be set up. A council of Iraqis was formed. There were British advisors to aid the council. The Iraqi council primarily was made up of Sunnis while Shiites were underrepresented. The council voted that there would be a monarchy formed that would be "constitutional, representative, and democratic."[77] The council decided that Prince Faisal Ibn al-Husayn I would be the first King. Faisal I was a direct descendant of Muhammad and was from a long line of powerful Arab leaders. "His ancestors had held political authority in the holy cities of Mecca and Medina since the tenth century."[78] The British worked with the Iraqis to set up a Constitution and representative Assembly. An Iraqi Army was also formed in support of the new monarchy. Note the eerie parallel between the attempt of Great Britain to set up a constitutional government and the attempt of the United States after the 2003 invasion. The U.S. correctly avoided any ties to a monarchy which was a definite improvement to the British attempt. In October 1922, "the first elections to the assembly were held."[79] Although an Iraqi monarchy was formed along with a representative assembly, King Faisal I was not from Iraq. The Iraqi people knew that Britain still exercised control over the new government. The Iraqi people were discontent and wanted a truly independent Iraqi Government. This also parallels the problems of the 21st century American backed Iraqi government despite the American avoidance of an imposed monarchy.

In October 1922, the British signed a treaty with Iraq. The treaty ensured that Britons held many high level administrative and advisory positions in the new Iraqi government. The treaty also assigned expenses to Iraq. One expense that was imposed on Iraq was to pay half of the living expenses of British officials who resided in Iraq. Cleverly the British added to the treaty that the "king would heed British advice on all matters affecting British interests and on fiscal policy as long as Iraq was in debt to Britain."[80] The treaty went on to state that "British officials would be appointed to specified posts in eighteen departments to act as advisers and inspectors."[81] The British were also beholden to Iraq. Britain was to provide aid to the new monarchy by providing military assistance and proposing to the League of Nations that Iraq become a member. Essentially the treaty made certain that Iraq would be fiscally, politically, and militarily dependent on Britain.

Defining the Iraqi border was an important issue that needed to be addressed by the new Iraqi Government. There were and still are three distinct ethnic and religious groups in Iraq. The Sunni Kurds are located in Northeast Iraq in Mosul. Although they are Sunni Muslims, they are a completely separate and distinct ethnic group from the surrounding populations. The Sunni Arabs inhabit Central Iraq in Baghdad. The Shiite Arabs inhabit Southern Iraq in Basra.[82]

The Mosul Province was the northern mountainous part of Iraq. This province was primarily Kurdish and oil rich. The Kurds wanted to secede and create their own Kurdish nation. In 1920, the Treaty of Sevres concluded that the Mosul Province should be an independent nation. The British were accepting of this as long as they could continue controlling the oil fields as they had under the Ottoman Empire. The treaty was disregarded when Mustafa Kamal, a nationalist leader in Turkey, came into power. He took control of the eastern part of the Mosul Province. Once this happened, Britain decided to include the Mosul Province as part of the Iraq nation. The Kurds would be able to represent themselves in the new Iraqi government and the Kurdish language would be protected. In 1925, the League of Nations officially considered the Mosul Province as part of the Iraq nation. Turkey was given concessions by receiving 10 percent of the oil revenues that came from the Mosul Province.[83]

Britain was determined to maintain control over Iraq's most important natural resource, the Iraqi oil fields. Britain had originally maintained control of the oil fields in Mosul during the Ottoman Empire. The Turkish Petroleum Company was a British oil company. Britain wanted to maintain the same control over the oil fields even though the new Iraqi government had been formed. During the 1916 Sykes-Picot Agreement, the Mosul Province would have gone to the French. France agreed to relinquish their rights to the oil fields to Britain, but asked for a 25 percent share of ownership in the Turkish Petroleum Company as compensation.[84] The Turkish Petroleum Company became the Iraq Petroleum Company. In 1923, Iraq wanted

20 percent ownership in the Iraq Petroleum Company. Britain refused to give them any share in it. Since Iraq wanted to become a member of the League of Nations which was coming up for a vote soon thereafter, Iraq relinquished any and all rights to the oil fields. Iraq agreed to give up control of the oil fields and acquiesce to Britain. An agreement was made to give the British full control of the Iraq Petroleum Company for the next 75 years.

Gradually over the years Britain's control of Iraq lessened. Later treaties were formed that officially reduced Britain's power in Iraq and moved Iraq closer to full independence. In 1930, a treaty was formed that eliminated the British advisory roles that were required in the 1922 treaty. In addition, British military bases in Iraq were to be maintained, and the British army would continue to train the Iraqi Army. Furthermore, the treaty stated that Iraq could perform its own foreign policy abroad independent of Britain. Iraq became a sovereign nation on October 3, 1932 which was the same day that Iraq was accepted into the League of Nations.[85] The treaty of 1932 was the beginning of Iraq loosening the grip that Britain had on it.

In 1933, King Faisal I died while receiving medical treatment in Switzerland. This was a major disruption to the fledgling new Iraqi nation. King Faisal I was a strong stabilizing force in uniting the various factions in Iraq into one nation. King Faisal's son Ghazi ibn al-Faisal would succeed him. Ghazi was only king for a few short years because he died in a car accident in 1939. His four year old son Faisal II ibn Ghazi succeeded him. Because Faisal II was only four years old, his uncle Amir Abd al-Illah was appointed as an intermediary ruler until Faisal II became old enough to assume being King. Nuri as Said was an influential leader that worked closely with an Amir Abd al-Illah. Said was an Ottoman trained officer that became a loyalist to Britain. In 1930, Said became Prime Minister. He had been instrumental in negotiating the 1932 treaty with Britain that made Iraq a sovereign nation. He was an aggressive leader that oppressed all political opposition.[86] Amir Abd al-Illah and Nuri as Said were British loyalists more so than any other Iraqi leaders that had preceded them. Husayn ibn Ali and Faisal I both worked for an independent Arab nation. They only sided with the British because at the time they needed their help in overthrowing the Ottoman Empire. An important distinction is that Amir Abd al-Illah and Nuri as Said began to support the "tribal shaykhs as a counterforce against the growing urban nationalist movement."[87] This was an entirely different direction in policy than had existed before. Both Faisal I and Ghazi were strong Arab nationalists and "opposed the British-supported tribal shaykhs."[88] Concerned about the new pro-British actions of the government, a group of young officers in the Iraqi Army formed the Free Officers. It was a secret organization that plotted to overthrow the monarchy.

After World War II, British Imperialism in the Middle East declined. The United States was concerned about increasing Soviet influence in the Middle East and Central Asia. In order to fill the void that was created with Britain's diminished role, the United States began working with NATO and SEATO on the Baghdad Pact. NATO was established in 1949 after World War II. It was an alliance of nations to counterbalance the Soviet expansion in Central and Eastern Europe.[89] SEATO was a similar organization but represented Southeast Asia countries that wanted to protect themselves against Communist expansion. The United States was instrumental in getting NATO and SEATO to sign the Baghdad Pact. The Baghdad Pact was an agreement that included Iraq, Britain, Turkey, Iran, and Pakistan. This agreement infuriated Iraqi Nationalists that felt it was too pro-Western. This led to the rise of the National Unity Front that eventually overthrew the Iraqi Monarchy. In 1955, Nuri as Said was instrumental in having Iraq join the Pact. This was seen as a direct act of opposition to the Egyptian government of Gamal Abdul Nasser.[90] On February 1, 1958 Egypt and Syria joined together to form one Arab country called the United Arab Republic. The pan-Arab movement wanted Iraq to unite with Egypt and Syria as part of the United Arab Republic. Both Iraq and Jordan which were Hashimite monarchies feared this new pan-Arab movement that threatened their own monarchies. The Jordanian King Hussein asked the Iraqi monarchy to join them in a Hashimite Pact to support each other's countries against the growing opposition.

Iraqi's were discontent with their monarchy. There was a great divide between the oligarchy and the rest of the people. The people were angry that Iraq signed the Baghdad Pact. "Consequently, the four main opposition parties, the National Democratic Party (NDP), the Iraqi Communist Party (ICP), the Istiqlal Party, and the Baath Party (all illegal parties functioning underground) coalesced to form the National

Unity Front (NUF)."[91] The primary goals of the National Unity Front were as follows:

1) Removal of Nuri as Said from office;
2) Iraqi withdrawal from the Baghdad Pact;
3) Release of all Iraqi political prisoners;
4) Freedom of all political parties;
5) Iraq joining the nonaligned movement (NAM).

The nonaligned movement was led by India in 1955 and was made up of 29 countries that wanted to remain neutral and not align themselves with the United States or the Soviet Union. In 1958, King Hussein of Jordan was concerned about an anti-Western movement that had led to a civil war in Lebanon. King Hussein was concerned that this anti-Western movement might spread to Jordan. As a result, King Hussein asked the Iraqi monarchy to help in defending Jordan from an impending Jordanian crisis. King Faisal II ordered troops to go into Jordan to help stabilize Jordan. Before dawn on July 14, 1958 Brigadier Abd al Karim Qasim and Colonel Abd as Salaam Arif, who were both members of the Free Officers, sent their battalion into Baghdad instead of Jordan. In the chaos, a mob ensued and King Faisal II, Amir Abd al-Illah, and Nuri as Said were all executed. Within two days, order was restored and the Iraqi military was in complete control of the government. A republic was declared with Brigadier Abd al Karim Qasim as the leader of the new government.[92]

Although the old oligarchy was destroyed, many problems that have historically plagued Iraq were still present. The rift between the Kurds and Arabs and the chasm between the Sunnis and Shias was prevalent. The chasm between the Sunnis and Shiites goes back hundreds of years to who would be the Prophet Muhammad's successor. The Shiites felt that Muhammad's successor should be his son-in-law, Ali ibn Abi Talib. However, the Sunni's felt that the successor should be an elected official and be run as a caliph. A caliph is the civil and religious leader of the Muslim community. Ali was passed over three times before he was chosen to be the caliph. Once he became the caliph, he was murdered five years later. The Shiites were outraged when Ali's son was not chosen to succeed him as caliph.[93] This solidified the rift between the Sunnis and Shiites which remains to this day after 13 centuries of strife and mistrust.

There are other theological differences between the Sunnis and Shiites. Sunnis believe that they can directly approach God in principle. There are religious figures that wield social, political, and religious power, but individual Sunnis do not have to go through an Imam to approach God. Sunni Imams do not require any formal training and are considered more like prayer leaders. In contrast, Shiites hold their Imams in a more exalted way. Shiite Imams must possess special spiritual guidance and be able to interpret the mysteries of the Quran and sharia law.[94]

In addition to the religious differences among Iraqis, there was a divisive power struggle along ideological lines. One was the pan-Arab movement, the second the Iraqi Nationalists, and the third the Communists. In general, Sunni Arabs were pro pan-Arab. The Shiite Arabs were Iraqi Nationalists untrusting of merging with other predominantly Sunni led nations. The Sunni Kurds were Communists.[95]

The two main leaders in this new republic were at odds. Brigadier Abd al Karim Qasim of Sunni and Shiite background was an anti-union person who was backed by the Iraqi Communist Party. The Communist Party was against a pan-Arab union because Nasser was anti-communist. Although Abd al Karim Qasim was not a communist, he also did not want to join the United Arab Republic. Colonel Abd as Salaam Arif, a Sunni, was pro-Nasser and wanted to join the United Arab Republic. The Baath and Istiqlal party were pro pan-Arab and threw their support behind Colonel Abd as Salaam Arif. Qasim outranked Arif and eventually his nationalist view won out. The first major task of Qasim and his aid Colonel Arif was to gain support across many of the differing political factions. Qasim created a council of sovereignty made up of Sunnis, Shias, and Kurds. Qasim became the prime minister and commander-in-chief of the armed forces. Arif became the deputy premier and deputy commander-in-chief.

As Qasim sought to unify Iraq behind the new government, he had to formally denounce the pan-Arab movement and dismiss any attempt at merging with the United Arab Republic. Soon after the council of sovereignty was formed, the pro pan-Arabs led by the Baath party, pressed for an immediate merger of Iraq with the United Arab Republic.[96] On September 12, 1958 Arif was removed from office. Arif was given a position as ambassador to Germany, but never assumed his post. He was arrested on November 4, 1958.

At this point the Baath and Istiqlal parties had little representation in the government. Consequently, the Baath, Istiqlal, and other pan-Arabists joined together to form a new organization called the National Front. Qasim was concerned about his opposition and relied heavily on the Iraqi Communist Party that supported him. As a result, the Iraqi Communist Party was able to infiltrate all levels of the Iraqi Government. In March 1959, concerned about the growing Communist influence, Colonel Abd al-Wahab al-Shawaf, a pan-Arabist, led a revolt against the new government. The revolt was quickly put down and an aggressive purging of all pan-Arabists from the new government was accomplished. As a result, the Communists felt empowered and pushed for more influence in the government. Qasim was not a communist and did not want the Communists to gain control over the government. Qasim took actions to subdue the communists. He removed two influential Communists from the cabinet and placed a strong nationalist as the military governor-general of Iraq.[97] Now Qasim had alienated the Communists who had previously supported him. At this point his only supporters were nationalists. Even the nationalists were suspicious of Qasim because he had previously allowed the Communists so much power in the government. On October 7, 1959, the Baath party made an attempt on Qasim's life, but he survived.

Two events occurred that led to Qasim being overthrown. One was the Kurdish revolt in the Northern part of Iraq. The Iraqi military was unable to regain control of the North. Second on June 25, 1962,

Qasim made a declaration that Kuwait was an extension of Iraq. Kuwait had been part of the Iraqi Province under the Ottoman Empire. Kuwait had been a British protectorate since 1913. In 1962, Britain relinquished its claims on Kuwait. June 19, 1962, Kuwait was declared to be a sovereign nation. Qasim saw this as an opportunity to forcibly bring Kuwait back into Iraq. The international community was outraged along with the Arab world.[98]

In 1963, Qasim was hugely unpopular at this point and was vulnerable to being overthrown. The Baath party used this as an opportunity to assemble all the nationalist groups and independent groups into a force to overrun the Kurdish communists and Qasim. On February 8, 1963, Qasim was overthrown by an alliance comprised of the Iraqi army, Baathists, and pan-Arab forces. On February 9, 1963 Qasim was executed. Upon seizing power of the government, the Baathists established the National Revolutionary Command Council (NRCC). Colonel Abd as Salaam Arif was made the president while Ahmad Hasan al Bakr, a Free Officer, was made prime minister.[99]

The Baath party was a socialist pan-Arab party that originated in Syria in 1943. Michel Aflaq was the founder and spiritual leader of the Arab Socialist Resurrection Party also known as the Baath party. He was the leader of the Baath party in Syria until 1966 when he was exiled. Once exiled, he assumed power of the Baath party from Baghdad, Iraq. While in college Aflaq won a scholarship to study in Paris, France. During his time in France, he was associated with the Communist party. He wrote several articles for various French

Communist papers. Aflaq became disillusioned with the Communist party and decided to form his own Socialist party, the Baath party.[100]

The Iraqi Baath party saw Iraq as a province of a much bigger pan-Arab nation. The Baathists viewed the arbitrary division of the Ottoman Empire after World War I as illegitimate. The borders assigned between the various Arab nations were seen as artificial boundaries that should be abolished and redrawn as provinces within a single Arab nation.[101] The desire to be a single Arab nation goes back to the beginning of the Muslim religion to the Arabian Prophet Muhammad. "The Arabs were to be united into one great community, the Community of the Faithful – the Ummah or the Arab Nation … born out of Islam."[102] Surprisingly the founder of the Baath party was a nominal Greek Orthodox Christian, but he still saw the importance of the pan-Arab nation rooted in Islam. Michel Aflaq uniquely separated the pan-Arab nationalism it so strongly embraced from Islam. The Baath party was a secular political organization, not religious, that intended to spread the gospel of socialism to the Arab world. The socialism that they created differed from pure communism because it respected religion, private property, and inheritance. The Baathists acknowledged the extreme differences between the wealthy and poor and followed two major principles of communism. First, they believed that income redistribution was necessary. Second, the Baathists believed that major industries must be nationalized.[103] Once in power, the Baathists swiftly moved to silence all political opposition. This paved the way for the most ruthless dictator to take control of Iraq, Saddam Hussein.[104]

5

Rise of Saddam

> We are ready to sacrifice our souls, our children and our families so as not to give up Iraq.
>
> **- Saddam Hussein**

By 1968 the Baath Party was determined more than ever to stay in power. In order to solidify their hold on the government, they quickly issued a new Iraq Constitution which favored the Baathist rule. The National Revolutionary Command Council (NRCC) was disbanded and a similar Revolutionary Command Council (RCC) was established. Ahmad Hasan al Bakr, the current prime minister, was made the chairman of the RCC.

The Israeli victory in the Six Day War of June 1967 against an Arab coalition comprised of Egypt, Syria, and Jordan was a devastating blow to the pan-Arab movement. As a result, an ideological shift occurred in the Baath Party. There was a move away from the pan-

Arab movement. The pressure for Iraq to join Egypt and Syria waned. This allowed the Baathists in Iraq to focus more on domestic issues.[105]

When Abd as Salaam Arif, the current president, was killed in a helicopter crash in 1967, his brother Abdul Rahman Arif became president of Iraq. Abdul Rahman Arif made a series of blunders that made him unpopular with the Iraqi people. Ahmad Hasan al Bakr, one of the Tikriti clan, saw this as an opportunity to overthrow Arif and take control of the Baathist party and Iraq.

With the overthrow of Arif, Iraq was now ruled by the Tikritis family clan. The Tikritis came from the Northwestern town of Tikrit and were Sunni Arabs. The RCC was made up of five total members. Three of these members were from the town of Tikrit. Two of these three were related, Ahmad Hasan al Bakr and Hammad Shihab. In addition, Tikritis were placed in the three most influential cabinet positions: president, Prime Minister, and Defense Minister. Saddam Hussein, who was a young civilian Baath leader, was also from Tikrit and was related to Bakr. Saddam was a key organizer of the coup that overthrew Arif. At the age of 31 Saddam was appointed to be the acting deputy chairman of the RCC. This meant Saddam Hussein had been appointed to the second most powerful position in Iraq.[106]

Saddam Hussein al Tikriti was born in 1937 to Subha Tulfah al Musallat and Hussein al Majid in a small town outside of Tikrit called Al Awja. In the 1930's Iraqis began to do away with family names and named themselves after their Father's first name and used their birthplace as their last name. Saddam chose to name himself after the larger nearby town of Tikrit. Tikrit is a poor town located Northwest of Baghdad. No one knows exactly what happened to Saddam's birth father, but most likely he died of natural causes or was killed before Saddam's birth. Although the death of Saddam's father is somewhat a mystery, the al Majid extended family accepted Saddam from his birth as Hussein's son. Biographers think the mystery of Saddam's Father is in the fact that he was not a successful person. Apparently his Mother was a strong woman who was outspoken for her time and surroundings. Women in the Al Awja were suppose to be subservient to men and were to remain quiet. Al Awja and Tikrit were extremely poor areas. The land was not fertile, so there were no large landowners in the area providing jobs. Saddam grew up in a one room mud brick dwelling with no electricity, running water, bathroom, or kitchen. Disease ran rampant causing life expectancy to be short. The Tikritis were known for secrecy, lies, revenge, and eliminating their enemies.[107] These became the same traits that Saddam used to run his Baathist Regime.

Just two short months after Bakr had secured his place as president of Iraq, a "coalition of pro-Nasser elements, Arif supporters, and conservatives from the military attempted another coup." This prompted Bakr and Hussein to begin a purging of the opposition within the newly formed Iraqi Government. "Between 1968 and 1973, through a series of sham trials, executions, assassinations, and intimidations, the party ruthlessly eliminated any group or person suspected of challenging Baath rule."[108] To solidify their Baathist rule, a Provisional Constitution was instituted in July 1970. This Provisional Constitution made it mandatory for any new members of the RCC to also be Regional Command members of the Baathist party. The Regional Command was the top policy making executive branch of the Baathist party. Essentially this ensured the Baathist party maintained control of the Iraqi Government.

Saddam volunteered to take over the security services for the Baathist party. He personally oversaw that all Baathist opposition was removed from the Iraqi Government. Any opposition leaders throughout the Iraqi Government and military were tortured, tried, and executed. Over the next five years all opposition to the Baathist party was eradicated. During this time Saddam was almost an invisible figure in the new government while quietly and brutally leading the cleansing. By 1973 the Baathist hold on the Iraqi Government was secured. Anyone seeking a government position knew that they had to be Baathist party members. As a result, the Baathist party grew in record numbers

In 1973 another coup attempt was made to overthrow the Bakr presidency. This was led by a civilian faction of the Baath Party. Bakr and Hussein quickly moved to solidify their hold on the Iraqi government. They again amended the Provisional Constitution to give the president more power. To further tighten its grip, the Regional Command of the Baathist party was made the official body for setting policy for the Iraqi Government. By 1977, the RCC was made up entirely of Regional Command members of the Baathist party. Finally to guarantee the Baathist party's hold on the Iraqi Government, a militia was established which numbered nearly 50,000 men. This militia was called the Popular Army and was also known as the Fedayeen Saddam. This was Saddam's personal army that answered directly to Saddam and operated separate from the regular Iraqi Army.[109] This personal army has a direct analogue to Caesar's Imperial Guard in ancient Rome. It protected the person of Saddam and inspired fear in his political enemies.

Hussein kept the Baathist Party in power not only through fear, but through progressive domestic policies. He nationalized the oil companies which provided Saddam and the Baathists with wealth. In addition, he provided tax breaks for the Iraqi people and free education from kindergarten through College. Saddam also enacted laws that were pro-women rights. He had laws passed that guaranteed women would be paid the same as a man doing the same job and allowed women to enter the workforce in more traditional male oriented jobs such as the military.[110]

By the mid 1970's, Saddam gained more power. Bakr became ill and delegated more and more responsibilities to Saddam. "By 1977 the party bureaus, the intelligence mechanisms, and even ministers who, according to the Provisional Constitution, should have reported to Bakr, reported to Saddam."[111] In 1979, Bakr resigned his position as president making way for Saddam to officially assume the Presidency. Along with the Presidency, Saddam assumed the following positions: "secretary general of the Baath Party Regional Command, chairman of the RCC, and commander in chief of the armed forces."[112] Once Saddam took over he was a dictator. He did not share his power with the RCC and Regional Command as his predecessor had.

Iran – Iraq War

Unrest in the neighboring country of Iran was of great concern to Saddam. There were riots in Iran against its current leader, Mohammad Reza Pahlavi, the Shah of Iran. Pahlavi's family had ruled Iran since the early 1900's. By 1977, it was clear that Iran's economy was in serious trouble with widespread corruption, runaway inflation, and an expanding gap between the richest and poorest. Socially Iran was becoming more influenced by Western culture in fashion, movies, and music. Many Muslims were concerned that the Islamic Religion and heritage of Iran may be lost. This intensified the criticism of the Shah who was seen as too Western.

Internationally Iran was criticized for human rights violations. In 1977, the Shah responded by releasing "political prisoners and announced new regulations to protect the legal rights of civilians brought before military courts." [113] With these changes, professionals such as lawyers, judges, and professors organized and pressured the Shah to adhere to the constitution and provide basic freedoms. Protests followed and the government responded by releasing an article that implied that the Ayatollah Ruhollah Khomeini was a British agent. This caused widespread riots. Khomeini was a Shiite cleric that had regularly spoken out against the monarchy and had been exiled to Iraq in the early 1960's. The situation continued to deteriorate until the Shah was asked to leave the country by Khomeini followers. Shortly thereafter Khomeini returned to Iran. He engineered the overthrow of the monarchy and established a new Islamic regime with the institution of sharia law.[114] The success of overthrowing a secular monarchy along with the imposition of sharia law in a modern Muslim country, lead directly to the state-sponsored Islamic terrorism movement that has threatened western democracies ever since - the Islamic revolution in Iran. Now the Islamic fundamentalists had a state to sponsor their fanatical "jihad" against the West.

In late 1979, Khomeini was declared the leader of Iran for life. This included both political and religious leadership. Shortly thereafter the Ayatollah Khomeini began broadcasting that the Shiites in Iraq should overthrow Saddam Hussein in order to establish an Islamic regime. Saddam saw the upheaval and change of leadership in Iran as both an opportunity and a threat. Saddam viewed the chaos in Iran as an opportunity because it would give him more power over the Gulf region. At the same time, Saddam saw it as a threat because it might shift the delicate balance of the Sunni and Shiites in Iraq. In Iran prior to the revolution a Sunni minority controlled a Shiite majority. Likewise in Iraq, a Sunni minority was in control of a Shiite majority.[115]

Saddam took the threat of revolution seriously. Dawa, a militant Shiite group in Iraq, began plotting terrorist actions against Saddam and his leaders. Tensions mounted as 20 Iraqi officials had been killed in Shiite bombing attacks. During this time there had been ongoing border skirmishes between Iran and Iraq. On September 2, 1980, Iran and Iraq exchanged heavy artillery fire near the Iranian town of Qasr-e Sharin. Iran retaliated by bombing two Iraqi towns,

Khanaqin and Mandali. This was the tipping point. On September 17, 1980 Saddam announced Iraq's treaty with Iran, the Algiers Accord, was no longer valid. Less than a week later the Iraqi air force bombed ten Iranian air bases "destroying fuel and ammunition depots, but much of Iran's aircraft inventory was left intact."[116] The bombing of the airfields failed because most of the Iranian jets were protected in reinforced aircraft hangers, and the bombs dropped on the runways failed to totally destroy them. Just a few hours later, Iran sent fighter jets from those same air bases to Iraq to strategically bomb Iraq's military targets. Concurrent to the Iraqi air force attacks, Saddam advanced his troops on three simultaneous fronts. The Northern and Central fronts were met with little resistance, but the Southern front was much more difficult. There was an important airbase in the South at Dezful that became increasingly difficult to take. The Iranians ended up releasing pilots that had been imprisoned in order to fight the Iraqis. The Iranian air force was able to hold off the Iraqi troops from taking the air base. The last Southern most front was Abadan. Although the Iraqi troops had Abadan surrounded on three sides, they were unable to take the city. At night the Iranians were receiving reinforcements by boat. Iraq was able to take a town just outside of Abadan called Khorramshahr after a difficult house to house and hand to hand combat that ended with high casualties, 6,000 for Iraq and more than 6,000 for the Iranians.[117]

Iran retaliated by using its Navy to blockade Basra, Iraq's only port access to the Persian Gulf. Iran further hindered Iraq, by taking aim at their oil fields. Iran ordered air strikes against Iraq's oil fields, pipelines, and refineries. The attacks were successful and reduced Iraq's exports to one-sixth their normal production. Although the Iranian air attacks were successful, several initiatives on the ground were unsuccessful. In 1981, two different Iranian counteroffensives, one in Khuzestan and Kurdistan proved unsuccessful. Iranian troops were "inadequately trained and undermanned, the result was a devastating defeat for the Iranians."[118] In 1982, Iranian forces were successful in ousting Iraqi forces from Abadan. Iranian forces went on to expel Iraqi forces from the Qasr-e Shirin area. Iraq was reluctant to continue sustaining high casualties; therefore, Saddam refused to reinitiate offensives to reclaim these areas.[119]

In March 1982, Tehran launched an aggressive assault, Operation Undeniable Victory, on Iraqi troops that split Iraqi troops and forced an Iraqi retreat. Saddam made a critical error by trying to negotiate a cease fire at too early a juncture. Iran refused the cease fire and instead launched a new offensive on Iraqi territory near Basra. Iran sustained high casualties, but was able to recapture some territory. In 1983, Iran launched three major yet unsuccessful offensives. Casualties were high and by the end of 1983 "an estimated 120,000 Iranians and 60,000 Iraqis had been killed."[120]

The Iran-Iraq War went on for a devastating eight years. Khomeini was vehement in his cause of spreading his radical Shiite brand of Islam throughout the Middle East. He encouraged his people to sacrifice themselves for the War cause. Khomeini told his people "We should sacrifice all our loved ones for the sake of Islam."[121] By

Spring 1988, the Iranians were worn down fighting the War. Saddam realized this weakness and maneuvered a fierce siege on major Iranian cities. People fled the cities in mass which severely harmed the Iranian government. In addition, there were not enough Iranians volunteering for the Iranian Army. At a point of weakness, Khomeini decided to accept the UN Security Council's cease fire. After two years of international involvement in the Iran-Iraq war, it was finally brought to a resolution on August 20, 1988.

One of the problems with both Iraq and Iran's handling of the war is that they did not use their military equipment properly or efficiently. Tanks were dug in when they could have been maneuvered during assaults. Soldiers were not trained properly to use, maneuver, and repair the sophisticated equipment. The war could have been over much sooner if either side had used the weapons and artillery properly. A crucial mistake that Saddam made is he insisted all military troops take orders directly from him. This put the Iraqi military in a precarious situation because military commanders in the field could not quickly maneuver their troops. This made the Iraqi military unable to quickly respond to Iranian assaults.

In February 1984, Iraq ordered the use of chemical weapons against Iran. Shortly thereafter in March 1984, Saddam again tried to negotiate a cease fire with Iran. Khomeini again refused to negotiate with Iraq. In March 1986, the UN formally charged Iraq with using chemical weapons against Iran. Iraq denied using chemical weapons, but Iranian troops that had sustained chemical burns were being flown to Europe for medical treatment.[122] The use of chemical weapons brought international attention to the war.

Chemical and Biological Weapons Admission

What does the Pentagon report on Saddam show regarding Iraq having biological and chemical weapons? In Volume 4, there is a taped transcript labeled as ISGQ-2003-M0006443. This transcript takes place in 1995 after the Gulf War. This transcript is relevant to our discussion of the Iran-Iraq war because Saddam admits to having both biological and chemical weapons developed during the Iran-Iraq War.

In 1990, Iraq invaded Kuwait in order to annex Kuwait. After the victory of the allied forces against Iraq, a cease fire was agreed upon. In April 1991, the Security Council of the United Nations (UN) decided the conditions of the cease fire and adopted Resolution 687.[123] Resolution 687 was an International affirmation by the UN that Kuwait was again an independent, sovereign nation. In addition, Iraq agreed to eliminate its biological and chemical stockpile of weapons. In 1991, Rolf Ekeus went to Iraq with a UN inspections team to disarm the biological and chemical weapons that Saddam had amassed during the Iran-Iraq War. The U.N. was well aware that Saddam had NEVER destroyed his cache of "weapons of mass destruction" and the international community was in agreement that these weapons should be removed and destroyed.

This discussion takes place in 1995. I base this on the fact that later in the conversation, Aziz says that the UN inspections team has been working for four and a half years. Aziz says "first of all [the UN Inspectors] saw... from [their] work during the last four and a half years that there was a big effort, but the history of that effort, when you go back to it, you find it entirely during the period of [the Iran-Iraq] war."[124] (Appendix, Figure 16, first text box)

In this transcript, Saddam meets with his command members to discuss the United Nations visit to disarm the biological and chemical stockpiles of Iraq. The command members present are as follows: Saddam Hussein, Tariq Aziz the deputy prime minister, and Dr. Amir Muhammad Rashid the minister of oil. This transcript proves that Iraq had both biological and chemical weapons. During the Iran-Iraq war, Iraq developed any and all forms of biological and chemical weapons to be used against Iran and Israel. Rolf Ekeus was the "executive chairman of the United Nations special commission responsible for disposing of Iraq's weapons of mass destruction."[125] Rolf Ekeus was in Iraq leading the UN team at the time of this discussion.

In order to not let the UN inspectors know the full truth about Iraq's chemical and biological weapons, Tariq Aziz has prepped his technicians to not disclose anything regarding quantities, goals, and whether they had been transformed into weapons. Aziz explains that Mr. Ekeus had very specific questions regarding the amount of biological weapons that were produced and why they were produced. Tariq Aziz says, "When he [Mr. Ekeus] asked that you have produced such amounts of the biological, so what was the goal of it, meaning what is the political or security meaning for its production. **Of course**

we had told the technical comrades that when they ask, tell them [to say] this is not our job. We have the duty of implementation. Ask us in the implementation matters and when you do have questions of this kind, when Ekeus comes he will present them to the political official with whom he will meet."[126] (Appendix, Figure 15, first text box)

Aziz continues by saying that he told Mr. Ekeus that prior to the Iran-Iraq War, Iraq did not have Chemical weapons or a developed armament industry. Aziz says, "I told him [Mr. Ekeus]... that the strategy or armament that we have was originally developed during the war with Iran, I mean, before entering the war with Iran we did not have neither chemical [weapons] nor missiles. We did not have a developed armament industry, we had a very simple armament industry and this industry was developed during the period of war with Iran due to the threat facing us."[127] (Appendix, Figure 15-16)

The truth is Iraq began its biological weapons laboratory in the mid-1970's. "At Saddam's request, Izzat al-Douri, a high-ranking Baath official who served on the Revolutionary Command Council as minister of agriculture, traveled to Paris in November 1974 where he signed a contract with France's Institut Merieux to set up Iraq's first bacteriological laboratory."[128] After getting the biological agent laboratory up and running, in 1975 Saddam began working on chemical weapons. Saddam sought the means to produce poison gases such as mustard, Tabun, and Sarin. Under the guise of agricultural development the manufacturing of lethal phosphorus based pesticides began. These pesticides had been banned in other Western countries due to their lethal qualities. It turns out Sarin and Tabun are made from phosphorus materials. Iraq had large natural phosphate deposits near the Syrian border.[129]

In response to Mr. Ekeus' question regarding why Iraq had such large amounts of chemical and biological weapons, Aziz explains that their enemy was an **"exceptional threat."**
Aziz goes to say that **"the people we wanted to fight are not people**, they do not live on this planet on which we live.... Hundreds of thousands of fanatics blind in their minds and in their hearts used to come to us who wanted to die. He would get upset when he does not die. Thus, a threat of this kind requires… special confrontation."**[130] (Appendix, Figure 17) The extremist ideological make up of the Iranian army is described in the Library of Congress Country Study of Iran. "Some members even carried their own shrouds to the front in the expectation of martyrdom."[131] The Iranians were sent into battle with inadequate armor and weapons, yet were driven by their allegiance to Khomeini. Furthermore, Saddam had a hatred for the Iranians who were Persians the same as the Nazis had for the Jews. This was seen in the engraved plaque that was on Saddam's desk which read **"Three Whom God Should Not Have Created: Persians, Jews, and Flies."**[132]

In order to save Iraq and its people from this fanatical enemy, the Iraqi leadership decided to find the cheapest most effective weapons which included chemical and biological weapons. Aziz explains, "when we were confronted we faced this type of aggression and this danger that threatened the existence of our people and our land, we I mean, took a decision as a political leadership, and I am a part of the political leadership, that whatever we can save to face this aggression, we saved. First in money." The UN inspections team wanted to see the money trail for buying these chemical and biological weapons. Aziz explains that Iraq gave bags of money to whomever in order to acquire the necessary weapons. "I told him we are an organized state, you [UN] come ask us that, okay you spent several million dollars. Where are its [Iraq's] documents and where are the accounts so we could know exactly?... **We, yes used to give bags, bags we would bring and put a bag in his hand and tell him here are ten million, twenty, fifty million, go get whatever you can, find tanks or artillery or equipment, go bring it, we did this.** Not all of this is orderly nor does the Iraqi state work this way, nor all the Iraqi army works this way. But for this performance especially it was required to face the exceptional aggression we encountered, we used to do it. Is it risky? It is risky. Are there losses? There are losses. **But when you measure it with the current situation we consider that it was good and necessary and we do not regret it.**" [133] (Appendix, Figure 17 last text box – Figure 18)

Saddam considered the Persians as less than human. As a result, Iraq disregarded all international humanitarian laws. Saddam authorized his workers to produce both chemical and biological weapons. Aziz says, "I told him [Mr. Ekeus] that, as a political leadership you now tell me about international charters…yes we are a state that respected international treaties. But Khomeini was not respecting any international treaty…. **International treaties are respected when warring parties respect them. But when a party does not respect it the other party finds itself obliged to behave to protect itself.** I told him [Mr. Ekeus] so we authorized the workers for the military production [of] **any weapon they could produce let them produce it. They asked, can we improve the missile? We told them to improve it. They said, can we produce chemical weapons? We told them to produce chemical weapons. They said can we produce biological weapons? We told them to produce biological weapons. Everything that the technicians and experts came and told us that they can produce, we told them, yes, produce it.**"[134] (Appendix, Figure 19, text box 1)

In Aziz's own words he is saying that Iraq produced chemical and biological weapons with complete disregard to international laws. Aziz says, "**our decision was that we produce any weapon which our experts and technicians can reach its production. Forbidden internationally, not forbidden internationally, a breach to international treaties or not, this is another subject because the party we were facing was an outlawed party, out of the treaties, out of the epoch, out of this planet.**" (Appendix, Figure 19, last text box)
The biological weapons were developed during the Iran-Iraq war, but were not available until the end of the war. Aziz goes on to say that Iraq kept the chemical and biological weapons after the Iran-Iraq war because of the Israeli threat. Aziz says, "until the war ended between us and Iran, were not producing biological weapons, had not reached

the production stage, and the production continued.... **Israel yes was always present on our minds and any weapon we produce after and along the defense against Iran we were thinking that Israel could attack us thus we would have the retaliatory weapon.**"[135]

In this transcript there is a clear admission from Iraq that they produced both chemical and biological weapons for the Iran-Iraq War. These weapons were produced disregarding all international laws. Chemical weapons were used against Iran. The biological weapons were produced, but not in time to be used during the Iran-Iraq War. Stockpiles of both the chemical and biological weapons were kept to be used in defense of an Israeli attack. In Aziz's own words, Iraq did indeed have illegal chemical and biological weapons.

Revenge on the Kurds

During the Iran-Iraq War the Kurds located in the Northern part of Iraq decided to fight with Iran against Iraq. The Kurds ultimate goal was to have its own sovereign nation. Khomeini had promised the Kurds that Iran would aid them in their struggle for an independent state as long as they fought with Iran and against Iraq. Many Kurds felt betrayed by their own government. Saddam did not take kindly to this kind of disloyalty. Instead of trying to seek out the Kurds that actually fought with Iran, Saddam decided to attack all of the Kurds including men, women, and children. This would also solve the long standing problems that Baghdad continued to have with the Kurds in their struggle for a sovereign nation. Many of the Kurds that had fought with Iran had already fled the country realizing that the end of the War was near. After the Iran-Iraq War had ended Saddam decided to solve the Kurdish problem in a brutal Tikriti style.

Saddam decided to use his biological and chemical weapons on the Kurds in a mass extermination. Saddam gave his cousin Ali Hassan al-Majid, also known as Ali Chemical, full power over Northern Iraq. It was Ali's responsibility to carry out the extermination which was called al-Anfal. Al-Anfal was implemented in a series of campaigns. Ali began the cleansing by razing villages. He ordered the Iraqi Army to destroy a line of villages in order to create a boundary between Central Iraq and the Northern Territory. In the villages that were targeted, the Army would bulldoze over all structures and dynamite any cement buildings. Wells were filled in and electrical lines were destroyed. When the Army was finished, the entire village was inhabitable. If the people of the village tried to resist, every person in the village was executed.[136]

The second wave of Ali's cleansing involved using biological weapons on the Kurds. The first attack was on a remote city named Sulaimanya. Typhoid spores were dumped in the water supply in and around the city. "A forensic medical probe of the epidemic in England revealed that the typhoid victims were all infected with one strain of the disease, unlike a natural outbreak that would consist of many typhoid strains, including cholera."[137]

The next wave of the cleansing involved the use of chemical weapons to wipe out entire village populations in a matter of mere moments. Several villages in the Balasan Valley were targeted for a gas attack.

When survivors tried to flee to a nearby city for medical treatment, they were intercepted by Iraqi troops who were told to shot any survivors – men, women, and children. In the final chemical weapons attack on the Kurds, Ali sent Iraqi warplanes and helicopters to 65 Kurdish villages. Ali ordered that nerve gases be dropped. The nerve gases included tabun, sarin, soman plus mustard gas. Thousands of Kurds were killed instantly. The Kurds that were not killed were rounded up. Men were separated from women. The women were sent to concentration camps while the men were executed.[138] "Three thousand villages were razed and five hundred thousand people were moved to concentration camps in Southern Iraq. By early 1988 the number of towns and villages depopulated was to reach four thousand and the number of Kurds moved south had risen to 1.5 million."[139] Now that Saddam had his biological and chemical weapon stockpiles, who or what would be his next target? With his blatant disregard for humanity, Saddam's reign of terror was just beginning.

Saddam's Nazi Connection

Saddam had ended his Kurdish rebellion with a mass extermination not seen since Adolf Hitler's Jewish concentration camps. It turns out Saddam was mentored from a very impressionable age by his maternal uncle, General Kharaillah Tulfah, who would later become Saddam's Father-in-law. General Kharaillah Tulfah was a Nazi. In 1941, during World War II, Kharaillah Tulfah was involved with a failed coup attempt to overthrow the Iraqi monarchy. The failed coup was backed by Nazi Germany. Nazi Germany sent aircraft and weapons in support of the coup. Tulfah was imprisoned for five years for his involvement with the coup. With his imprisonment, Saddam had to return to live with his Mother. She had remarried to an awful man that regularly abused Saddam both physically and verbally.[140]

Saddam idolized his uncle who became a formidable force in Saddam's life. Tulfah's Nazi beliefs can be seen in a pamphlet that he wrote titled "Three Whom God Should Not Have Created: Persians, Jews, and Flies." Saddam was so enamored with the pamphlet that he had the title engraved on a plaque that he kept on his desk. Within the pamphlet Tulfah wrote that "Persians were 'animals God created in the shape of humans' while Jews were 'a mixture of dirt and the leftovers of diverse people.' Flies, by contrast, were poor, misunderstood creatures 'whom we do not understand God's purpose in creating.'"[141] This vehement Nazi hatred of the Jews and Persians was passed on to Saddam by his beloved uncle. When Saddam finally became President of Iraq, he appointed his uncle as Mayor of Baghdad.

Kharaillah Tulfah was a strong nationalist who was actively involved in politics in Iraq. After his release from jail, he was angry and bitter due to being stripped of his military rank and harsh treatment by the British in jail. Tulfah decided to become a teacher at a private school in Tikrit. This was the perfect setting for him to indoctrinate young impressionable students with his Nazi, nationalistic, and socialist views. A student who attended the school said Tulfah was "a very tough man, a Nazi and a Fascist. All the pupils were in awe of him, both because of his record in fighting the British and because of his political views."¹⁴² It was at this time that a young Saddam went to live with his uncle in Tikrit.

Kharaillah Tulfah was the right hand man of Amin al Husseini, a radical Nazi that was the Mufti of Jerusalem. The Mufti, Amin al Husseini, was the religious and political leader of the Palestinian Muslims.¹⁴³ He was an extremely influential leader in the Muslim World. He had previously served in the Army of the Ottoman Empire during World War I. During his service, the Ottoman Empire was engaged in a mass genocide of the indigenous Armenian Christian population. Millions of Armenians were slaughtered by the Ottoman Empire. It was a lesson in the extermination of your enemy through genocide for al Husseini. The Armenian men were executed and the women and children were forced from their homes and country. Most of the women and children died as a result of their harsh and brutal treatment. Does this sound familiar? This is the exact method that Saddam used to exterminate the Kurds. At the time, the Ottoman Empire was allied with Germany.¹⁴⁴

In 1937, Amin al Husseini met with the German consul in Jerusalem. Husseini sought the cooperation of the Nazis in his goal of extermination of Jews in Arab lands and establishing a Palestinian state in Jerusalem. In September 1937, Hitler sent representatives to Jerusalem to meet with Husseini. Soon after this September meeting, the Nazis sent financial and military assistance to Husseini to carry out the 1941 coup against the Iraqi Monarchy. After the unsuccessful 1941 coup, Husseini fled to Germany. On November 28, 1941 Amin al Husseini met with Adolph Hitler. Afterwards, Husseini became the

Islamic arm of the Nazis. He was paid a regular salary by the Nazis and began to recruit Muslims for the Nazi cause. He assumed the following duties for the Nazis:

1) "radio propaganda on behalf of Nazi Germany;

2) espionage and fifth column activities in Muslim regions of Europe and the Middle East;

3) the formation of Muslim Waffen SS and Wehrmacht units in Bosnia-Hercegovina, Kosovo-Metohija, Western Macedonia, North Africa, and Nazi-occupied areas of the Soviet Union; and,

4) the formation of schools and training centers for Muslim imams and mullahs who would accompany the Muslim SS and Wehrmacht units."[145]

Amin al Husseini was instrumental in the "systematic extermination of European Jewry."[146] Husseini convinced Hitler that the European Jews should not simply be expelled from Europe. Nothing less than extermination was suitable for the European Jews. Hitler was considering allowing the Polish Jews to move to Palestine. Husseini convinced Hitler that the Jews should be sent to concentration camps. In radio addresses, Husseini routinely said to "kill the Jews wherever you find them."[147] Doesn't this sound familiar to statements Usama Bin Laden has made? This could easily be reworded to say kill the Americans wherever you find them. Amin al Husseini was waiting for Germany to be triumphant in Europe in order to begin the mass extermination of the Jews from all Arab lands.

After World War II, Husseini played a major role in implementing Project Odessa which was an escape route for Nazis. This allowed Nazis to avoid prosecution and to flee to Arab and South American countries. Many Nazis relocated to Egypt. They converted to Islam and changed their names to Muslim names.[148] The Nazis assimilated to Arab lands efficiently and many were recruited into the military and intelligence agencies. An example of this is "an SS General who had commanded mobile Einsatzgruppen units in charge of murdering Ukrainian Jews and who would become a close friend and bodyguard for Egyptian President Abdel Gammel Nasser."[149] Isn't it interesting that so many Nazis relocated to Egypt which became a hot bed for Islamic terrorism.

Amin al Husseini was a Nazi and is at the root of the Islamic Jihad of today. Husseini was infuriated when he realized that Britain wanted to establish a Jewish nation in Palestine. It was called the Balfour Declaration of 1917. Husseini formed a radical Islamic group called the Society of Palestinian Youth. He also wrote articles that were published in Arab newspapers denouncing the Balfour Declaration. Husseini incited riots and encouraged the killing of Jews. He hated Western society and was a radical Islamic fundamentalist. He was the precursor to Seyyid Qutb, the so called father of jihad. From Amin al Husseini's radical form of Nazi Islamofacism sprang up several radical terrorist organizations. The founder of the Muslim Brotherhood, Hassan el Banna, had ties to Husseini. "In Pakistan, Syed Abdul Ala Maududi founded the Jamaat Islami movement with the goal of establishing Muslim theocratic states based on Koranic law.

Egyptian Sayed Qutb of the Muslim Brotherhood continued the movement after World War II. The Muslim Brotherhood had offshoots: the Egyptian Islamic Jihad and Hamas. Haj Amin el Husseini, the Muslim Brotherhood, Jamaat Islami, Islamic Jihad, all form the roots and historical background for the emergence of the Al Qaeda network, the mujahedeen of Afghanistan, and Usama Bin Laden." [150]

    Interestingly enough Yasir Arafat was related to Amin al Husseini. Yasir Arafat's birth name was Mohammed Abd al-Rauf Arafat al Qudwa al-Husseini. Arafat's Mother was a cousin of Husseini. Arafat's Father was a member of the Muslim Brotherhood. As a teenager, Arafat joined a youth organization which was affiliated with Husseini.[151] The radical Islamic terrorism that the West is battling today has its origins from Nazi Germany.

6

Gulf War

"[America] will not be excluded from the operations and explosions of the Arab and Muslim mujahidin and all the honest struggglers in the world."

- Saddam Hussein January 30, 1991

Setting the Stage

After the Iran-Iraq War, Iraq had sustained large population and financial losses. Over the eight years of the war, Iraq lost 105,000 men and sustained 300,000 wounded. This was over 2.5% of Iraq's population. To put this in perspective, this would be the equivalent of six million people in the United States compared with 1989 census data. In addition, Iraq incurred massive financial costs due to the war. By the end of the war, Iraq was in serious debt to foreign countries. "Iraqi reserves had disappeared: $35 billion was owed to the West, $11 billion to the USSR and … more than $40 billion to Kuwait and Saudi Arabia."[152] To further understand the severity of the debt, Iraq's annual oil revenue at the time was estimated to be less than $14 billion. Iraq owed $86 billion to other countries while its largest source of revenue came from oil. Interest on the $86 billion was on the order of $10 billion since the Iraqi dinar was a weak currency and lenders charged higher interest to offset the currency risk. This meant that most of the oil earnings were going to service the Iraqi debt, leaving Saddam very little room to maneuver financially. There was no way for Saddam to sustain his economy without further borrowing from other countries and for the price of oil to increase. In addition to the debt, Saddam had to pay money to the families who sustained losses from the War. The families of soldiers who died in the War were owed entitlements for their sacrifice.

In addition to the debt incurred from the Iran-Iraq War, Saddam had begun the huge undertaking of rebuilding Babylon. To Saddam, Iraq was the leader of the Arab world.
"Its people, history, and resources combined with his leadership made it the inevitable leader in the region - perhaps not without struggle, but struggle contributes to the overall glory." Saddam saw himself as the new Nebuchadnezzar. "In Babylon, where Iraq was reconstructing the historical city, the bricks were molded with the phrase, 'Made in the era of Saddam Hussein' -mimicking the ancient bricks forged in ancient Babylon and demonstrating his assumption that he will be similarly remembered over the millennia."[153] King Nebuchadnezzar had left instructions for future kings to rebuild his temples and palaces. Royal scribes had written instructions on clay tablets. The various buildings and palaces had inscribed bricks which read this building was built by

"Nebuchadnezzar, King of Babylon from far sea to far sea."[154] Saddam Hussein had taken on this audacious task. Starting in 1986, Saddam began importing Sudanese laborers since so many Iraqi men were fighting in the Iran-Iraq War. These Sudanese laborers "worked seven days a week through wet winters and scorching summers to rebuild what archeologists call King Nebuchadnezzar's Southern Palace - a vast complex of some 500 rooms and the reputed site of the legendary Hanging Gardens of Babylon. Walls of yellow brick, 40 feet high and topped with pointed crenelations, have replaced the mounds that once marked the Palace foundations. And as Babylon's walls rise again, the builders insert inscribed bricks recording how Nebuchadnezzar's palace was 'rebuilt in the era of the leader Saddam Hussein.'"[155] Saddam ordered that the Southern Palace must be finished by September 1989. Saddam saw Iraq as the cradle of civilization and "as heirs to the great cultures of Babylon, Nineveh and Ur, which flourished thousands of years ago in Mesopotamia, between the Tigris and Euphrates." Experts said that Saddam was doing this to strengthen Iraqi nationalism. Could this be something even more insidious? Could Saddam be trying to mirror the old Babylon Empire which stretched from the Persian Gulf to the Mediterranean encompassing present day Kuwait, Syria, Jordan, and Israel. I think this was what Saddam was planning. The Iraqi Baath party saw Iraq as a province of a much bigger pan-Arab nation. The Baathists viewed the arbitrary division of the Ottoman Empire after World War I as illegitimate. The borders assigned between the various Arab nations were seen as artificial boundaries that should be abolished and redrawn as provinces within a single Arab nation.[156]

Even after the Gulf War, in the transcript labeled ISGQ-2003-M0003964 Saddam says "we must concentrate on our Arab nation". Saddam still held the goal for one Arab nation with Iraq at the helm. (See Appendix, Figure 52, last text box)

In light of Iraq's dire economic situation, Saddam increased Iraq's oil production in order to increase Iraqi revenues. This plan backfired because increasing the supply of oil led to a lower oil price. To make matters worse Kuwait and the United Arab Emirates (UAE) also increased oil production which further inflated the supply of oil, thus lowering the oil price. Next Saddam sought to privatize many industries that had previously been nationalized. This increased revenues slightly, but did not make a dent in Saddam's overall debt.

Saddam lobbied for Saudi Arabia and Kuwait to write off the $40 billion in debt that Iraq amassed during the Iran-Iraq War. On February 23, 1990 at a summit meeting for the Arab Cooperation Council (ACC) Saddam reiterated his demands on the Arab World. It was a celebration of the one year anniversary of the ACC. Both King Hussein Bin Talal of Jordan and the Egyptian President Hosni Mubarak were present. At the celebration, Saddam brazenly made an anti-U.S. and anti-Israel speech. He criticized the U.S. presence in the Gulf Region and declared his purpose of attacking Israel in order to reverse the "rape of Palestine." Saddam declared that he would lead the Arab world in a fight against Israel and the U.S. Here Saddam is declaring himself the leader of the Arab world in the fight against the West and Israel. This is just a prelude to his true intentions of reestablishing the

Babylon Empire and creating one pan-Arab nation. Saddam did not differentiate between the U.S. and Israel in his hate-filled speech. He also announced that all Arab nations should forgive Iraq's War time debt. In addition to the written off debt, Saddam wanted $30 billion to pay for rebuilding Iraq. Saddam is quoted as saying, "Let the Gulf States know, that if they did not give this money to me, I would know how to get it."[157] Essentially Saddam is saying, forgive the debts or I will take what is mine by force as the true leader of the pan-Arab nation. The Gulf States ignored Saddam's threats, and OPEC continued with their increased production of oil which further depressed oil prices. Saddam especially felt that Kuwait should forgive Iraq's debts because he saw Kuwait as an extension of Iraq. The Kuwaiti emir refused to forgive Iraq's war time debt and to provide additional loans to Iraq for reconstruction.[158] The Egyptian President Hosni Mubarak was outraged at Saddam's blatant anti-U.S. speech. President Mubarak did not want to violate the Camp David Accords between Egypt and Israel. Also Egypt relied on U.S. aid. President Mubarak strongly rebuked Saddam for making such a hate filled anti-U.S. and anti-Israel speech. Furthermore, Mubarak told Saddam that asking the Arab countries to forgive his debt was "unjustified." This created a rift between Saddam and Mubarak that would never be repaired.[159]

In Saddam's desperation, he saw the Kuwaiti oil fields as a solution to Iraq's bankrupt economy. Historically Iraq had ties to Kuwait. Under the Ottoman Empire, Kuwait had been an Iraqi Province. After World War I with the fall of the Ottoman Empire, which was a German ally, Kuwait became a British protectorate. In 1962, Britain relinquished its rights to Kuwait which then became a sovereign nation. On June 25, 1962, Brigadier Abd al Karim Qasim, the Iraqi Prime Minister, made a declaration that Kuwait was an extension of Iraq. Geographically Iraq was at a huge disadvantage without the Kuwait territory. Without Kuwait as an Iraqi Province, Iraq had a very limited shoreline and shipping port.[160]

Evidence that Saddam was still working on the pursuit of a nuclear weapon became evident on March 28, 1990 when "five people were arrested at Heathrow Airport while trying to smuggle krytons or triggering devices that could be used in triggering an atomic device.... Two days later Saddam Hussein, proudly holding a kryton, told the world that Iraq had all the krytons it needed."[161] The British were tipped off by U.S. Intelligence about the smuggled krytons. Saddam was certain that the U.S. and Israel were plotting against him. This just motivated Saddam even more to continue on his anti-Israeli mission and his search for the possession of an atomic bomb.

At this sensitive time, President George Herbert Walker Bush sent a Congressional delegation led by Senator Dole to calm Saddam's fears that the U.S. was not plotting against Iraq. Saddam was terrified that sanctions would be enacted against Iraq at this vulnerable economic time for Iraq. The U.S. Congress was working on legislation that would suspend loans to Iraq.[162] This was due to the UN releasing information about the genocide of the Kurds. This put considerable economic pressure on Iraq, which made the forcible annexation of Kuwait seem more plausible.

On July 17, 1990 on the twenty-second anniversary of the Baath Revolution, Saddam gave Kuwait a written ultimatum. The ultimatum made the following demands on Kuwait:

1. Forgive Iraq's war debt,
2. Aid Iraq in its reconstruction,
3. Lessen oil production.

If Kuwait did not meet these demands, then Saddam would take action against Kuwait. On July 21 Saddam began deploying eight Republican Guard divisions, an estimated 120,000 troops, and 1,000 tanks to the Iraq-Kuwait border. Although the Saudis and Kuwaitis did not expect to be repaid for the war debt, they also did not think it would look good to publicly excuse the loans. The Saudis were deeply concerned about Saddam's threat and were willing to excuse the debt. The Saudis worked to convince the Kuwaiti emir to agree to Saddam's demands. Finally the Kuwaitis were persuaded to accept. On July 26 at an OPEC meeting, both Kuwait and the UAE agreed to lower oil production and to increasing oil prices. By this time it was too late. Saddam had already decided to invade Kuwait. Although Saddam was visibly preparing to invade Kuwait, on July 31, he still assured President George H.W. Bush and President Mubarak that he was not going to invade Kuwait.[163] The fact that Kuwait gave into Saddam's demands, and he still invaded, makes it obvious that Saddam was going to invade Kuwait no matter what.

In Saddam's Words

On April 3, 1990, Saddam Hussein made a threat on Iraqi radio to Israel "'Because by God, we will make the fire eat up half of Israel if it tries to do anything against Iraq.... We have the dual chemical. Whoever threatens us with the atomic bomb, we will annihilate him with the dual chemical."[164] There is a transcript (ISGQ-2003-M0006248) within the Pentagon report on Saddam that is a discussion about Iraq going to War with the U.S. This conversation took place on April 19, 1990 between Saddam Hussein, his cabinet members, Yasir Arafat, and a Palestinian delegation. The interesting thing is that at this time, Saddam had not yet invaded Kuwait. This was three months prior to Saddam's invasion of Kuwait. Saddam had made demands at the Arab conference three months earlier that Iraq's debts be forgiven, reconstruction funding be provided, and for a decrease in oil production. At the time, Saudi Arabia and Kuwait had not agreed to Saddam's demands. Saddam was already planning to invade Kuwait. He knew that when he invaded Kuwait, the U.S. would get involved. Saddam wanted the U.S. to attack Iraq. In this conversation Saddam says to Yasir Arafat, "As you said, when you were in Beirut..., 'it is time to die, and now I can smell the breeze of heavens', it is the same for us, as long as the small players are gone, and it is the time for America to play [directly], we are ready for it, we will fight America, and with God's [will] we will defeat it and kick it out of the whole region...." (Appendix, Figure 30) Remember that this is three months prior to Saddam giving Kuwait the written ultimatum. Here it is clear that Saddam has already decided to invade Kuwait and is planning for the inevitable battle with the U.S. that will follow. Saddam goes on to say that "if America strikes us, we will hit back. We said that before, you know us, we are not that talkative type of people that holds the microphone to say things only, we do what we say. **Maybe we cannot reach Washington but we can send someone who has explosive belt to reach Washington. Our missiles do not reach America, but I swear if it does! I would strike it.** We can't keep silent like this, while the Americans are hitting Arabs or Iraqis and say we can do nothing, yes we can, **we can send a lot [of] people to Washington just like the old days, for instance; the person with explosives' belt around him would throw himself on Bush's car.**" (Appendix, Figure 30) *Here Saddam is threatening the U.S. with terrorist attacks as retaliation to a U.S. strike against Iraq.* This is a prelude to the 1993 and 2001 World Trade Center attacks. Saddam is saying since I don't have missiles that can reach the American homeland, I will use terrorist attacks. Saddam continues by saying, "However, the American Bases, which are all over the world, in Turkey... etc, we can sweep them. We have to be ready for that level." Saddam's goals clearly are defined as follows:

1. Attack Kuwait and wait for the U.S. to strike Iraq;
2. Retaliate against the U.S and drive the U.S. military out of all Arab lands;
3. Attack all U.S. military bases in the world;
4. Attack Israel once and for all using chemical weapons.

Saddam says, "Iraq has Chemical weapon and successfully used it on Iranians, and Iraq won't think twice about Striking Israel with Chemical weapons."(Appendix, Figure 32) Saddam continues, "Maybe we [can] stop for 20 days, and then we hit back once upon time with rockets and Air Forces hitting Tel Aviv, we don't have to strike them daily; we will cho[o]se times so they will never [k]now [the] meaning of sleeping, we are a disaster, good and flexible people but once, if someone is stuck with us, we will not let him go unless he got on his knees, or crawl on the ground, we don't have something in the middle, **we don't want to negotiate, we don't want any mediators**, (looking at Yasir Arafat and Saying: Right Abu-'Ammar?, **Yasir Arafat Replies saying: yes 100%**). …**you either have an enemy or friend, you can't have something in the middle, they are two, to be a brother and friend on Arab level, or a friend on the world wide level, or enemy on world level."** Next Saddam says "coordinate with the Intelligence System Director and our Palestinian brothers to **check every single place that the Americans exist in, within the Middle East area, even if some American man came to Greek for trade, we have to know about him also. This is the battle; we have to be beasts in the battles, to remain beasts to the next**, (Yasir Arafat Says: Yes …**Beast**.)." (Appendix, Figure 31) This brings to mind the memo in chapter 1, Figure 2 which is a directive to hunt Americans on Arab soil. The memo is dated three years later, but the idea originated here before the Kuwait invasion. Here Saddam and Arafat are saying they want to know about every American that is on Arab soil, so they can hunt them down if necessary. Clearly Saddam wants a war with the U.S.

This transcript shows that Saddam invading Kuwait was much more insidious than just gaining new territory. Saddam knew in advance that the U.S. would intervene and most likely strike Iraq after it invaded Kuwait. Saddam was already planning on attacking the U.S., driving all Americans off Arab soil, and then when the time was right using chemical weapons on Israel. Saddam, in his own words, said that if Iraq had missiles that would reach the U.S., he would have used them. Since Iraq did not possess missiles that could reach the U.S., he would use terrorists to strike the U.S. Saddam was committed to using terrorism to attack the U.S. He had both the will and the means to coordinate with terrorists and attack the U.S. homeland. Both Saddam and Arafat made it clear that there is no negotiating with them. You are either with them or against them. Since Israel was an ally of the U.S., the U.S. was also the enemy of Iraq and the Palestinians.

Invasion of Kuwait

On August 2, 1990, Saddam invaded Kuwait. The 100,000 Iraqi troops overwhelmed the Kuwaiti forces and took control of the country. There was no resistance at the Kuwaiti border and minimal resistance once the Iraqi forces invaded Kuwait City. The Kuwait Air Force and Navy did not engage the enemy.[165] The Kuwaiti emir and his family were able to escape before troops arrived at the palace. Since Saddam had been making threats to Kuwait for months, the

Central Intelligence Agency (CIA) had worked out an escape plan for the emir and his family months prior. An elite Republican Guard unit had been ordered to go to the palace and take the emir and his family hostage. The emir would have been given an ultimatum to either stand down and allow Saddam to remotely rule Kuwait while the emir remains a figure head leader or be executed. The emir's brother, Sheik Fahd was at the palace when the troops arrived. He was shot to death by one of the Iraqi troops.

Soon after the initial invasion, Saddam announced that there was a provisional revolutionary government being set up. Saddam said that as soon as the provisional government was stable, the Iraqi troops would withdraw. Essentially Saddam was setting up a satellite government which would be run from Baghdad. On August 8, Saddam announced on his Baghdad Radio Network that the annexation of Kuwait was "irreversible" and it would be incorporating Kuwait into Iraq as its "19th Province." Saddam began to convert the Kuwaiti government agencies over to Iraq, while plundering Kuwait in the process. Kuwaiti citizens were encouraged to leave the country while Iraqi and Palestinian citizens relocated in Kuwait. Kuwait's administration services were reorganized while cities and streets were renamed to Iraqi names. Saddam ordered all "foreign embassies be closed, Iraqi currency substituted for Kuwaiti currency, and Iraqi identity cards, licenses, and personal papers issued to all residents. In addition, a great deal of equipment belonging to the Kuwaiti armed forces was removed to Iraq, as was about $4 billion in gold bars and foreign currency reserves from the central bank, 50,000 cars, the country's eighteen-month supply of foodstuffs, consumer goods, and valuables from shops and private homes."[166]

Now that Saddam had invaded Kuwait his goal was to delay any military action against Iraq and Kuwait for as long as possible. The international community was outraged by Saddam's invasion of Kuwait. Soon after the invasion, the U.S. imposed an economic embargo on Iraq. President George Herbert Walker Bush had all of Iraq's monies and investments in American companies frozen. The European nations and Japan soon followed by imposing economic sanctions on Iraq. Even the Communist countries, the Soviet Union and China, stopped all arms shipments to Iraq. The UN passed Resolution 660 which condemned Iraq's invasion of Kuwait. The UN wanted an unconditional cease-fire and for Iraq to withdraw from Kuwait. Early on, the Egyptian President Hosni Mubarak was the first Arab leader to denounce Saddam and call for an unconditional withdrawal of troops. Of course this infuriated Saddam. This would lead to Saddam ordering his Fedayeen troops along with al Qaida to execute missions against Egypt in order to destabilize the government. Next the UN passed Resolution 661 which imposed worldwide economic sanctions and an arms embargo on Iraq.[167] Although Saddam was in an extremely dire economic situation, his plan was coming into focus. Remember the transcript (ISGQ-2003-M0006248) where Saddam had met with Arafat three months prior to the invasion to discuss the upcoming war with the U.S. and Israel. Saddam knew all along that in taking action against Kuwait, America would strike Iraq.

This is exactly what Saddam wanted. Once Saddam had driven the Americans out of the Middle East what was his plan? Saddam planned on attacking Israel with chemical weapons that Iraq had perfected during the Iran-Iraq War. "Iraq has Chemical weapon and successfully used it on Iranians, and Iraq won't think twice about Striking Israel with Chemical weapons."

On August 3, 1990, President George H. W. Bush declared a national emergency with respect to Iraq. He quickly levied strict economic sanctions on Iraq. He issued two Executive Orders that "

- prohibit exports and imports of goods and services between the United States and Iraq and the purchase of Iraqi goods by U.S. persons for sale in third countries;
- prohibit transactions related to travel to or from Iraq, except for transactions necessary for journalistic travel or prompt departure from Iraq;
- prohibit transactions related to transportation to or from Iraq, or the use of vessels or aircraft registered in Iraq by U.S. persons;
- prohibit the performance of any contract in support of Government of Iraq projects;
- ban all extensions of credit and loans by U.S. persons to the Government of Iraq;
- block all property of the Government of Iraq now or hereafter located in the United States or in the

> possession or control of U.S. persons, including their foreign branches; and
> - prohibit all transfers or other transactions involving assets belonging to the Government of Kuwait now or hereafter located in the United States or in the possession or control of U.S. persons, including their foreign branches."[168]

President George H.W. Bush took decisive action to quickly impede Iraq's invasion of Kuwait. He explained to the U.S. Congress that "The measures we are taking to block Iraqi assets will have the effect of expressing our outrage at Iraq's actions, and will prevent that government from drawing on monies and properties within U.S. control to support its campaign of military aggression against a neighboring state. Our ban on exports to Iraq will prevent the Iraqi government from profiting from the receipt of U.S. goods and technology. Our ban on imports, while not preventing sales of Iraqi oil to third countries, denies Iraq access to the lucrative U.S. market for its most important product. We are calling upon our friends and allies, and all members of the world community who share our interest in the peaceful resolution of international disputes, to join us in similar actions against Iraq and for the protection of Kuwait."[169]

With international pressure mounting, Saddam announced that he would begin to withdraw troops on August 5, "unless something emerges that threatens the security of Kuwait and Iraq."[170] This was just another ploy to buy time. Saddam wanted to "to fracture and undermine the U.S.-led coalition… and undermine or circumvent the sanctions which had been imposed after the invasion of Kuwait."[171] Although Saddam was saying he would withdraw troops, he was secretly planning for war. "In August, Iraq dispersed its inventory of Al-Hussein missiles from the central missile support facility at Taji to deployment areas in western and southern Iraq as a defensive measure and to ready them for possible retaliatory strikes. In addition, the army transferred chemical munitions to air bases and storage bunkers in southern Iraq, and established several decontamination facilities."[172] Saddam threatened that any attacks on Iraq or Kuwait would be addressed with force. He went on to assure the U.S. and Saudi Arabia that Iraq would not invade Saudi Arabia. Saudi Arabia did not trust Saddam and was concerned about Iraqi troops that had been advancing near their border. Both the Saudi King and the Kuwaiti emir asked President George H. W. Bush for U.S. troops to be deployed to Saudi Arabia in order to protect Saudi Arabia from further Iraqi aggression. On August 8, 1990, President Bush addressed the nation and announced that he would deploy U.S. troops to Saudi Arabia to protect them from Iraq. "In the life of a nation, we're called upon to define who we are and what we believe. Sometimes these choices are not easy. But today as President, I ask for your support in a decision I've made to stand up for what's right and condemn what's wrong, all in the cause of peace. Four simple principles guide our policy:

- First, we seek the immediate, unconditional, and complete withdrawal of all Iraqi forces from Kuwait.

- Second, Kuwait's legitimate government must be restored to replace the puppet regime.
- And third, my administration, as has been the case with every President from President Roosevelt to President Reagan, is committed to the security and stability of the Persian Gulf.
- And fourth, I am determined to protect the lives of American citizens abroad....

But we must recognize that Iraq may not stop using force to advance its ambitions. Iraq has massed an enormous war machine on the Saudi border capable of initiating hostilities with little or no additional preparation. Given the Iraqi government's history of aggression against its own citizens as well as its neighbors, to assume Iraq will not attack again would be unwise and unrealistic. And therefore, after consulting with King Fahd, I sent Secretary of Defense Dick Cheney to discuss cooperative measures we could take. Following those meetings, the Saudi Government requested our help, and I responded to that request by ordering U.S. air and ground forces to deploy to the Kingdom of Saudi Arabia.... Let me be clear: The sovereign independence of Saudi Arabia is of vital interest to the United States. This decision, which I shared with the congressional leadership, grows out of the longstanding friendship and security relationship between the United States and Saudi Arabia. U.S. forces will work together with those of Saudi Arabia and other nations to preserve the integrity of Saudi Arabia and to deter further Iraqi aggression. Through their presence, as well as through training and exercises, these multinational forces will enhance the overall capability of Saudi Armed Forces to defend the Kingdom. I want to be clear about what we are doing and why. America does not seek conflict, nor do we seek to chart the destiny of other nations. But America will stand by her friends. The mission of our troops is wholly defensive. Hopefully, they will not be needed long. They will not initiate hostilities, but they will defend themselves, the Kingdom of Saudi Arabia, and other friends in the Persian Gulf."[173]

Saddam began to publicly tie the Kuwait invasion to the Palestinian-Israeli conflict. On August 13, 1990, Saddam made a public address on Iraqi radio about the Persian Gulf Crisis. Saddam said, "I propose that all cases of occupation, and those cases that have been portrayed as occupation, in the region, be resolved simultaneously and on the same principles and basis that should be laid down by the Security Council, as follows:

- preparation for an immediate and unconditional Israeli withdrawal from occupied Arab lands in Palestine, Syria and Lebanon;
- a Syrian withdrawal from Lebanon;
- mutual withdrawals by Iraq and Iran and arrangement for the situation in Kuwait.

All military withdrawals and all related political arrangements should take into consideration *Iraq's historical territorial rights* and guarantee the Kuwaiti people's right to decide on their future. Should the United States, its allies and its agents fail to respond to our initiative, then we as the people of Iraq along with our brethren in the Arab world will resist its evil intentions and aggressive schemes. We will fight America's evil plans, with help from the good people of our Arab nation and our great Iraqi people, and we will be victorious with God's help. The evil-doers will regret their acts when they are *driven out in shame from the region*."[174] Here we see that Saddam was boldly proclaiming his true intentions. Saddam is reiterating Iraq's territorial rights on Kuwait.

Yes he wanted Kuwait annexed, but he also wanted to lead the Arab world in a fight against the U.S and ultimately Israel. Saddam was trying to pit himself against the evil U.S in order to rally the Arab world. Saddam was saying Iraq will withdraw from Kuwait if Israel withdraws from Palestine. This goes back to his speech made in Jordan where he proclaimed to reverse the "rape of Palestine" and would lead the Arab world in a war against the U.S. and Israel. Prior to having access to the transcript (ISGQ-2003-M0006248) between Saddam and Arafat made public, the pundits saw Saddam's actions as changing frantically as the stakes increased with the U.S. and international community imposing harsh embargos and limits on Iraq. Now with this transcript, we know that Saddam's ultimate goal was war with the U.S. and the annihilation of Israel. Even beyond the destruction of Israel, Saddam wanted to recreate the Babylon Empire. If Saddam was able to destroy Israel he then would be able to rally the Arab world behind him as the true leader of the Arabs. If they did not accept him, he would forcefully take the territory that he believed belonged to Iraq and the Babylon Empire. Then Saddam could become the leader of one pan-Arab nation. With the West out of the Persian Gulf, he could actually recreate the Babylon Empire. Saddam would not have stopped with Kuwait, this was just the beginning.

Saddam began to openly warn the West that terrorist attacks would be made against the West in the event of a military attack on Iraq. Abu al-Abbas, head of the Palestine Liberation Front, vowed to attack Western targets in Europe and the Middle East if the West attacked Iraq. The Palestinian Liberation Front is affiliated with the Palestinian Liberation Organization (PLO) that Arafat led. Abu al-Abbas was a known terrorist who had "fled to Iraq to avoid an Italian warrant imposing five life terms for his part in the 1985 hijacking of the Italian cruise liner *Achille Lauro* and the murder of an American citizen."[175] Saddam gave Abu al-Abbas sanctuary in Iraq. Saddam allowed Abu al-Abbas and his wife to live in Iraq under Saddam's protection. Both Abbas and his wife were issued Iraqi diplomatic passports so they could travel the Middle East freely.

On August 19, 1990, Saddam announced that he would hold all foreign nationals that were currently in Iraq and Kuwait. This amounted to nearly two million foreigners being held hostage in Iraq and Kuwait.[176] In a radio address Saddam said that particularly "in the case of those 'whose governments have a hostile position and are taking part in the preparations for aggression and the economic embargo against Iraq,' was designed to open 'a deep dialogue' for a peaceful resolution of the crisis and the averting of war."[177] While Saddam was taking thousands of men, women, and children hostage, he was trying to mask it by saying this is a means to a peaceful resolution.

On August 21, Saddam began moving the hostages to strategic military and industrial installations in order to use them as "human shields."[178] Saddam was first and foremost using the hostages to protect important industrial and military installations from attack. Saddam was also using the hostages to threaten the alliance of nations that was against him. He wanted to use the hostages as bargaining chips in order to drive a wedge between the coalition nations that were against him. On August 25, the Austrian President, Kurt Waldheim, traveled to Baghdad to negotiate the release of the Austrian hostages. President Waldheim was the only Western president to visit Baghdad. Waldheim was shunned by the other Western leaders because he had tried to cover up the fact that he fought with the German Army in the Balkans during World War II. He kept close ties to Middle Eastern leaders while being alienated by Western leaders. Since Waldheim had been a Nazi, it is no wonder he traveled to Baghdad and gave Saddam a chance at relaying his position on Kuwait. Saddam used the opportunity to conduct a press conference and announced that he would release all 140 Austrians that were being held in Iraq and Kuwait.[179]

On August 24, 1990 Saddam made a propaganda video of him visiting with English speaking hostages. He wanted to show that the hostages were being treated well. Saddam used the opportunity to explain his point of view in invading Kuwait. Saddam said "In any case, the Arab nation is one nation. It's a single nation. British colonial rule scissored away - cut away - the Arab nation. All that happened was for this spot, this particular part, called Kuwait, has now come back to its motherland."[180] During his visit with the hostages he spoke directly to a child who had the look of fear on his face. The international community was outraged so Saddam decided to release all women and children on August 29, 1990.[181]

On August 20 President George H. W. Bush issued the National Security Directive 45 regarding the U.S policy in Response to the Iraqi invasion of Kuwait. In the directive, President H. W. Bush reiterated the principles he issued in his national address and that he wanted to try to find a peaceful solution to the Kuwait invasion. He asked for the Secretary of State to continue to work bilaterally with U.S. allies and the international community to "find a peaceful solution to end the Iraqi occupation of Kuwait and to restore Kuwait's legitimate government."[182] Looking at the situation, Saddam seemed to be in a very difficult place. Once the U.S. demands are met, Iraq would be back in the dire economic state it was in before Iraq invaded Kuwait. Knowing what we now know from the transcript between Saddam and Arafat three months prior to the invasion, Saddam was right where he wanted to be in the prelude of a war with the U.S.

In preparation for war against the U.S., Saddam rallied Arab nations into a jihad against Saudi Arabia and the U.S. Saddam said that Saudi Arabia had "defiled Islam's holiest shrines by allowing the presence of Western troops on their territory: 'Arab, Muslims, believers in God, wherever you are. This is the day for you to stand up and defend Mecca, which is the captive of the spears of the Americans and Zionists.... The rulers there not only disregarded their people and the Arab nation; not only challenged their people and the Arab nation; but challenged God when they placed Mecca and the tomb of the prophet Muhammad under foreign protection.'"[183] By changing the focus into a holy war against the West, Saddam hoped to rally the Arab nations around him to his cause.

In order to give himself time to maneuver, Saddam began to renew relations with old allies. First he negotiated with the Soviet Union. At a time when the Soviet Union was on the brink of its own economic collapse, Saddam offered them free oil supplies. On September 4, the Soviet Foreign Minister, Edward Shevardnadze, specifically linked the invasion of Kuwait to the Arab-Israeli conflict that had long plagued the Middle East. He asked that Israel participate in an international peace conference. The Soviets argued on Saddam's behalf that he be given maneuvering room.[184]

Next Saddam negotiated with France who had been an ally in the past. Remember that during the mid-1970's Saddam sent a high ranking Baath official to Paris. Under the guise of agricultural development, Saddam set up its first bacteriological laboratory. In a very public display, Saddam released all French workers that were being held in Kuwait. On September 24, President Francois Mitterrand addressed the UN General Assembly and proclaimed that the invasion of Kuwait was linked to the Arab-Israeli conflict. President Mitterrand demanded that Iraq comply with the UN resolution to pull out of Kuwait. He also pronounced that Iraq may have some legitimate territorial claims on Kuwait. Finally, President Mitterrand announced that a Middle East peace conference would follow the resolution of the Iraq-Kuwait conflict. The fact that France had negotiated a private deal with Iraq outraged the international community especially the U.S. Saddam even released information regarding the meeting he had with France in hopes this would turn the other countries against each other. It actually backfired and made France's claims illegitimate. France embarrassingly removed itself from the negotiations regarding Iraq.[185]

On October 1, 1990, President George H. W. Bush reiterated in an address to the United Nations that there must be an unconditional withdrawal from Kuwait. He said that Kuwait must be restored to its previous government. President George H. W. Bush said "Let me take this opportunity to make the policy of my government clear. The United States supports the use of sanctions to compel Iraq's leaders to withdraw immediately and without condition from Kuwait. We also support the provision of medicine and food for humanitarian purposes, so long as distribution can be properly monitored. Our quarrel is not with the people of Iraq. We do not wish for them to suffer. The world's quarrel is with the dictator who ordered that invasion.

Along with others, we have dispatched military forces to the region to enforce sanctions, to deter and, if need be, defend against further aggression. And we seek no advantage for ourselves, nor do we seek to maintain our military forces in Saudi Arabia for 1 day longer than is necessary. U.S. forces were sent at the request of the Saudi Government, and the American people and this President want every single American soldier brought home as soon as this mission is completed.

Let me also emphasize that all of us here at the U.N. hope that military force will never be used. We seek a peaceful outcome, a diplomatic outcome. And one more thing: In the aftermath of Iraq's unconditional departure from Kuwait, I truly believe there may be opportunities for Iraq and Kuwait to settle their differences permanently, for the states of the Gulf themselves to build new arrangements for stability, and for all the states and the peoples of the region to settle the conflicts that divide the Arabs from Israel."[186]

Saddam's plan to shift the impasse of the invasion of Kuwait to the Arab-Israeli conflict had seemingly worked. We know that the invasion of Kuwait was about the Palestinian-Israeli conflict because of the transcript (ISGQ-2003-M0006248) where Saddam had met with Arafat three months prior to the Kuwait invasion. Saddam talked about driving the U.S out of the Persian Gulf region and then attacking Israel with chemical weapons. Ultimately Saddam wanted to create one pan-Arab nation with him at the helm. Kuwait was just the beginning of his recreation of the Babylon Empire.

Saddam continued to maneuver his position by limiting the coalition against him. He only wanted Western countries in alliance against him. In order to get other countries out of the Western alliance, he offered financial incentives to other nations. In September he offered to supply Third World Nations with free oil. Similar financial incentives were given to the Soviet Union and China.[187] These bribes were made to narrow the coalition.

While publicly Saddam was trying to diplomatically negotiate with the coalition, secretly he was planning for war and terrorist attacks against the coalition forces. From the Pentagon report on Saddam we know that secretly Saddam was ordering his Fedayeen troops to begin infiltrating Saudi Arabia for terrorist activities. The Fedayeen was Saddam's personal army that answered directly to him and operated separate from the regular Iraqi Army. In a memo dated November 28, 1990 (see Appendix, Figure 34, 35) Saddam ordered his Fedayeen forces to sabotage an American Oil Company in Saudi Arabia called ARAMCO. In the same memo, it describes sending a Fedayeen member to Saudi Arabia in order to create a secure base for Unit (999) members. Unit (999) was a Fedayeen battalion dedicated to deep reconnaissance and private missions.[188] Members of Unit 999 were trained in the following:

a) "Introduction to explosives and other elements pertaining to terrorism."
b) Use of dough and plastic explosives.
c) Practical training on use of explosives and timed electronic devices.
d) Ways to destroy buildings, oil refineries, pipes, and planting car explosives. (see Appendix, Figure 41)

While Saddam was publicly releasing hostages and trying to negotiate with various countries, he was secretly contacting Anti-American terrorist groups around the globe to perform terrorist acts against the U.S. In a memo dated September 14, 1990 (ISGP-2003-00011487), it says that representatives of the Iraqi Intelligence Service (IIS) in Bangkok, Thailand met with two representatives of the Sri

Lankan Socialist Student federation that were willing to carry out "suicidal activities against American targets in Thailand." (see Appendix, Figure 42)

<u>The Stage Is Set</u>

Now Saddam has set the stage for his true plan. We know from the transcript between Saddam and Arafat that Kuwait was just one part of Saddam's plan. Saddam wanted a war with the U.S. and ultimately with Israel. On November 19, 1990, Saddam announced that he would release all Western hostages by the end of March 1991. By doing this, Saddam was attempting to delay any attacks on Iraq until the end of March. This would have given him an advantage because he would have more time to prepare. In addition, Iraq gets extremely hot during the Spring season which would work to their advantage. The Iraqi troops would be used to these harsh conditions while the coalition troops would not. On November 29, the United Nations Security Council adopted Resolution 678 (S/RES/0678 (1990)) which reaffirmed previous resolutions (660-677) and demanded that Saddam withdraw Iraqi troops from Kuwait by January 15, 1991. If Saddam did not comply, then the coalition nations could use force to remove Iraqi troops from Kuwait. On December 6, Saddam announced that he would release all hostages in the hopes to gain international support. In late December in a televised interview, Saddam said that "In the event of war, he would attack Israel, launch terrorist attacks against U.S. interests around the world, use foreign detainees as human shields at strategic installations, and destroy oil installations in Saudi Arabia and elsewhere in the region leading to economic chaos and environmental disaster."[189] These threats did not deter President George H. W. Bush from standing firm in his resolve for Saddam to withdraw unconditionally from Kuwait. On January 9, President George H. W. Bush called on the U.S. Congress to adopt a resolution for the use of force against Iraq if it did not withdraw unconditionally from Kuwait by January 15.[190]

In Appendix, Figure 7, memo 110/2/43 says that Saddam met with an organizational representative of al Qaida on December 14, 1990. Let's take a closer look at this. Saddam met with an al Qaida representative during this Kuwait crisis after he had invaded Kuwait and was trying to delay any attacks on Iraq. We see here in the midst of this crisis, Saddam was scheming with al Qaida. Here the plan was "to move against the Egyptian regime through Fedayeen operations, provided we guarantee them (TC:Financial) aid training and whatever they need." The Fedayeen and al Qaida were working together to destabilize Egypt. They wanted Mubarak removed from office. Al Qaida wanted to overthrow Mubarak to institute an Islamic regime. Remember Saddam was furious with Mubarak for siding with the U.S. against him.

In a related memo (see Appendix, Figure 43) dated March 18, 1993, it says that Iraq "stopped targeting Egypt Promptly after the cease fire." Instead Saddam ordered that the Fedayeen forces along with al Qaida work together "**to execute Fedayeen operations against the coalition countries that are against us.**" This is a directive from

Saddam to his Fedayeen forces and al Qaida. Isn't it interesting that al Qaida is the same group that carried out the 1993 World Trade Center bombing? This is just three years before the attack on the World Trade Center. First Saddam worked with al Qaida to attack the Egyptian regime during the Kuwait invasion. Once the cease-fire was agreed upon, he reassigned them to **attack the coalition countries**. Clearly in this memo we see that Saddam was not only financing and training al Qaida, but he was giving them directives. More importantly he gave this directive *after* the Kuwait cease fire only three years before the 1993 World Trade Center bombing. Even more interesting is the fact that Iraq had agreed on the cease fire to begin February 26, 1990. The 1993 World Trade Center bombing occurred on February 26, 1993. Some experts think Iraq was sending a message to America. Now that we have access to memo 110/2/43, we see that Saddam gave the order to attack **coalition countries** and this order was given to the same al Qaida affiliate (IG) that carried out the 1993 World Trade Center bombing.

On January 12, 1991 Saddam spoke at an Islamic conference held in Baghdad in order to continue his call for *jihad* against the West. When Saddam entered the convention hall, he was given a standing ovation while attendees yelled "God is Great!" in Arabic. Many of the attendees embraced Saddam. "A Sudanese delegate said, 'We are with you,' while a tearful Bangladeshi delegate said, 'You must defeat the Israelis and drive the American infidels out of Saudi Arabia.' One American delegate, the Rev. Louis Farrakhan, leader of the Chicago-based Nation of Islam, also delivered a personal greeting to Mr.

Hussein and warned in a news conference that Mr. Hussein and President Bush were on a 'collision course.' Mr. Farrakhan later called on the United States to step back and allow a court of Islamic scholars to settle the dispute between Iraq and Kuwait and save 'thousands of American lives.' ... Baghdad's mosques were filled with worshipers who heard uniformly militant sermons from prayer leaders calling for a jihad, or holy war, against the Western 'infidels' and 'atheists sullying the land of the holy shrines' in Western Saudi Arabia, as one sermon put it." In Saddam's speech he "defended his invasion of Kuwait as an attempt to end the 'corruption' of the Kuwaiti royal family and to 'purify Islam.' Again he tied the Palestinian-Israeli issue to the Kuwait invasion. Saddam continued by saying "If the international community behaved in a balanced manner all things would be open for application of international legitimacy.... Whether they solve the problem according to international law or not, Palestine will return to the Palestinians."[191] Brilliantly Saddam has turned his illegal and immoral invasion of Kuwait into an *Islamic jihad*. We know this was his intention from the beginning. He was prepared to bring War to the region in order to drive out the U.S. from the Persian Gulf and then attack Israel. Saddam declared *jihad* against America and the West. This was just the beginning of the declaration of jihad that Usama Bin Laden and al Qaida would echo in years to come. Is it any surprise that Saddam and al Qaida were working together? They had the same goals, to attack America and Israel.

Mother of All Battles

On January 15, 1991 Baghdad was eerily silent for two days. Coalition forces had been routinely carrying out training operations near the Iraq-Saudi border. As a result, when the actual attack started, the Iraqis were taken by surprise. On January 17, "At 2:39 AM …Army Apache helicopters, led by three Air Force MH-53s, attacked two Iraqi early warning sites up on the frontier."[192] This created an opening for other aircraft to carry out their missions. F-15E jets were then able to attack several Scud missile sites in Western Iraq. Two EF-111 aircrafts supported the F-15E aircraft by providing electronic support. The EF-111's jammed the Iraqi radar. As the first Apache helicopters crossed the border at 2:39 AM, two F-117's were already on their way to Baghdad. At 2:51 AM, their first Baghdad target was the Nukhayb Intercept Operations Center. This was the central reporting station that would most likely detect the F-15E strikes. In Baghdad, one of the first sites bombed was the AT&T Building and the Telecommunications Center. This resulted in all telephone and television communications being destroyed. Five minutes later six more F-117's bombed the Baghdad air force headquarters, the air defense operating center, the presidential palace, the Tallil Sector Operations Center, and the Salman Pak Intercept Operations Center.[193]

In an extraordinary execution of air power, the coalition air forces had successfully crippled Iraq's defenses. Within 48 hours of Desert Storm, most of Iraq's electricity and telecommunications were shutdown. Its air defenses were severely disabled. Coalition air losses were extremely low. On January 19, bad weather hampered the coalition air forces success. Even with the bad weather, a significant number of strikes occurred. The Ministry of Defense and the Air Defense Operations Center were primary targets that required several bombing runs to be completely destroyed.

    The primary targets on day three were Scud missile and air defense targets. Through U.S. intelligence, the locations of 64 scud missile fixed launch sites had been discovered. These scud missile sites were bombed by the U.S. In addition to the fixed launch sites, the Iraqis also possessed several mobile missile launchers. Estimates were in the high twenties. They also possessed decoy mobile launchers to throw off U.S. bombers. On January 18, Iraq launched eight scud missiles at Israel. The missiles did not cause much damage, but concern over chemical weapons being used raised fears. Saddam had threatened to attack Israel if Iraq was attacked and he did. He hoped Israel would retaliate to change the War from Iraq against the world to the Arab nations against Israel and the West. His tactic failed. President George H. W. Bush was able to convince Israel not to retaliate. Bush knew the danger if Israel entered the War. The coalition including the Arab nations stood firm against Saddam. During the War, Iraq launched missiles at Saudi Arabia and Israel. The U.S. Army deployed Patriot batteries to Israel and Saudi Arabia. Although the anti-scud Patriot batteries proved unsuccessful during the War, they did provide psychological support. An estimated 13 scuds launched against Israel were destroyed by the Patriot batteries.[194]

The second defensive move that Saddam took was to sabotage the Kuwait oil fields. Saddam ordered that the oil pipeline from the Kuwait oil fields be opened up so that the oil would drain out into the open sea. This was the Kuwaiti pipeline that filled tanker ships. In response, Lieutenant General Horner and Brigadier General Buster Glosson derived a plan to use precision guided missiles to blow up the pumping stations and shut off valves. Within a few days, F-111Fs destroyed the pumping stations and severed the pipeline itself preventing an ecological catastrophe.[195]

By January 23, the coalition forces had control of the air. In addition, the electrical power had been shut off to most of Iraq and the military and telecommunications infrastructure had been severely damaged. Even with this allied success, Saddam showed no sign of surrender.

Although the allied air campaign had been successful, there was a concern that the Iraqi Air Force might try to exercise an all out offensive on the coalition troops. Thus far, most of the Iraqi aircraft remained intact. They had been protected by hardened shelters which Saddam had acquired from the Soviets. In early 1991, Iraq made an agreement with Iran to move military and civilian aircraft to Iran for safekeeping. In order to prevent an Iraqi air assault, on January 21 coalition aircraft began bombing these shelters. Coalition forces "dropped 2,000-pound, laser guided bombs"[196] on the shelters. By the end of the war, the coalition forces had destroyed or damaged 63% of the shelters. With the increasing number of shelters being hit, Iraq decided to fly the remaining aircraft to Iran. Except for the first week of the war,

Iraqi aircraft had not engaged the coalition forces in the air. With this large scale movement of Iraqi aircraft to Iran, the coalition fighter pilots began to engage the Iraqi pilots. The coalition fighter pilots were quite successful in shooting down many of the Iraqi planes. The "shelter-busting campaign" successfully obliterated the Iraqi Air Force from being a threat.[197]

General H. Norman Schwarzkopf, Commander-in-Chief of the US Central Command, wanted to move the coalition forces focus onto preparing for the ground campaign. Now that the coalition forces were in full control of the air, Lieutenant General Horner was prepared to engage the Republican Guard. In order to attack the Republican Guard, Lieutenant General Horner, decided to "rely on 'penetration and heavy bombers' to attack the enemy's artillery, supplies, and armor."[198] By January 26, Lieutenant General Horner said "We are where we need to be to shift the emphasis to the Republican Guards."[199] F-111F crews were able to use their infrared receivers to pick up distinct signatures of tanks and other military equipment in the desert. The metal of the vehicles and equipment cooled at a different rate than the sand in the evening. The F-111Fs successfully launched laser guided bombs targeting dug-in Republican Guard armor and artillery. On February 24, the F111Fs concentrated their attacks on ground forces. More specifically the Republican Guard ground troops that were located along the Iraq-Kuwait border were targeted. In addition, the Iraqi leadership and command and control units were targeted. These had changed from the beginning of the war. The centers of command and control would relocate as needed. These strikes were to hit the command and control locations that were currently in use. In all wars mistakes are made. The Al Firdos bunker was targeted. U.S. intelligence said it was an activated command post, but it was also being used as a civilian bomb shelter. It turns out the shelter was actually a command post and a civilian shelter. Saddam had built large bunkers used as military command posts below bunkers used as civilian shelters. This is a direct violation of the "Geneva Convention to hide military commanders behind women and children."[200] These bunkers were not being used by common people, but by the Iraqi elite. Once the U.S. realized they had hit a bunker being used as a civilian shelter, they ended the strikes at these command post bunkers. Next the political Baath leadership headquarters were targeted. Targets such as the Ministry of Defense, Baath Party Headquarters, and Baghdad Presidential Bunker were hit.[201]

The ground offensive lasted only 100 hours. The Soviet Union had been negotiating a cease fire plan with Iraq. At the United Nations, the Soviet Union delegates announced that Iraq had submitted a letter to the Soviets saying that Iraq would comply with all twelve UN Security Resolutions. "By noon on February 26 the Iraqi troops had withdrawn from Kuwait City and its suburbs." On February 27, 1991, Bush declared a cease-fire. President George H. W. Bush said that as long as Iraq did not fire any missiles at coalition forces or neighboring countries, the cease fire would remain intact.[202]

Let's see what the Pentagon Report on Saddam has to say about the terms of the cease fire. In a transcript labeled as ISGQ-2003-

M0003964, Saddam has a conversation with his command members discussing the cease-fire and withdrawal. The command members in the conversation are Saddam, Abu Usama, and Abu Ahmad. Saddam begins by saying that if the U.S. and its allies do not accept the initiation of the cease fire by the Soviet Union, then "Iraq will cooperate with the Kuwaiti political and religious organizations in order to erect a national democratic rule." (See Appendix, Figure 46) Saddam is still trying to find a way to influence the government of Kuwait.

Later in the conversation the command members discuss that all traces of the West need to be erased as soon as possible. Abu Usama says "we need to launch a celebration and a victory campaign, in a positive method, in order to execute the enemy traces, which affected our people. I mean launching campaigns to remove the traces as fast as possible, for example, just like ... [after] World War II, to erase the war effect on the Armenian women's behaviors." (Appendix, Figures 46 and 47) In order to accomplish this Saddam replies that "We must first erase the negativity, sins and then the other issues." Abu Usama goes on to say that "By the name of Allah sir, you should engrave at every city entrance, and on every rock, how many attacks were launched on it by the enemy..." Saddam replies "Wow Abu-Usama! I am impressed with your way of thinking. You are right. Why do you think we trusted the prophets? It is because they recorded every incident." Abu Usama says that each attack should be recorded so that a museum can be built to remember what the U.S. did to Iraq. Abu Usama says "Every city keeps its record, in order to record the martyrs, numbers of the children and the numbers of the women. Every city will obtain photos of the destroyed buildings, in the event we build a museum, in the future." Saddam agrees that this will be a good way to memorialize and show the Arab world how terrible America has been. Saddam says "**As well as improving negativity among them. Let the Arabs, when they come to visit the first time, to observe what the betrayer Americans have done.**"

His command members discuss making a movie to show how evil the Americans were in their attacks of Iraq. They also discuss creating a radio station that will be used to explain to the Arab world the horrible things that America and the West perpetrated on Iraq. Specifically they want to make Saudi Arabia and Egypt look bad since they fought against Iraq. Abu Usama says, "We must establish... a radio station.... We need to establish a research center, as well, connected to this radio station, its main task is to search for numbers, facts and documents in regards to the Gulf corruptions. **Moreover, it will broadcast to the region regularly, in connection to their [Saudi Arabia and Egypt] budget, their money, their scandals and their Western investments... then we end the truce period**. Lately, when the Gulf was granted truce, his [Saudi Arabia and Egypt] corruption and his money were in peace, and everything else." Saddam replies "On a political and diplomatic level, it is considered inappropriate; however, we may wait for a while, a year or six months. I suggest that we think this over." A little later in the conversation Abu Usama again brings up the radio station and says "We will expose them [Saudi

Arabia] to the Arab Nation and to the whole world, in order for the world to hear…" An unidentified male voice says "Even the Shiite countries, we created banners asking them to listen to our station." Saddam replies, **"Okay, then we must concentrate on our Arab nation. Am I right? In addition, to our [Baath] party and all the good people, I mean not just our party. Whoever is following the same path; we must support him and help him**." This clearly shows that Saddam wants to work with any group that is against America, Egypt, or Saudi Arabia. When Saddam says "we must concentrate on our Arab nation", he is reiterating his goal for one pan-Arab nation with Iraq at the helm. This was the Baathist pan-Arab goal to have one Arab nation.

Next the conversation turns to withdrawing troops from Kuwait. They are concerned the coalition forces may try to attack the Iraqis upon withdrawal. Saddam says "I do not believe that the Americans will accept this project easily as it is, they might try to agitate the situation, through other tricks, and this is the first aspect. The other aspect is I am not comfortable with the Kuwaiti's restraint in the first four days, in Qazim City. It is a very devastating situation, since Kuwait is located by the ocean, if we withdraw in the first four days, the opening area will be inside our region. Kuwait or the American army could enter through it; therefore, we are not sure of what they might use as an excuse, in the event we withdraw." Saddam says that the troops will be withdrawn on the last day at night. He says "They will withdraw from Kuwait City, on the fourth day." Abu Usama suggests assassinating the Prince of Kuwait. Abu Usama says "Sir, could we assassinate the Prince of Kuwait upon his entrance to Kuwait?" All of the command members laugh.

Having the Pentagon report on Saddam revealed to us shows that Saddam's intentions toward Kuwait were much more insidious than just adding new territory to Iraq. Yes Saddam wanted the Kuwaiti oil fields, but this was just the beginning. In his mind, this invasion would bring about war with the U.S. and Israel. Saddam wanted to drive the Americans out of the Middle East and destroy Israel.

Taking into context the huge effort Saddam was taking to rebuild the Babylon Empire, it only makes sense that next he would have invaded and tried to further incorporate more Arab territory into Iraq. One thing is for sure nothing was going to stop Saddam except force. He was prepared to suffer through any and all embargos. He had such a grip on the nation of Iraq, no other group was able to overthrow him. Saddam did not see the cease fire as the end of the Gulf War. He was already plotting terrorist attacks against America. This is clear in memo 140/D1/4/1 where it says that after the cease fire Saddam made an agreement with al Qaida for Fedayeen operations to be carried out against the **coalition countries.** "On 24 December 1990, we agreed with the representative of the Islamic Organized Group in Egypt on a plan to move against the Egyptian Regime through conducting Fedayeen operations provided we secure for them financial aid, training, and other things, **based upon orders from the esteemed Presidency to execute Fedayeen operations against the coalition**

countries that are against us. We stopped targeting Egypt Promptly after the cease fire." (Appendix, Figure 43)

Although the cease fire for the first Gulf War had been agreed upon, Saddam was still determined to not comply with *all* of the UN Resolutions. On the 26th, at a UN Security council session, the Soviet delegation announced that Saddam had formerly notified Mr. Gorbachev that he was willing to withdraw his troops from Kuwait and comply only with the UN Resolution 660. Essentially UN Resolution 660 condemned the invasion of Kuwait, called for an unconditional withdrawal from Kuwait, and called upon Kuwait and Iraq to diplomatically negotiate a resolution. It did not specify that Kuwait was a sovereign nation. More specifically, it was UN Resolution 661 that declared Kuwait's sovereignty and demanded that the legitimate Kuwaiti government be reinstated. Saddam refused to accept Kuwait as a sovereign nation. As a result, the U.S. and other coalition nations did not recognize his withdrawal as a cease fire.[203]

As the Iraqi troops were withdrawing, they were still engaging the coalition forces. In fact Saddam launched a scud attack on U.S. military barracks after he made the announcement that his troops were withdrawing. This scud attack was the deadliest attack for coalition forces of all engagements in the Gulf War. The scud attack was on U.S. military barracks located in Saudi Arabia. In the attack, twenty-seven Americans were killed along with ninety-eight wounded. As coalition forces moved into Kuwait and reached the Kuwait International Airport, Iraqi troops led a stiff resistance. As a result,

President George H. W. Bush addressed the nation on February 26, 1991 and said that Saddam would not accept the coalition terms and was still engaging coalition forces. Until Saddam accepted all of the UN Resolutions, the coalition would still engage the enemy. President George H. W. Bush asked that the Iraqi soldiers lay down their arms and withdraw.[204]

On February 27, 1991, President George H.W. Bush addressed the nation by saying "Kuwait is liberated." He went on to say in order for the cease fire to become permanent, the following demands must be met: "Iraq must release immediately all coalition prisoners of war, third country nationals, and the remains of all who have fallen. Iraq must release all Kuwaiti detainees. Iraq also must inform Kuwaiti authorities of the location and nature of all land and sea mines. Iraq must comply fully with all relevant United Nations Security Council resolutions. This includes a rescinding of Iraq's August decision to annex Kuwait and acceptance in principle of Iraq's responsibility to pay compensation for the loss, damage, and injury its aggression has caused. The coalition calls upon the Iraqi Government to designate military commanders to meet within 48 hours with their coalition counterparts at a place in the theater of operations to be specified to arrange for military aspects of the cease-fire. Further, I have asked Secretary of State Baker to request that the United Nations Security Council meet to formulate the necessary arrangements for this war to be ended. This suspension of offensive combat operations is contingent upon Iraq's not firing upon any coalition forces and not launching Scud missiles against any other country. If Iraq violates these terms, coalition forces will be free to resume military operations."[205]

Saddam did not attack coalition forces after this cease fire was agreed upon. What Saddam did do was unconscionable. He purposefully destroyed Kuwait buildings, monuments, and oil wells. Hundreds of oil wells were sabotaged. Saddam's war crimes were many and did not stop as his troops withdrew. The Iraqi troops had tortured and murdered Kuwait civilians. Civilian and cultural property was looted. Scud missiles were primarily launched against civilian cities, not military targets.[206] The handling of the Iraq war showed how diabolical Saddam was. He knew he had lost the war. He publicly announced on February 25 that his troops were withdrawing. In the meantime he launched a scud attack on U.S. barracks. Iraqi troops continued to loot and destroy Kuwait property. Saddam tried to agree only to the UN Resolution 660. His plan was for his troops to withdraw to just outside Kuwait where they were deployed as of August 1st. President George H. W. Bush and the coalition forces saw through Saddam's empty agreements. Finally after two more days of pounding by the coalition forces, Saddam was ready to agree to all of the UN Resolutions. This type of underhanded, unethical behavior was the way Saddam ran Iraq and his regime.

On March 4, 1991 the coalition military commanders met with the Iraqi military commanders to make the cease fire permanent. The meeting was held in Safwan, Iraq just three miles north of the Kuwait border. The eight member Iraqi delegation agreed to all of the coalition terms. "General Schwarzkopf said in a brief statement after the meeting…that the Iraqis had agreed to allied demands on prisoners of war, including a 'symbolic release' of a few prisoners almost immediately, as well as requests for charts of minefields on land and in the gulf and the delineation of zones of influence to prevent accidental clashes." General Schwarzkopf went on to say that 'We have also made it very clear… that upon the signing of a cease-fire, but not before, all coalition forces will be drawn back from Iraqi territory that we currently occupy.'"[207] On April 7, 1991, Saddam formally agreed to the United Nations conditions for a cease-fire. Saddam said the conditions were "unjust." This allowed the UN to continue its peace keeping mission. The UN wanted to set up a peacekeeping force in order to force the destruction of all biological and chemical weapons, and Iraq's long range missiles. Also, Iraq agreed to pay reparations to Kuwait for damage done during the invasion.[208]

Crushing the Resistance

After the war with the coalition forces, Saddam brutally put down any resistance in the country. In the South there were Shiite Muslim forces fighting against Saddam. Saddam used his usual mode of operation and used chemical weapons on the rebels. Refugees from the attacks made their way to an US Army camp and told of atrocities. Doctors who were treating the gas victims were stabbed to death. Refugees told of the "use of napalm and chemical weapons, people hanged from electricity poles, bodies dragged through the street behind tanks, and patients and doctors slain in hospitals." A doctor explained how he had treated numerous people for chemical burns. "'It was not a normal burn', he said. 'It only affected the exposed parts, the face and hands. There was extreme sloughing off of the skin in blisters. The covered parts, where there were clothes, were just reddened.' Another technician who helped dress the wounds "described the patients as yellow-colored and unable to move."[209] Saddam was at it again using his chemical weapons and brutality to put down any opposition to his rule.

7

State of Terror

"One chemical weapon fired in a moment of despair could cause the deaths of hundreds of thousands."

- Saddam Hussein

On April 3, 1991, the UN passed Resolution 687 which specified that Iraq must destroy *all* biological, chemical, and nuclear weapons. All research and development programs in these areas must be halted. In addition, it called for the destruction of all ballistic missiles that had a range of greater than 150 kilometers. Iraq had to submit to UN weapons inspections within fifteen days. UN Resolution 687 also required that *Iraq not sponsor terrorism*. In addition, it mandated that *Iraq cannot allow any terrorist organization to operate within its borders*. Saddam was "**to condemn unequivocally and renounce all acts, methods, and practices of terrorism.**" The resolution went on to specify that all of these demands must be met before the economic embargos would be lifted. Saddam **never** fully complied with UN Resolution 687. As a result, the economic embargos were never lifted. The memos, transcripts, and documents included in the Pentagon report on Saddam clearly prove that Saddam was in violation of ***all*** of the above measures up until Operation Iraqi Freedom.[210]

Partnering with Terrorism

After the Iran-Iraq War, Iraq was in serious financial trouble. Now add to that the devastating defeat Iraq suffered from the 1991 Gulf War. Iraq's economy was worse off than before the War. Now Iraq was facing the costs associated with paying reparations to Kuwait and rebuilding its own infrastructure. The UN sanctions imposed after the 1991 Gulf War, "reduced Saddam's ability to shape regional and world events, steadily draining his military, economic, and military powers. The rise of Islamist fundamentalism in the region gave Saddam the opportunity to make terrorism, one of the few tools remaining in Saddam's "coercion" toolbox, not only cost effective but a formal instrument of state power."[211]

Terrorist Training in Iraq

Saddam's alliance with terrorist organizations is clearly seen in memo 110/2/43 (Appendix, Figure 4-8). Memo 110/2/43 dated January 25, 1993, lists ten terrorist organizations that were affiliated with Iraq. Prior to the 1991 Gulf War, Saddam was already partnering with terrorists. He was actively working with the PLO, IG, and Abu al-Abbas. His alliance with terrorists expanded during and after the first Gulf War. He saw Islamic terrorism as a means to further his own ambitions. After the first Gulf War, Iraq became aligned with even more terrorist organizations including al Qaida.

During the 1991 Gulf War, one hundred Arabs (non-Iraqis) were trained in Fedayeen training camps located in Iraq. Saddam was using his Fedayeen training camps to train terrorists. The Fedayeen was Saddam's personal Army that answered directly to him and operated separate from the regular Iraqi Army. In memo M4/7/3/586, Saddam sent a memo to the director of M4 Iraqi Intelligence Service (IIS). M4 was a section of the IIS that was responsible for gathering foreign intelligence information and for directing foreign operations. The memo requested that a detailed inventory of all non-Iraqis that had been trained in Fedayeen training camps during the first Gulf War. (see Appendix, Figure 62) Apparently the training of these non-Iraqis to carry out terrorist operations during the first Gulf War was called the "Fedayeen Operation."[212]

The response to memo M4/7/3/586 included a detailed listing of the names of one hundred non-Iraqi foreign national fighters that were categorized by country. The list provided can be categorized as follows:

"[Foreign national fighters by country]

- Palestine 38
- Lebanon 10
- Tunisia 8
- Egypt 4

- Libya 1
- Sudan 18
- Syria 10
- Eritrea 7
- Morocco 3
- Unknown 1"[213]

Keep in mind this was just the list of foreign nationals trained to fight during the first Gulf War. There were many more terrorists trained in Fedayeen training camps. This just establishes that Saddam was training non-Iraqis inside of Iraq to carry out terrorist operations against the U.S. and its allies.[214]

Volume 1 of the Pentagon report on Saddam says "under Saddam, the Iraqi regime used its paramilitary Fedayeen Saddam training camps to train terrorists for use inside and outside Iraq. In 1999, the top ten graduates of each Fedayeen Saddam class were specifically chosen for assignment to London, from there to be ready to conduct operations anywhere in Europe."[215] Essentially, Saddam was training non-Iraqi's to carry out terrorist actions anywhere in the world. Great Britain has been a strong ally of America and has been a favorite target for al Qaida. It just so happened that the top ten graduates were sent to London. The Pentagon report on Saddam describes what was taught in these Iraqi Fedayeen training camps:

a) Use of all kinds of weapons.

b) Use of all kinds of explosives.

c) How to plant car bombs.

d) "Introduction to explosives and other elements pertaining to terrorism."

e) Use of dough and plastic explosives.

f) Practical training on use of explosives and timed electronic devices.

g) Ways to destroy buildings, oil refineries, pipes, and planting car explosives. (see Appendix, Figure 41, Figures 57-59)

Passports Issued to Terrorists

Saddam provided support to terrorists that only a nation state could provide such as the issuing of passports. The Pentagon report on Saddam says that Iraq issued passports, renewals, and other official documentation to known terrorists.[216] A specific example of Saddam issuing passports to and harboring a known terrorist is Abu al-Abbas, a Palestinian Liberation Front leader. Saddam allowed Abu al-Abbas and his wife to live in Iraq under Saddam's protection. Saddam went so far as to issue both Abu al-Abbas and his wife diplomatic passports so they could travel the Middle East freely. "Abu al-Abbas originally fled to Iraq to avoid an Italian warrant imposing five life terms for his part in the 1985 hijacking of the Italian cruise liner *Achille Lauro* and the murder of an American citizen."[217] Once Abu al-Abbas was given sanctuary in Iraq, he began heading terrorist attacks from Iraq. During the 1991 Gulf War he carried out several international terrorist attacks:

a- "Burning of the Japanese embassy in Manilla- Philippine[s].

b- Burning of the American Airlines office in the Philippine[s].

c- Placing an explosive device near an American army base in Azmiir.

d- Placing an explosive device on the pipe lines that carry oil to an American base in Southern Spain.

e- Placing gliding airplanes (including their pilots) under the command of the Service (IIS) and an agreement was reached with the Iraqi Special Work Team to use these planes.

f- Abu al-'Abbas has provided a team of his organization to carry out some of the operations in the Saudi territories; this team [he] has is now under the command of the Iraqi Special Work Team."[218]

Here we have a known terrorist who was given safe haven in Iraq. Iraq issued him and his wife passports which allowed them to freely move about and lead these terrorist attacks against the U.S and its allies.

Furthermore, two of the 1993 World Trade Center bombers had Iraqi passports. Both Ramzi Yousef and Abdul Rahman Yasin entered the U.S. with Iraqi passports. Ramzi Yousef was the tactical mastermind behind the 1993 WTC bombing. Abdul Yasin, an Iraqi with U.S. citizenship, played a supportive role by mixing the chemicals and teaching Mohammed Salameh how to drive.

Al Qaida terrorists were masters at obtaining legal identification papers and passports and then cleaning their trail. "According to Khalid Sheikh Mohammed, [9/11 mastermind of the planes operation], [the hijackers] were to use Yemeni documents to fly to Malaysia, then proceed to the United States using their Saudi passports to conceal their prior travels to and from Pakistan."²¹⁹ Al Qaida had a passport division which created false trails on passports to conceal past travel.

In Laurie Mylorie's book <u>Study of Revenge Saddam Hussein's Unfinished War Against America</u>, she presents a valid case that Ramzi Yousef is actually an Iraqi spy. The Iraqi passport he presented was valid, but contained a Kuwaiti identity that traced back to the time when Iraq had invaded Kuwait. After Iraq invaded Kuwait, new Iraqi identification cards were issued to all Kuwait citizens. This means that Iraq was tampering with Kuwait's official documentation such as passport files and visas. Why destroy these documents, when they could be used to aid Iraqi Fedayeen members? This was a perfect opportunity for Iraq to obtain new identities for its Fedayeen members that would be deep under cover for Iraq.

Laurie has reviewed Ramzi Yousef's original passport file and noticed some irregularities that are detailed in her book. For instance the identity in the passport is Abdul Basit, a Kuwaiti, who was 4' 7" at age sixteen, and is described as being 5' 8" at age twenty. "Thus, he grew 13 inches between the ages of sixteen and twenty."²²⁰ Ramzi Yousef was noted as being 6' tall by U.S. Immigration officials in 1992. Another irregularity is that the last official mark on Abdul Basit's passport is dated May 22, 1990 made by the Pakistan Embassy located in Kuwait. This is two months before Iraq invaded Kuwait. Laurie goes to say that although Ramzi Yousef presented himself as a Pakistani while receiving his passport in New York, the Arabs who knew him described him as "Rashid, the Iraqi." Yousef got a new temporary passport from the Pakistani consulate in New York with the name Abdul Basit in preparation for his escape after the bombing. "On November 11, 1992, Yousef went to a Jersey City police station claiming to be Abdul Basit and reporting that he had lost his passport two days before. On December 31, he went to the Pakistani consulate in New York to get a new passport. Yousef presented Xerox copies of Abdul Basit's 1984 and 1988 passports."[221] Ramzi Yousef is not even his real name. To this day U.S. officials do not know Yousef's true identity. Was Ramzi Yousef an Iraqi agent sent to the U.S. to lead the bombing team? Indeed, the preponderance of evidence suggests that Yousef was actually an Iraqi agent.

WMDs?

Saddam's partnership with terrorists is known, but what about the weapons of mass destruction? Weapons of mass destruction are chemical, biological, and nuclear. These are weapons that kill military personnel as well as civilians when used. They have a widespread devastation and killing effect. Saddam never fully disarmed his biological, chemical, and nuclear weapons as described in the UN Resolution 687. There is a memo (ISGQ-2003-00003598) that was contained in a personnel file that describes Iraq having both biological and chemical weapons as late as January 4, 2001. (See Appendix, Figure 56) In the memo it says that the U.S. is developing weapons that are able to "penetrate deeply into the ground or concrete." Their concern is that storage facilities for chemical and biological weapons may be targeted. In the event that one of these facilities is attacked, chemical and biological weapons may be spewed into the air and then be detected. It says that these weapons could be "detected from the air by some hazardous airborne substances." The memo goes on to say that it would be hard to strike the *mobile storage facilities*. Here is an admission to hiding weapons of mass destruction from UN weapons inspectors. In describing the mobile storage facilities the memo says "Iraq has proven that it moved [chemical and biological weapons] throughout the country [with] very expansive equipment and data to evade United Nations' weapons inspection teams." U.S. intelligence was correct in its belief that Saddam had highly sophisticated mobile units that were able to produce, store, and move these weapons.

What about nuclear weapons? On July 6, 2008 the Los Angelos Times reported that "550 tons of 'yellowcake'-- the seed material for high-grade nuclear enrichment" was found in Iraq and shipped to Canada to be demilitarized. "The Iraqi government sold the yellowcake to a Canadian uranium producer, Cameco Corp. A Cameco spokesman, Lyle Krahn, said the yellowcake would be processed at facilities in Ontario for use in nuclear power plants. The deal culminated more than a year of diplomatic and military initiatives, kept hushed in fear of ambushes or attacks once the convoys were underway: first carrying 3,500 barrels by road to Baghdad, then on 37 military flights to the Indian Ocean atoll of Diego Garcia and finally aboard a U.S.-flagged ship for a 8,500-mile trip to Montreal."[222] The 550 tons of yellowcake if refined could make an estimated 142 nuclear weapons.[223]

We also know Saddam still had his nuclear weapons program as late as October 22, 2000. This is because of memo ISGQ-2005-00034061, which is addressed to the Deputy Director of Intelligence Service regarding scientific ideas and is from the General Security Section Director. The General Security Section Director asks that the biologist named Uday Salim Mahdi destroy all documents he has in regards to his biological weapons research. The memo states that Mahdi should "**destroy all of the documents related to his research to avoid any inconvenience with the inspection groups or the possibility of it reaching the country's enemies.**" (see Appendix, Figure 63) The response letter from the Deputy Director of Intelligence Service to the General Security Section Director explains that the biologist has been working on the "**production of viruses and bacteria that could be used to contaminate enemy water supplies in American military bases in Kuwait and Saudi Arabia.**" Most interesting is the fact that in the letter it says that one of the biologist's ideas will be forwarded to the *nuclear energy organization*. This provides evidence that Saddam was continuing his nuclear energy program as late as October 22, 2000. Rolf Ekeus, the first lead UN inspector, said that "The Iraqi nuclear weapons projects lacked access to fissile material but were advanced with regard to weapon design."[224]

Salman Pak

Salman Pak was a top secret location in Iraq that housed both biological and chemical weapons laboratories. In addition, there was a terrorist training camp located there. It was the nexus of terrorist training and WMDs. What training was provided at Salman Pak? Three Iraqi defectors testified and U.S. satellite imagery showed that there was an airplane parked at the Salman Pak camp with no runway. The trainees were taught how to highjack planes with small knives and utensils. The Iraqi memos already prove that Saddam was training non-Iraq's in terrorism. Could this be one of the camps where the 9/11 hijackers were trained? Considering Saddam's longstanding relationship with al Qaida this is quite possible.

The director of Salman Pak was Muhammad Munim al-Azmerli. "A former Iraqi Intelligence officer with direct access to the information said that Dr. Munim obtained the equations for producing chemical weapons and established laboratories in Salman Pak during the 1980-82 timeframe where he worked on sarin, sulfur mustard, nitrogen mustard, and tear gas (CS)." Biological weapons were also developed at Salman Pak. The following biological agents were produced and weaponized:

- anthrax,
- botulinum toxin,
- anthrax,
- gas gangrene,
- ricin,
- cholera.

The following weapons delivery systems were also available:
- missile warheads,
- aerial bombs, and
- commercial spray devices.

To understand the seriousness of these agents an explanation of the two most deadly agents is needed. First ricin is an extremely deadly poison. A person that consumes less than a pinch of ricin would die within 72 hours. Ricin causes shock followed by circulatory failure. There is no known antidote for ricin poisoning. Anthrax is also quite deadly. In the fall of 2001, less than a teaspoon of dry anthrax shutdown the United States Senate. As a result, several hundred people went to the emergency room to seek treatment. Two postal workers died from handling the tainted envelope. As you can see these biological agents are proven to be quite deadly and could kill large numbers of civilians in the hands of Islamic terrorists.[225]

Conclusion

In the Pentagon report on Saddam we see that Saddam was producing and storing biological, chemical, and nuclear weapons. In fact, Saddam was the most powerful *state sponsor of terrorism* in the world because of the oil resources that he had access to. In addition, he was using his Fedayeen training camps to train foreign terrorists. He was providing them with passports and identification papers. Most importantly of all, he had direct operational ties to al Qaida. Saddam was a dire threat to the U.S. that had to be addressed at an early point in the War on Terror if the U.S. was serious about destroying the terror network!

8

The Missing Link

فجرنا القنبلة قبل ما
"We pulled the trigger."
- Tariq Aziz

فجرناها وخليناها عاشيه
"Yes, will be pulled…"
- Saddam Hussein

Motives for the 1993 WTC bombing

In discussing who was behind the 1993 World Trade Center bombing, two factors must be considered: Saddam Hussein and al Qaida. Saddam Hussein threatened the U.S. in 1990 with terrorist attacks. Saddam invaded Kuwait in August 1990, and said that he would use terrorism to strike the U.S. homeland if the U.S. strikes Iraq. Saddam's threat is clearly seen in transcript (ISGQ-2003-M0006248). Saddam says **"if America strikes us, we will hit back.... Maybe we cannot reach Washington but we can send someone who has [an] explosive belt to reach Washington. Our missiles do not reach America, but I swear if [they did]! I would strike it."** (Appendix, Figure 30) At the same time, al Qaida was angry with the U.S. for deploying troops to Saudi Arabia on sacred land. "Bin Laden and his associates believed that Islamic doctrine explicitly prohibited the presence of infidels, or non-Muslims, in the 'Land of the Two Holy Places' (the Arabian Peninsula), home to the sacred Muslim cities of Mecca and Medina."[226] In 1991, Usama Bin Laden issued a fatwah "indicating that the United States was the 'head of the snake' and the enemy and should be attacked in Somalia and elsewhere."[227] Both Saddam Hussein and al Qaida had the motives and means to attack the U.S. on February 26, 1993. As we know already Saddam and al Qaida had been working together prior to this heinous attack.

1993 World Trade Center Bombing

On February 26, 1993 *the second anniversary of the ending of the first Gulf War*, a devastating car bomb exploded in the parking garage below the World Trade Towers. "The explosion created a crater five stories deep, killed 6 people, injured more than 1,000, and trapped thousands of office workers in the twin-towers complex in lower Manhattan."[228] The FBI was able to trace the VIN number of the van that was used in the car bomb explosion to Mohammed A. Salameh.[229]

Mohammed A. Salameh was the nephew of Kadri Abu Bakr. Abu Bakr was a prominent leader in the western sector of the PLO and worked out of the Baghdad office. The original bomb plot was a less sophisticated attack using pipe bombs. From court documents, we know that Salameh made forty-six calls to Iraq from June 10, 1992 to July 9, 1992. We also know from the Pentagon report on Saddam that Saddam had a close relationship with the PLO. (see Appendix, Figure 30) Saddam must have found out about Salameh's bomb plot and decided to lend Iraq's support.[230]

Within two months, three operatives arrived in New York to aid Salameh in his endeavor. On September 1, 1992, both Ramzi Yousef and Ahmad Mohammad Ajaj arrived from Pakistan. They had met at an al Qaida training camp in Afghanistan. A third support person, Abdul Rahman Yasin, arrived shortly thereafter from Iraq. He was an Iraqi who held dual U.S. citizenship. Here we see a nexus of al Qaida and Iraqi operatives coming together to aid Salameh with his planned attack. Once these individuals arrived, the plan became much more sinister.

Investigators discovered that Salameh attended the Farouq Mosque where Sheik Umar Abed al Rahman taught. At this Mosque, Rahman was teaching that the United States was the "oppressor of Muslims worldwide and asserting that it was their religious duty to fight against God's enemies"[231] The Farouq Mosque was operating as part of the "Services Office" in the al Qaida network.[232]

Umar Abed al Rahman had pledged an oath to Usama Bin Laden and al Qaida in 1989. When he moved to the United States in 1990, he was operating as al Qaida operative under the direction of Usama Bin Laden. From the Pentagon report on Saddam, we know that Saddam had close ties to Umar Abed al Rahman. Saddam met with a representative of the al Qaida's IG subsidiary on December 14, 1990 (see Appendix, Figure 6-7). Saddam was providing training, financing, and support to al Qaida since 1990. Here again we see the nexus of al Qaida and Saddam Hussein working behind the scenes to give aid to the 1993 World Trade Center bombers.

Prior to Rahman's arrival in the U.S., the team of bombers was being assembled and trained in New Jersey. In 1989, three of the bombers Mahmoud Abouhalima, Mohammad Salameh, and Nidal Ayyad were receiving training in weapons such as AK-47's. "Although Rahman was in Egypt at the time, Nosair and Abouhalima called him there to discuss various issues including the progress of their military training, tape-recording these conversations for distribution among Rahman's followers. Nosair told Rahman 'we have organized an encampment, we are concentrating here' [in New Jersey]."[233]

In 1990, Sheik Umar Abed al Rahman was readily accepted by the Brooklyn Muslim community and moved into the Alkifah Refugee Center. The Alkifah Refugee Center was an American branch of the al Qaida recruiting center called the "Services Office". For nearly 10 years the Center had recruited and trained young men for the Afghan mujahideen. Before the recruits were sent to Afghanistan, they were provided training in weapons and explosive handling at a nearby camp in Connecticut. Known al Qaida operatives such as Ali Mohamed frequently visited the Alikifah Refugee Center to provide training to the recruits. Ali provided trainees with "military training in survival techniques, map reading and how to recognize tanks and other Soviet weapons." In addition, Mohamed gave the trainees "Army manuals that described how to throw grenades while kneeling and make booby traps with explosives."[234]

Two of the World Trade Center bombers, Ahmad Mohammad Ajaj and Ramzi Ahmed Yousef, had traveled to a known al Qaida terrorist training camp located in Afghanistan called Camp Khaldan. The camp trained terrorists in guerilla warfare, weapons, and explosives. For example, one guerilla warfare tactic taught at Camp Khaldan was "how to place cyanide near the air intake of a building to achieve maximum lethality at minimum personal risk"[235] Ajaj was trained specifically in how to make bombs and carry out a bombing. Flight records show that on April 24, 1992 Ahmad Mohammad Ajaj flew from Houston, Texas to the Middle East to attend Camp Khaldan.[236]

Apparently Ajaj and Yousef met at Camp Khaldan. On September 1, 1992 both Ajaj and Yousef flew from Peshawar, Pakistan to New York City and arrived at JKF International Airport. Yousef was being financed by Usama Bin Laden and flew first class to JFK. Ajaj went through customs and presented a legal Swedish passport that had been altered with Ajaj's picture affixed on top of the original picture.[237] The INS inspector recognized that the passport had been altered and proceeded to search his belongings. Meanwhile, Yousef proceeded to another INS checkpoint acting as if he did not know Ajaj. Yousef showed the INS inspector his Iraqi passport. Although his passport appeared to be legitimate, he did not have a visa. The INS inspector arrested Yousef for not having a visa, but he was later released.[238]

While inspectors searched Ajaj's belongings, they found his terrorist kit. Ajaj became angry, and INS inspectors arrested him. "The kit included, among other things, handwritten notes Ajaj had taken while attending explosives courses, manuals containing formulae and instructions for manufacturing bombs, materials describing how to carry-off a successful terrorist operation, videotapes advocating terrorist action against the United States, and fraudulent identification documents."[239] More specifically, the terrorist kit included a video of a suicide bomber using a van to blow up an U.S. embassy. Both Ajaj and Yousef obtained assumed names for themselves before entering the U.S. Ajaj's alias was "Khurram Khan" and Yousef's was "Azan Mohammad." In order to legitimize their new assumed names, they assembled multiple identification documents. In addition to their passports, they possessed identification cards, bank accounts, education records, and medical records under their assumed names. The importance of this is that both Ajaj and Yousef obviously had sophisticated training and support in order to obtain these identification records.[240]

Ajaj ended up being arrested and convicted for passport fraud, and served six months in prison. Although Ajaj was in prison when the World Trade Center was bombed, he was able to communicate with the other bombers in code over the telephone. In order to hide his co-conspirators, Ajaj would call a friend in Texas, Mohammad Abukhdeir, who would then either relay the message to Yousef or would conference Yousef into the call. While Ajaj was serving his six month sentence, the United States District Court for the Eastern District of New York ordered that Ajaj's belongings *including his terrorist kit* to be returned to him. Ajaj then contacted Yousef via Abukhdeir to make sure one of his co-conspirators could pick up his belongings. The point here is that one of Ajaj's co-conspirators was able to pick up his terrorist kit in order to carry out the bombing of the World Trade Center.[241]

Yousef was allowed into the U.S. and proceeded to assemble a team of bombers through the Alkifah Refugee Center. The team included the following individuals: Mohammed Salameh, Nidal Ayyad, Mahmoud Abouhalima, and Abdul Rahman Yasin. The team implemented the bombing plot of the World Trade Center that Yousef and Ajaj had plotted in Pakistan. They rented a storage facility where they assembled the chemicals to create the bomb. They followed the instructions that Ajaj provided from Camp Khaldan. Ayyad worked as an engineer at a large New Jersey chemical company which gave him access to the chemicals necessary to build the bombs. Yasin, an Iraqi with U.S. citizenship, helped mix the chemicals for the bomb. He also taught Salameh, another co-conspirator in the 1993 bombing how to drive, so he could rent the van that would be used in the World Trade Center bombing. Although Salameh was the planned driver of the bomb laden van, Eyad Ismoil took his place at the last minute due to Salameh's poor driving skills. Salameh failed his driving test four times and was in an accident a few weeks before the WTC bombing. Yousef was so unsure of his driving skills that he called a long time friend, Eyad Ismoil, who was living in Dallas to be the driver.[242]

On February 23, 1993, Salameh went to a Jersey City Ryder dealership and rented a van. The terrorists loaded the homemade bomb in the van and on February 26, 1993. Eyad Ismoil drove the van with Yousef to the below-ground parking lot in the World Trade Center. They set a timer used to activate the bomb after they had vacated the area. "At 12:18 p.m., the bomb exploded, killing six people, injuring over a thousand others, and causing hundreds of millions of dollars in damage."[243]

Yousef, Abouhalima, Ismoil, and Yasin fled the country. Abouhalima was arrested in Egypt. Salameh attempted to leave the country, but was apprehended after returning to the Ryder rental company to receive his deposit. Although Ajaj was released from prison on March 9, 1993, he was arrested shortly thereafter as a conspirator in the bomb plot of the World Trade Center. In 1995, Yousef was arrested in Pakistan while staying at one of Usama Bin Laden's guest houses. Ismoil was arrested in Jordan two years after the bombing while Yasin remained a fugitive.[244]

In Saddam's Words

Within the Pentagon report on Saddam there is transcript that proves Iraq was behind the 1993 World Trade Center bombing. Transcript ISGQ-2003-M0007419 (see Volume 4, p.63-83) is a conversation with Saddam Hussein, his younger son Quasy Saddam Hussein, Abid Hamad Mahmoud al-Tikriti the Presidential Secretary, Tariq Aziz the Deputy Prime Minister, and Staff Lieutenant General Saber Abdul Aziz, the Head of Military Intelligence.[245] The unknown participants are labeled as MV for male voice. The transcript takes places just days after the 1993 World Trade Center bombing. Iraq has Abdul Rahman Yasin in custody. Yasin is an American citizen of Iraqi descent. He was involved in the 1993 World Trade Center bombing and shortly thereafter fled to Baghdad.[246] This is a long transcript that is basically split into three topics:

1) Saddam wants a scapegoat for the 1993 World Trade Center (WTC) bombing;
2) Saddam has Abdul Rahman Yasin, one of the 1993 WTC bombers in custody;
3) Saddam has relatives of Umar Abed al Rahman in custody that "know" something.

Finding a Scapegoat

Saddam begins the discussion with the possibility that a nation state sponsored the 1993 World Trade Center bombing. Saddam is paranoid that Iraq will ultimately be blamed as being responsible for the 1993 World Trade Center bombing. **Why is Saddam worried that Iraq will be blamed for this terrorist attack if Iraq was not involved with the bombing?** Saddam's paranoia seems like an admission of guilt. There are several hints in this conversation that Iraq was indeed involved with the 1993 World Trade Center bombing. Saddam begins by going through several scenarios of which other nations could logically be blamed. He needs a scapegoat. His scapegoat essentially planned and implemented the 1993 WTC bombing just to have Iraq blamed so that the United Nations (UN) sanctions would be worsened. First Saddam discusses the United States, but then says the losses were too great for it to have been behind it. Saddam begins by saying, "Yes, this issue [1993 WTC bombing] from the preliminaries before us there has obviously been a special technical arrangement where the US seems to have a hand in. These dirty games are games that the American intelligence would play if it had a bigger purpose, which would be bigger than the losses and sacrifices it would have to suffer. But this issue concerns the American public-you would expect losses in the bombing of the [1993] World Trade Center... And they had losses; the media announced it and you remember it. So how could/would the American intelligence do such a thing [bomb WTC] even though they knew there would be American human losses?"[247] (Appendix, Figure 74, text box 1)

The next statement that Saddam makes implies that Iraq was complicit in the preparation of the 1993 World Trade Center bombing. Saddam is saying that the plan has been implemented, and they must think carefully who will be the scapegoat. Next Saddam discusses the possibility of Israel being the scapegoat and how that would benefit the Arab world. **"Because this [WTC bombing] is not in the prep stage for us [Iraq] to claim that it is just a technical tactic intended for a certain party**. It [1993 WTC bombing] must be done by a party whose heart would not break over the loss of American lives and who would not suffer direct political consequences. Of course we immediately think of Israel.... So this is one of the options [of a possible scapegoat]."[248] (Appendix, Figure 74, text boxes 2 and 3)

Next Saddam discusses the motivation that caused all these different factions to work together to carry out the 1993 WTC bombing. How come Saddam knows that all these different factions worked together? Aren't we all supposed to think that Umar Abed al Rahman and his radical mosque members were to blame for the 1993 WTC bombing? *Was Saddam the one who organized all these factions to work together to accomplish the 1993 World Trade Center bombing?* **"But what tempted all these other factions to show such cooperation,** especially if its [al Qaida's] contact with Saudi Arabia is correct. Because when he [Abdul Rahman Yasin] says he contacted

[Saudi Arabia] then he really has contacted Saudi Arabia in the name of Abdullah like Nouri said."[249] (Appendix, Figure 75, text box 1)

Saddam has Abdul Rahman Yasin in custody. Yasin, an Iraqi, was involved with the 1993 World Trade Center bombings and had fled to Baghdad. Yasin helped mix the chemicals for the bomb. He also taught Salameh, another co-conspirator in the 1993 bombing how to drive, so he could rent the van that would be used in the World Trade Center bombing. Yasin told the Iraqis that he contacted Saudi Arabia via Abdullah. Abdullah Umar Abed al Rahman is the son of the blind cleric, Umar Abed al Rahman. Abdullah has followed in his father's footsteps.

During the discussion regarding Yasin, Saddam says something that implies he had discussed the 1993 WTC bombing with Umar Abed al Rahman, the blind cleric, previous to the bombing. In this previous discussion, Umar Abed al Rahman must have suggested that he could be the scapegoat of the 1993 WTC attack. Saddam says, "**Like Abed al Rahman said, this whole matter [1993 WTC bombing] could be thought up by Abed Al Rahman**." [250] We know Umar Abed al Rahman met with Saddam on December 14, 1990 from the Pentagon Report on Saddam (see Appendix, Figures 6 and 7). Could this meeting have been the precursor to the 1993 WTC bombing? Saddam is agreeing with Rahman's previous suggestion that Rahman be the scapegoat. Saddam is saying Umar Abed al Rahman brought all the factions together. He is the perfect scapegoat because he was located in New Jersey at the Mosque where many of the bombers attended. Use him as the scapegoat, and get the blame off of Saddam and Iraq. Saddam realizes that this scenario could be sold to the U.S. as a possibility to remove all suspicions from Iraq. Apparently this worked because Umar Abed al Rahman was ultimately blamed as being the mastermind of the 1993 World Trade Center bombing. At the time the role that Usama Bin Laden and al Qaida played was not even investigated let alone the possible responsibilities of a nation state such as Iraq. The Clinton administration always seemed afraid that any confrontation with Usama Bin Laden would bring an increase in terrorist attacks. Saddam got what he wanted which was Umar Abed al Rahman was blamed. In actuality Rahman was not arrested and tried on participating in the 1993 World Trade Center bombing, but on the Holland and Lincoln Tunnels bombing that was planned as the next attack.[251] However, we should remember that Rahman actually issued the fatwah for the 1993 and 2001 World Trade Center attacks.

Yasin and the Announcement

Saddam is concerned about the possibility that Abdul Rahman Yasin had been apprehended by the FBI and is acting as a double agent trying to get evidence on Iraq and its role in the 1993 WTC bombing. This is certainly a possibility since Yasin is an American citizen who was actually born in Indiana. Saddam is questioning whether Yasin contacted another faction possibly Gulbuddin Hekmatyar who then informed Abed al Rahman. Hekmatyar had a close relationship with Umar Abed al Rahman and had met with him twice in Peshawar in 1988 and 1990.[252] Many recruits that came from the Alkifah Refugee

Center were sent to Afghanistan and fought with Hekmatyar' forces in the mujahideen. Saddam thinks that Yasin may have actually contacted U.S. intelligence acting as though it was the Saudi consulate. I think Saddam is concerned that Yasin is working for U.S. intelligence. Saddam says "he [Yasin] could have possibly contacted another faction and informed Abed al Rahman. One of the tricks and games of such people [U.S. intelligence] would be for him [Yasin] to pretend that he is contacting the Saudi consulate but maybe he is contacting a different party [U.S. intelligence].

Saddam is wondering if Saudi Arabia or Egypt is working with U.S. Intelligence. Saddam thinks maybe Saudi Arabia is secretly tape recording the conversation that Yasin had with the Saudi consulate in order to aid the U.S. Next Saddam thinks about the possibility of Egypt being involved with this secret tape recording. Umar Abed al Rahman has a history of trying to undermine the Egyptian government and has actively tried to overthrow the Egyptian government. Saddam thinks that Egypt would want Umar Abed al Rahman blamed for the 1993 WTC attack and has a motive to aid the U.S. Saddam says, "What kind of temptation would they [U.S. intelligence] offer Saudi Arabia to participate in such an operation or know of it? Nothing would be as effective as bringing harm to Iraq. Is it possible for Saudi Arabia to enter into such an operation [covert tape recording] without the official knowledge of the US? What could tempt Egypt? Because it [al Qaida] also sent signals to Egypt. Well, Egypt would primarily be tempted to involve the cleric [Umar Abed al Rahman] who is carrying the banner of resistance against it. Whose name is Omar Abed al Rahman. And it [Egypt] also tempted to harm Iraq. And I mean by that the Egyptian government. But it also can not take steps of this nature with out the knowledge and even the official request of the US." [253] (Appendix, Figure 75)

Here Saddam admits that he does not know everything about the 1993 World Trade Center bombing operation. Saddam says "**not the whole truth has been revealed to us as it is**." Saddam had been working with al Qaida since the early 1990s, but did not know everything about al Qaida and its operations. This amount of secrecy would be required to give both Usama Bin Laden and Saddam protection. Now Saddam wants to learn more details about how al Qaida was able to carry out this daring day-light attack on America. In Appendix, Figure 6 and chapter 1, Figure 4, the way the Sudanese leader of the Islamic National Front, Sheik Ali Uthman Taha, was acting as an intermediary between Saddam and al Qaida demonstrates the secrecy used in their relationship. Taha negotiated between Saddam and al Qaida to renew their relations prior to the 1993 World Trade Center bombing (see Appendix, Figure 6). Taha also arranged to have an al Qaida leader flown into Baghdad on a meat cargo ship two weeks after the 1993 World Trade Center bombing (see ch 1, Figure 2). Saddam goes on to say that "**the suspect [Abdul Rahman Yasin] we have in our custody is too organized in what he is saying and is playing games** (Appendix, Figure 74, last text box)." Saddam was paranoid that Yasin's story seemed "too organized" which made Saddam think that Yasin was working as a spy for the United States.

Saddam did not realize that the FBI had questioned Yasin about the World Trade Center bombing and released him believing he was not involved in the bombing. When Yasin fled to Baghdad, the FBI knew he had been involved with the bombing, but by then it was too late to apprehend him.[254] Saddam says, "So with all this you would see that…constantly at this stage **we offer conflicting factors because not the whole truth is revealed to us as it is**. Because the suspect [Yasin] we have in our custody is too organized in what he is saying and is playing games, playing games and influencing scenario."[255] (Appendix, Figure 74)

As part of Saddam's plan to find a scapegoat, Saddam is considering releasing information about the prisoner Iraq has in custody, Abdul Rahman Yasin. Saddam wants to release information that would make it look like the United States was behind the 1993 World Trade Center bombing. Since Abdul Rahman Yasin held both U.S. and Iraqi citizenship, Saddam was contemplating using him as a scapegoat in order to tie the U.S. into the 1993 WTC bombing. Yasin was born in Bloomington, Indiana, but grew up in Baghdad.[256] Saddam wants to preempt any announcement that America would make accusing Iraq of being behind the bombing. Saddam continues by saying "The conclusion of this matter, I [want] to issue a surprise statement and say that we have become privy to dangerous information that concerns the attacks that occurred in the US. And that the initial investigation has uncovered factions involved in this matter and up to now we do not know if there are American parties in cooperation with this tactic. Because we have not yet found out if there are American official or semi official parties involved in this arrangement, however we have indication to that end and we have our suspicions that are supported by some evidence that there are several factions involved in this matter. The initial persons involved in this matter are not necessarily the complete picture of the situation.... By us announcing first we would preempt the Americans independent announcement. Because if they do announce and we try to defend ourselves no one will listen to us."[257] (Appendix, Figure 75)

Saddam goes on to explain more about the announcement that Iraq will make. Saddam says that Iraq will release information about the **"initial set up of the operation**." Was Saddam involved with the initial setup? It is very interesting that Saddam says the announcement **"would not give the full picture**." This begs the question, did Saddam have the whole picture because he was involved with the 1993 World Trade Center bombing from its initial setup? Why was Saddam releasing this information? Because he wants to **"kill any dramatic announcement they [the U.S.] intended to make**." Saddam goes on to explain more about his planned announcement. Saddam will say that **"important information was uncovered, which has to do with the attack that happened and we have documents that are sufficient to indicate the initial set up of the operation that occurred and that we do not know, nor are we able to determine if there were entities in the US who knew of this operation**. Put it is [in] a smart way **that would not give the full picture** but at the same time would **kill any dramatic announcement they intended to make** to confuse the public opinion. And the opposite will happen... the **doubts will start being directed to the target [U.S.]**."²⁵⁸ (Appendix, Figure 76, text box 1 and 2)

Saddam begins to question his plan of announcing information about the initial setup of the 1993 WTC bombing. He knows once he makes the announcement and makes public the information he has regarding the initial setup of the 1993 World Trade Center bombing that this might bring more attention to Iraq's involvement. The U.S. would be suspicious of how Saddam had this information if Iraq was not involved in the bombing plot. Finally he admits that making this information public may hinder Iraq's *latest operation*. Since Saddam never made this announcement, he must have concluded that it would raise too many questions and would hamper any further terrorist operations that were planned. This shows in Saddam's own words that he was actively participating with al Qaida in their attacks against the West. Saddam says "**Well with this announcement, when they say anything about Iraq- that Iraq supports terrorism and then they have to say that Iraq has documents on this issue and they** [U.S.] **don't have** [documents] **it reaches the issues of terrorism, trouble making and the** *latest operation*."

Saddam is adamant that Yasin remain alive. Saddam wants to use Yasin as a diplomatic tool to aid the U.S. in their investigation of the 1993 World Trade Center bombing. Saddam thinks that if he helps the U.S., then the UN sanctions may be lifted. Saddam wants Yasin isolated from other inmates and guards. He wants a special guard unit to watch him. Saddam does not want Yasin to hear the news reports about him. **"We must also not allow him to hear or read the papers and to hear from no one."** Saddam is afraid that Yasin may hear that they are using him as a pawn to indict the United States in the 1993 World Trade Center bombing since Yasin is a U.S. citizen. If Yasin were to hear one of these broadcasts, he would be angry and might tell the guard everything about how he was sent to the U.S. by the Iraqi government to participate in the 1993 bombing. Saddam says about Yasin **"then he goes off and tells him [the guard] everything..."** Once Yasin was cleared by Saddam's security forces, he was given a job in the Iraqi Government.[259] This shows that even though he was working directly for al Qaida in the 1993 attack, it took many months before Saddam was satisfied as to his true loyalties to Iraq. Staff Lieutenant General Saber Abdul Aziz says "They need to watch him so that he doesn't commit suicide. There is a possibility." Saddam responds "He could commit suicide and someone might kill him. They mustn't the guards, and whipping and then they die... But the most important thing is that they [Saddam and his command members] keep it to themselves and the persons he [Yasin] sees and we must be very careful that he [Yasin] is not killed in jail in one way or another or commit suicide. We must also not allow him to hear or read the papers and to hear from no one to 'what did you hear in the news today?' you know, how we the Iraqis are 'hey the TV today announced news about you so and so' and then he **[Yasin] goes off and tells him [the guard] everything [about being sent to the U.S. by Saddam]** and then he

[Yasin] hears unintentionally what we don't want him to hear."[260] (Appendix, Figure 77)

Next Tariq Aziz, the Deputy Prime Minister, wants to review with Saddam the announcement that will be made regarding the 1993 World Trade Center bombing. Aziz says that Iraq has "**serious information**" regarding the 1993 World Trade Center attack. *How can Iraq have this information and not have been involved in the 1993 World Trade Center bombing?* This implies that Iraq was indeed behind the attack. Aziz begins by saying "**Iraqi intelligence organizations have documented and [have] serious information regarding the attack which occurred on the World Trade Center in New York. This information raises several questions regarding the entities that cooperated in this operation or who were behind it.**"

Aziz goes on to say Iraq will cooperate with the U.S. provided the American Congress is involved with the investigation. Saddam agrees that making sure the American Congress is involved is imperative. Aziz says that Iraq will "**cooperate with the American people to identify the facts. On the condition ... this is done with the knowledge of the American Congress or under its supervision.**" Saddam replies, "**Yes, I wanted to ... make it [Congress] an issue.**"

Aziz cautions that releasing this "**serious information**" to the U.S. is going to cause people "**to start to make up stories.**" Saddam agrees, "**Yes make up stories and as for us [Iraq] in all cases the purpose of harming us [Iraq being blamed for the attack and increased sanctions] after [this] is over.**" Saddam thinks that once

Iraq works with the U.S. officials and releases this "**serious information**" regarding the "**initial setup of the operation**," that all blame directed at Iraq will be directed at the U.S. and other entities. The serious information released will include information about Yasin. Since Yasin is a U.S. citizen, Iraq will imply that the U.S. was behind the 1993 World Trade Center bombing. Remember how Saddam was so concerned that Yasin may slip up and tell the truth about the whole operation to a guard if Yasin found out he was being used as the scapegoat for Iraq. It is interesting that Saddam says "**the purpose of harming us [Iraq] after the [1993 WTC bombing] is over.**" Why is it over? Because suspicion will then be on the U.S. not Iraq since Yasin was a U.S. citizen. Aziz cautions that releasing this "**serious information**" to the U.S. is going to cause people "**to start to make up stories.**" Saddam agrees, "**Yes make up stories and as for us [Iraq] in all cases the purpose of harming us [Iraq being blamed for the attack] after [this] is over.**"

The most telling statement is made next by Aziz, "**We pulled the trigger [on the 1993 WTC attack].**" Saddam's response is: "**Yes, will be pulled.**" Saddam is saying let them make up stories about Iraq, but not say that Iraq was behind the 1993 World Trade Center bombing. Saddam knows that if the U.S. figures out Iraq sponsored the 1993 WTC attack from the *initial setup*, then the UN sanctions may be worsened or the U.S. may invade Iraq. Aziz says, "**We pulled the trigger [on the 1993 WTC attack].**" Saddam's response is: "**Yes, will be pulled and let it be but not allow them to make up stories about**

people and Iraqis - preferred but not on the basis of [being responsible for the 1993 WTC attack]... preferred ... preferred."

Umar Abed al Rahman's relatives being interrogated

The final section of the transcript says that Saddam has relatives of Umar Abed al Rahman in custody. Saddam has been interrogating them twice a week. The relatives were in the United States during the planning and implementation of the 1993 World Trade Center bombings. An unidentified male voice says, "Sir, if you please, concerning Abed al Rahman family we issued directives to the secretary to bring them in and hold them. Sir, I don't support that Sir, he doesn't want to and he is an old man and if we let them go at least we can see when we keep them here."[261] (Appendix, Figure 79)

Saddam is trying to get more information from these individuals that he has in custody. Maybe he can use it to his advantage by putting the blame on the U.S. or another nation. Although Saddam has the big picture about the attack, he does not have all the details. He is trying to find out more details about the bombing. Also these individuals may prove useful to Saddam in aiding the U.S. in their investigation. Again this proved Saddam was involved with the 1993 World Trade Center bombing. Saddam responds by saying, **"Well she is a female there in the US and she saw who comes and who goes and the brother also knows what is up and what is not.** We must, he is a brother at home, impossible for something like this to pass by him, there was talk on the phone **'ability and this was bombed and this we wanted to do'** and

on the phones, the brother could have just put the phone down and didn't say anything. He must have something useful - call him in for interrogation."

The interrogation tactics of Saddam were not simply questioning these individuals. Saddam had 107 different torture techniques. Everything from setting victims limbs on fire to putting them in ice cold cells naked and allowing their limbs to freeze. Rape of the person being interrogated or the rape of their relatives was routinely carried out in Saddam's torture chambers.[262] These were the torture chambers of Saddam and how he dealt with his enemies.

Criminal Justice Failures

The 1993 World Trade Center investigation was prosecuted under the criminal justice system. The 9/11 Commission says one problem that resulted from the legal system handling the prosecution of the 1993 bombings is that "it created an impression that the law enforcement system was well-equipped to cope with terrorism. Neither President Clinton, his principle advisors, the Congress, nor the news media felt prompted, until later, to press the question of whether the procedures to put the Blind Sheik and Ramzi Yousef behind bars would really protect Americans against the new virus of which these individuals were just the first symptoms." The 9/11 Commission goes to say that the "successful use of the legal system to address the first World Trade Center bombing had the side effect of obscuring the need to examine the character and extent of the new threat facing the United

States. The trials did not bring the Bin Laden network to the attention of the public and policymakers."[263] The 9/11 Commission concluded correctly that this was a mistake that prepared the way for a much bigger tragedy – the September 11 2001 World Trade Center attacks.

The failure of the criminal justice system can clearly be seen in the handling of the Ahmad Mohammad Ajaj case. Ajaj, one of the 1993 World Trade Center bombing conspirators, was arrested in 1992 at the JFK airport for presenting a fraudulent passport. While Ajaj was serving his six month sentence, the United States District Court for the Eastern District of New York ordered that Ajaj's belongings **including his terrorist kit** be returned to him. This enabled the bombing team to have the instructions to carry out the bombing.[264] Thus we see that the judicial system failed in keeping America safe and actually aided the terrorists in the 1993 bombing.

Historical Perspectives

During World War II, Franklin D. Roosevelt was much less forgiving than President Clinton. "During World War II, eight Nazi saboteurs secretly landed in New York to attack factories and plants. Two of them were American citizens. After their capture, FDR sent them to military detention, where they were tried and most of them executed. In *Ex Parte Quirin*, the Supreme Court upheld the detention and trial by military authorities of American citizens who 'associate' with 'the military arm of the enemy' and 'enter this country bent on hostile acts.'"[265] If Roosevelt's judgment prevailed today, these terrorists would be incarcerated in military prison as enemy combatants and most likely executed under military tribunal.

Conclusion

Since Rahman had pledged an oath to Usama Bin Laden and al Qaida in 1989, he was acting as an al Qaida operative in the 1993 WTC bombing. Therefore, the 1993 World Trade Center bombing most certainly is the first al Qaida attack on U.S. soil. What about Iraq's role in the bombing? First of all we have the admission from Saddam within the Pentagon report. Other links to Iraq must be considered. From court documents, we know that Salameh made forty-six calls to Iraq from June 10, 1992 to July 9, 1992. Salameh was the nephew of Kadri Abu Bakr, a prominent leader in the western sector of the PLO that worked out of the Baghdad office. We also know from the Pentagon report on Saddam that Saddam had a close relationship with the PLO.[266] The other prominent group involved was the IG al Qaida subsidiary led by Umar Abed al Rahman. We know Saddam had a relationship with the IG and was supplying them with training, financing, and support from December 1990. Yousef presented an Iraqi passport upon arrival at JFK. We know that Saddam was issuing passports to known terrorists. Abdul Rahman Yasin was an Iraqi who held dual U.S. – Iraq citizenship. He safely fled to Iraq after the 1993 WTC bombing. Here we clearly see the links to Iraq in the 1993 World Trade Center bombing. Now taking into account the transcript described above, it is clear that Saddam gave the order for the attack.

9

Never Forget

"We will chase [Americans] to every corner at all times. No high tower of steel will protect them against the fire of truth."

- Saddam Hussein, Baghdad Radio, February 8, 1991

On September 11, 2001 at 8:46 AM American Airlines Flight 11 crashed into the World Trade Center's North Tower. America changed at this moment. No longer were terrorist attacks just a far away occurrence. For the first time a major terrorist attack was on American soil. Of course we had the 1993 World Trade Center bombing, but it was not this devastating or monumental. At 9:03 AM United Airlines Flight 175 flew into the South Tower and with it America's innocence was gone. Shortly thereafter at 9:37 AM American Airlines Flight 77 crashed into the west wall of the Pentagon. Finally at 10:03 AM United Airlines Flight 93 crashed in a field in Pennsylvania. Nearly 3,000 Americans died that day and it changed America forever.

Rootless Operatives?

We know the horror of that day, but where did it all start? Well it turn out that Ramzi Yousef, the mastermind of the 1993 World Trade bombing, came up with the idea to highjack airplanes and use them as missiles. He and his alleged uncle, Khalid Sheikh Mohammed (KSM), came up with the idea in 1995. Both Ramzi Yousef and Khalid Sheikh Mohammed are described as **"rootless yet experienced operatives"** in the 9/11 Commission report.[267] Could Ramzi Yousef and Khalid Sheikh Mohammed have been Iraqi agents? Neither Yousef nor Khalid was particularly devout in their Muslim religion. Neither of them actually participated in suicide operations themselves. In fact they always had an escape route or operated remotely. They were the masterminds behind the 1993 and 2001 WTC attacks. Yousef and Khalid would lead the operations and train the other terrorists. As described previously, Ramzi Yousef's identification documents are suspect. Both Yousef and Khalid were extremely knowledgeable and well trained. Knowing that Saddam was training, financing, and giving orders to al Qaida, it is very likely both Yousef and Khalid were highly trained Fedayeen operatives. We saw in memo 110/2/43 where it says **"We've previously met with the [IG] Organization's representative on December 14, 1990, and we agreed on a plan to move against the Egyptian regime through Fedayeen operations, provided that we guarantee them [financial] aid, training and whatever they need."** This clearly shows that Saddam's Fedayeen operatives were directly working with the IG. By the writing of this memo Rahman, the leader of the IG, was the spiritual leader of al Qaida. Add to this the fact that they had support from a nation state - Iraq that was issuing passports to known terrorists as well as providing training and financing to the IG operating under the al Qaida umbrella. Could these "rootless operatives" have been highly trained Iraqi Fedayeen agents that were sent to aid al Qaida in its war against the U.S.? Indeed, the preponderance of evidence suggests that both Yousef and Khalid were actually highly trained Iraqi Fedayeen agents working deep under cover. It seems inconceivable that these two masterminds would have come to this knowledge completely on their own as some sort of rogue "rootless" terrorists.

Precursor to 9/11

After the 1993 World Trade Center (WTC) bombing, Ramzi Yousef returned to Quetta which is the capital of the Pakistani province of Baluchistan and stayed in an al Qaida safe house. Khalid played a background role in the 1993 bombing. Khalid and Yousef first met in 1992 in Afghanistan at an al Qaida training camp. While Yousef was in New York planning the 1993 WTC bombing, telephone records showed that Yousef had called Khalid numerous times for support. Khalid even wired Yousef money to aid him in the 93 WTC bomb plot.
268

In 1994, Khalid and Yousef traveled to the Philippines to begin planning several more terrorist plots. Yousef and Khalid shared an apartment in Manila while plotting more terrorist attacks. Their next terrorist operation that echoed the 9/11 attacks was the "Bojinka" plot. This attack was an elaborate plan to blow up twelve U.S. airplanes while in flight over the Pacific Ocean. In addition, they were planning the assassination of President Clinton and Pope John Paul II. In preparation for the "Bojinka" plot, Yousef perfected a bomb timer that he had developed. He tested his new timer by using it to blow up a movie theatre in Manila and a Philippine airline that was on its way to Tokyo. Yousef and Khalid bought chemicals to build the bombs. They were also doing flight preparation work by checking out airport security and flight paths. On January 6, 1995 while Yousef was working on the bombs in his Manila apartment a fire accidentally started. The fire produced a billowing gaseous fire that raised suspicions. A neighbor in his apartment building called the building security guard who entered Yousef's apartment and saw his bomb making materials. The fire department and local police were called. Although Yousef calmly left the building and escaped, he had left his laptop, notes, manuals, and identification papers in the apartment. He had to get back in the apartment to retrieve these items. He asked an accomplice, Abdul Hakim Murad, to go back and get his belongings. Since the police and fire department had vacated the building, Murad thought it was safe to return to the apartment to get Yousef's belongings. When Murad entered the apartment, the police who had been monitoring it, swept in and arrested Murad before he could recover the items. In Yousef's apartment, they found the plans for the U.S. airlines bombing, the assassination of the Pope and President

Clinton. Yousef fled, but his days of freedom were numbered. Khalid had moved back to Qatar in September 1994. Once he got notice that Yousef's belongings had been apprehended, he also became a fugitive. On February 7, 1995 Yousef was arrested while staying at an Usama Bin Laden guest house in Islamabad, Pakistan.[269]

In Stephen Hayes' book <u>The Connection</u> he explains that a 9/11 planning meeting took place in Malaysia on January 5, 2000. In this meeting the planning of the October 12, 2000 U.S. Cole and September 11, 2001 attacks were planned. Representatives from Iraqi Intelligence and al Qaida were present. It was a three day planning meeting with one of the 9/11 hijackers present. Ahmed Hikmat Shakir was an Iraqi Intelligence Service (IIS) Agent that worked undercover as greeter at the Kuala Lumpur International Airport in Malaysia. The Malaysian government has pictures of Ahmed Hikmat Shakir meeting with Khalid al Mihdhar, a 9/11 hijacker, at the airport. Instead of simply greeting Mihdhar, Shakir got into the vehicle with Mihdhar and went with him to a condominium owned by a known al Qaida associate named Yazid Sufaat. Shakir, an IIS agent, is also mentioned in a memo in the Pentagon Report on Saddam. In Volume 2, p.154 a memo dated June 10, 2001 states that "Shakir headed to Malaysia." (See Appendix, Figure 85) This memo is addressed to the Director of the 4th Directorate. The 4th Directorate is also referred to as M4. M4 was the Directorate of Foreign Clandestine Operations, IIS. Clearly this memo shows that Shakir was indeed an Iraqi Intelligence agent working for the Iraqi Government. This meeting between Shakir and Mihdhar one of the American Airlines Flight 77 hijackers is the most compelling evidence tying Iraq to September 11. This along with the other compelling evidence given throughout this book of Saddam Hussein's ongoing support and relationship with al Qaida since December 1990.[270]

Planes Operation

In January 1996, Khalid left Qatar and moved to Afghanistan. Khalid met with Bin Laden and offered up a variety ideas for terrorist attacks. One of the ideas discussed was the 9/11 plot. Sometime in 1998 or 1999, Usama Bin Laden gave Khalid the green light to begin preparing for the 9/11 attacks on America. According to Khalid, the 9/11 attack plans originally included nine planes that would crash into targets on both coasts of the U.S. The targets included the World Trade Center, Pentagon, White House, U.S. Capitol, "CIA and FBI headquarters, nuclear power plants, and the tallest buildings in California and the state of Washington."[271]

Bin Laden began to select al Qaida members that would be used to hijack the planes. Mainly Saudis were selected to participate because they could easily travel the world with Saudi Arabia passports. Four men were selected to be part of the first group of trainees for the planes operation. The men selected were Nawaf al Hamzi, Tawfiq Bin Attash known as Khallad, Khalid al Mihdhar, and Abu Bara. Their first phase of training took place at an al Qaida training camp in Afghanistan. They were given top training in all forms of weapons, close quarters combat, and night operations. Once this training was complete, Hamzi, Khallad, and Abu Bara were moved to a safe house in Karachi, Pakistan where Khalid gave them briefings on Western culture and travel. He taught the recruits English words and phrases. He briefed them on how to rent an apartment and make travel plans. They used computer flight simulators to begin their flight training. "According to KSM, they were to use Yemeni documents to fly to Malaysia, then proceed to the United States using their Saudi passports to conceal their prior travels to and from Pakistan."[272]

In December 1999, Khallad and Hamzi began taking flights in Asia to review U.S. airline security. They tested things like taking a box cutter onto the flight in Hong Kong and observing cockpit security in flight. While the first group of recruits - Hamzi, Khallad, Mihdhar, and Abu Bara - was sent to the U.S., a second group of recruits was sent to Afghanistan to begin their training. These trainees had Western educations, spoke fluent English, and were familiar with Western culture. These recruits included Mohamed Atta, Ramzi Binalshibh, Marwan al Shehhi, and Ziad Jarrah who quickly became central figures in the 9/11 attacks. Because this group of recruits was from a close knit Islamic student group from Hamburg, Germany, they were referred to as the Hamburg group. Muhamed Atta would become the lead hijacker of the planes operation. Once the Hamburg group completed their training in Afghanistan, they began researching aviation schools where they could learn to be pilots. In preparation for their relocation to the U.S, they tried to get new visas claiming their passports had been lost.

Binalshibh was unable to obtain a visa, so he stayed behind. He ended up aiding his fellow terrorists from abroad.

Hazmi and Mihdhar arrived in Los Angelos on January 15, 2000. They were told to pose as "Saudi students and seek assistance at local mosques."[273] They ended up making contact with the King Fahd mosque. There was a radical cleric at the mosque named Fahad al Thumairy. He was reported to be an extreme Islamic fundamentalist that followed a strict orthodox Wahhabi doctrine.

In February, Hazmi and Mihdhar moved to San Diego. They made connections in the Muslim Community through the Islamic Center of San Diego. Now they turned their focus onto learning to become pilots as quickly as possible. Both Hazmi and Mihdhar were learning how to speak English, but were unable to learn how to read and write in English. This became a major obstacle to them becoming pilots. They enrolled at the Sorbi Flying Club in San Diego, where they found an instructor that spoke Arabic. When first attending the flight school, they asked to learn to fly Boeing jets. The flight instructor told them there was no such school, and they would have to begin their training with small planes. Other flight instructors at the school described Hazmi and Mihdhar as poor students that were only interested in learning how pilot the plane once it was in mid air. They were not interested in learning how to take off and land the planes. After a few short months, they decided to give up on becoming pilots. Mihdhar got word that his first child had been born, so he decided to leave the U.S and return to Yemen. Mindhar just wanted to abandon the operation entirely. Khalid Sheikh Mohammed was furious when he heard that Mihdhar had left San Diego without receiving permission from his al Qaida leadership. Khalid feared that Mihdhar might compromise the entire operation. Although Mindhar was allowed to visit his family in Yemen, he was not allowed to abandon the planes operation. When Usama Bin Laden heard what happened, he said that Mihdhar had to continue with the operation.

Hamzi was left in San Diego alone. At this point he completely gave up on learning English and becoming a pilot. He got a job and waited for another al Qaida recruit to join him in San Diego. In December 2000 Hani Hanjour arrived to partner with Hamzi on the planes operation. Soon after his arrival, Hani and Hamzi left San Diego and traveled to Arizona to attend flight school.

In May and June 2000, the Hamburg group arrived in the U.S. to attend flight school. Upon arrival Atta and Shehhi had to decide on what flight school to attend. Ziad Jarrah had already enrolled in the Florida Flight Training Center (FFTC) flight school in Venice, Florida. Atta and Shehhi ended up attending another flight training school in Venice, Florida called Huffman Aviation. Both Atta and Shehhi enrolled in the Accelerated Pilot Program that was offered and excelled in their training. By the end of the summer, they had both passed the private pilot airman test. Meanwhile, Jarrah completed his training at the FFTC and received his single engine private pilot license.

Ramzi Binalshibh was supposed to join his partner Jarrah in the U.S. He had been trying to obtain a visa all Summer and Fall of 2000. Once he and his superiors, namely Khalid Sheikh Mohammed heard of his unsuccessful tries at getting a U.S. visa, he became a plot coordinator and aid to Khalid. He would wire money to Atta and Shehhi. Zacarias Moussaoui became Binalshibh's replacement in the planes operaion. Now Binalshibh was to aid Moussaoui in becoming a trained pilot by helping him find a flight school. Binalshibh enrolled Moussaoui in a flight school in Norman, Oklahoma.[274]

Since it was now Fall of 2000 and they needed a fourth pilot for the planes operation, Hani Hanjour was selected. He was fluent in English and had attended the University of Arizona in the early 1990's. Hanjour was selected while training at an al Qaida training camp in Afghanistan. When news got up to the higher ranks that he already had his commercial pilot license and was fluent in English, he was selected as the fourth pilot. By December 2000, Atta, Shehhi, and Jarrah, the Hamburg group, had received their commercial pilot licenses. By the end of the year, they were training at flight simulators on how to fly large jumbo jets.[275]

Muscle Hijackers

By May 2000, muscle hijackers were sent to the U.S. to meet up with the pilots that had already been training in the U.S. These were the hijackers that would help commandeer the planes. The first ones to arrive were Ahmed al Ghamdi and Majed Moqed who were partnered up with Hazmi and Hanjour in Connecticut. Salem al Hazmi was Nawaf's younger brother who also arrived. In Florida, Atta was awaiting the arrival of his team of muscle hijackers. "Twelve of the thirteen muscle hijackers (excluding Nawaf al Hazmi and Mihdhar) came from Saudi Arabia: Satam al Suqami, Wail al Shehri, Waleed al Shehri, Abdul Aziz al Omari, Ahmed al Ghamdi, Hamza al Ghamdi, Mohand al Shehri, Majed Moqed, Salem al Hazmi, Saeed al Ghamdi, Ahmad al Haznawi, and Ahmed al Nami."[276] The muscle highjackers were between the ages of 20 and 28, and were unmarried. They were unemployed and had no more than a high school education. Most of the muscle hijackers went through a boot camp the same as any other al Qaida recruits. The boot camp they attended tested the recruits physically and mentally to assure their readiness and commitment to jihad. They received training in "firearms, heavy weapons, explosives, and topography."[277] Each one of the 9/11 highjackers were personally selected by Usama Bin Laden. He would frequently visit the al Qaida training camps to give lectures and meet the recruits. Once a recruit was selected by Usama, the recruit would swear a suicide oath and then would be sent to Khalid Sheikh Mohammed for further training.

KSM had all of the muscle hijackers obtain U.S. visas in Saudi Arabia. He instructed them to apply for new passports. This way the passports would be clean and would not have entries for Pakistan and Afghanistan which would raise suspicions upon entry into the U.S. Once these new passports were obtained, the passports would be sent to the al Qaida passport division to have entries added in order to create false trails.[278]

Once all of the muscle hijackers had obtained their visas, they went through further specialized training. They were taught specifically how to highjack a plane. All the necessary skills were taught from disarming air marshals to storming the cockpit. They also were trained in the use of knives to kill. Apparently the trainees had to butcher a sheep and camel in preparation for using box cutters and small knives during the hijackings. In addition, the handling of explosives and truck bombings were taught. Apparently they were taught more than just hijacking skills in case one of them was detained by authorities, they would not compromise the planes operation. In addition, they received bodybuilding training and were taught English words and phrases.[279]

Final Preparation

Beginning in May 2001 the Hamburg pilots, Atta, Shehhi, and Jarrah, began taking surveillance flights. Each one of them flew on planes similar to what they would be flying on September 11th. Summer of 2001, Jarrah flew to Philadelphia to receive more training on flying the Hudson Corridor. This flight path allowed him to fly by the World Trade Center. The flight instructor deemed Jarrah to not be experienced enough to fly this route solo, so the instructor flew with him. Hanjour went to another flight school in the area that also allowed students to fly the Hudson Corridor. Hanjour with Hazmi rented a plane together and flew near Washington D.C. In July, Zacarias Moussaoui enrolled in a flight school in Minnesota to learn to fly Boeing 747s. Since he only had 50 hours of solo flight time, an instructor at the school became suspicious and alerted authorities. Shortly thereafter, the INS arrested Moussaoui on immigration charges. Usama Bin Laden and Khalid Sheikh Mohammed did not find out that Moussaoui had been arrested until after September 11th. If they had heard about his arrest, it is possible they might have aborted the mission.^{280}

On August 3, final targets were being decided on by Atta and Binalshibh. Usama Bin Laden wanted the White House hit, but Atta said it would be difficult. Atta agreed but said the Capital would be a secondary target. In addition they decided which muscle hijackers would be grouped with which pilots. In early August Atta, Hazmi, and Hanjour bought tickets for another set of surveillance flights this time to Las Vegas. Each one bought a ticket for the type of plane that they would be hijacking on September 11. During the month of August the hijackers worked out in the gym and the pilots flew frequent practice fights. The hijackers also bought small knives, GPS units, and aeronautical charts. In final preparation 19 tickets were purchased two weeks before September 11th.^{281}

The Attacks

Two flights were boarded in Boston, flights American Airlines 11 and United Airlines 175. Atta, Omari, Satam al Suqami, Wail al Shehri, and Waleed al Shehri boarded American Airlines Flight 11, bound for Los Angelos. In another terminal at Logan airport, Shehhi, joined by Fayez Banihammad, Mohand al Shehri, Ahmed al Ghamdi, and Hamza al Ghamdi, checked in for United Airlines Flight 175, also bound for Los Angeles. In Washington D.C. at the Dulles airport, American Airlines 77 which was bound for Los Angelos was being boarded. Khalid al Mihdhar, Majed Moqed, Hani Hanjour and two brothers, Nawaf al Hamzi and Salem al Hazmi were the members of the third highjack team. The fourth hijack team boarded Flight United Airlines 93 bound for Los Angelos. Saeed al Ghamdi, Ahmed al Nami, Ahmad al Haznawi, and Ziad Jarrah were members of the fourth hijack team. By 8:00 AM, all nineteen hijackers had successfully boarded their planes to be hijacked. Each plane that was selected was bound for Los Angelos. Larger planes were chosen due to the larger size and thus more jet fuel. Each one of these planes was to become guided missiles. This time Ramzi Yousef's plan to bring down the World Trade Center would work. Ramzi Yousef was the mastermind of the 1993 World Trade Center bombing. He had hoped to kill 250,000 people in the 1993 World Trade Center bombing. Although he would not succeed in his kill numbers, his plan of using airplanes as missiles would succeed in destroying the twin towers.

The hijacking of American Airlines Flight 11 began at around 29,000 feet. The last communication Air Traffic Control had with Flight 11 was just after the fasten seat belt sign was illuminated. Up until that time, American 11 radioed Air Traffic Control and all seemed well. The Air Traffic Control told the pilots to go to 35,000 feet. This was the last communication Flight 11 had with Air Traffic Control. The two flight attendants from coach were able to relay information to the American Airlines headquarters. Apparently the two muscle hijackers sitting in first class stabbed the two first class flight attendants. One of the flight attendants was seriously injured and given oxygen while the other attendant had minor injuries. How the hijackers gained access to the cockpit is unknown. Atta soon gained access to the cockpit. Apparently Daniel Lewin who had been an officer in the Israeli Army, tried to attack Atta and Omari. Lewin did not know that another hijacker was sitting behind him. Lewin's throat was slashed presumably by Satam al Suqami who was seated behind him. Betty Ong, a flight attendant, contacted American Airlines Southeastern Reservations Office. She relayed that the hijackers said they had a bomb. The first class passengers were forced to the rear of the plane with mace, pepper spray, or some other irritant. The flight attendant said they could not breathe. Air Traffic Control in Boston overheard one of the hijackers trying to tell the passengers "Nobody move. Everything will be okay. If you try to make any moves, you'll endanger yourself and the airplane. Just stay quiet."[282] Mistakenly the hijacker radioed Air Traffic Control and not the cabin. A few minutes later the flight attendant relayed that the plane was flying erratically and too low. Within minutes American Airlines Flight 11 hit the North Tower of the World Trade Center. All eighty-one passengers, nine flight attendants, and two pilots were killed instantly.

United Airlines Flight 175 took off just as American Airlines flight 11 was being hijacked. The plane reached 31,000 feet. The flight crew had overheard a suspicious transmission from Flight 11 and reported this to Air Traffic Control. This was the last transmission from Flight 175. The hijackers used knives, mace, and a bomb threat to commandeer the plane. Members of the flight crew were stabbed as well as the pilots. The passengers were discussing storming the cockpit. Before they could take action, the plane crashed into the South Tower of the World Trade Center. All fifty-six passengers, seven flight attendants, and two pilots were killed instantly.

American Airlines Flight 77 took off from the Washington Dulles airport and reached a cruising altitude of 35,000 feet. Within a few minutes the plane had been commandeered by the hijackers. The passengers and possibly the pilots were moved to the back of the plane. A passenger reported that the hijackers had knives and box cutters. The pilot announced for everyone to stay calm and that the plane was being hijacked. There were no reports of people being stabbed or mace being used. At 9:37 AM American Airlines Flight 77 crashed into the Pentagon killing 184 people inside the Pentagon. All fifty-eight passengers, 4 flight attendants, and 2 pilots were killed instantly.

United Airlines Flight 93 took off from Newark, New Jersey twenty-five minutes late. By 9:10 American Airlines and United Airlines issued that all planes be grounded. American Airlines did not send an alert to planes already in the air. United sent an alert at 9:19 AM for planes already in the air who were not alerted. The following message was sent "Beware any cockpit intrusion - Two a/c [aircraft] hit World Trade Center." One of the flights that received the warning was United 93." United 93 did not receive the alert until 9:24 AM. At 9:26 AM the pilot asked for the alert to be repeated. At 9:28 AM the hijackers attacked the cockpit. Air Traffic Control could here one of the pilots yelling mayday. A fight ensued for several minutes between the pilots and hijackers. By 9:32 AM the plane had been commandeered. One of the hijackers said over the intercom "Ladies and Gentlemen: Here the captain, please sit down keep remaining sitting. We have a bomb on board. So, sit."[283] One of the flight attendants tried to fight the hijackers in the cockpit and was killed. Passengers began making calls on their cell phones. This gave authorities a lot of information of what was occurring on board. Apparently a passenger had been stabbed along with the captain and first officer who were either injured or dead. The passengers found out from loved ones about the other planes that had been hijacked and used as missiles. The passengers discussed rushing the terrorists and retaking the plane. They voted and decided to act. In mass the passengers rushed to the front of the plane and attacked the terrorists. From the cockpit voice recorder, a revolt could be heard. Jarrah began to roll the plane to the left and right in order to knock the passengers down. Next Jarrah told another hijacker to block the cockpit door while Jarrah threw the nose of the airplane up and down. Loud thumps and noises were heard on the cockpit recorder. Jarrah stabilized the plane and asked the other hijacker in the cockpit "Shall we finish it off?" The other hijacker replied "No. Not yet. When they all come, we finish it off." The fighting sounds continued. A passenger was heard saying "In the cockpit. If we don't we'll die!" A few second later a passenger yelled, "Roll it!" Jarrah says "Is that it? I mean, shall we put it down?" and the other hijacker replies "Yes, put it in it, and pull it down."[284] For the next two minutes the passengers continued their assault. Jarrah knew that the passengers were about to overtake the cockpit, so he turned the control wheel hard to the right. The airplane was turned over onto its back as one hijacker yelled "Allah is the greatest. Allah is the greatest."[285] The sounds of the passengers attacking the cockpit were heard up until the plane crashed into vacant field in Shanksville, Pennsylvania. All thirty-seven passengers, five flight attendants, and two pilots were instantly killed on impact. This plane crashed, but the bravery of the passengers fighting back foiled the hijackers' plans. This plane was not used as a missile as it was intended. The lives of many were saved by the heroism of these passengers.

September 11, 2001 changed every Americans life. No longer was terrorism in a far way country. It was here in our backyard. Usama Bin Laden had been attacking the U.S. for years and years prior to this attack. These attacks were in other countries and far from home. 9/11 changed all this. Now Usama Bin Laden had brought his treachery to our homeland.

Was Saddam Hussein behind the 9/11 attacks? There are links to Iraq. For one Saddam had been working with al Qaida subsidiaries such as the IG and EIJ since 1990. Al Qaida was carrying out operations on Saddam's orders. Definitely Saddam was involved based on his financing, training, and support given to al Qaida. We know as early as 1995 that Saddam was giving al Qaida a safe haven within the borders of Iraq allowing them to operate freely. Whether Saddam gave the order for the 9/11 attacks is unknown, but he was financing, training, and giving support to al Qaida which makes him complicit in the attacks. Remember only a percentage of the memos, transcripts, and documents from Iraq have been translated. I fully expect more evidence regarding Saddam's involvement in the September 11 attacks to be revealed.

10

Master of Deception

"If the attacks of September 11 cost the lives of 3,000 civilians, how much will the size of losses in 50 states within 100 cities if it were attacked in the same way in which New York and Washington were? What would happen if hundreds of planes attacked American cities?"

- Saddam Hussein, September 11, 2002

Saddam was the master of deception. We see in the Iraqi memos and transcripts that Saddam was financing, training, supporting, and providing a safe haven for al Qaida. Saddam was able to conceal his relationship with al Qaida through secrecy and intermediaries. Likewise Saddam was able to conceal his weapons of mass destruction. First let's address the definition of weapons of mass destruction. Weapons of mass destruction (WMD) can be biological, chemical, or nuclear. These are weapons that will kill civilians as well as military personnel when used. When we discuss WMD we are not just talking about nuclear, but biological and chemical weapons as well. The Pentagon report on Saddam is clear that Saddam had biological, chemical, and nuclear weapons long after he was supposed to have dismantled these weapons and halt these programs.

On February 5, 2003 the Secretary of State, Colin Powell addressed the United Nations Security Council. It turns out that everything he discussed in his address can be seen in the memos, documents, and transcripts within the Pentagon report on Saddam. Contrary to what the media has said, Colin Powell spoke the truth, and the intelligence he presented was good. First let's review the major points from Colin Powell's UN address:

- Iraq had a history of concealing its biological, chemical, and nuclear weapons programs.
- Iraq had a special committee that oversaw the UN inspections. Its job was to deceive and undermine the inspectors.
- Iraq had developed mobile units so that the WMD weapons and research could be moved easily to evade UN inspectors.
- Saddam had ties to terrorism, and was giving al Qaida safe haven in Iraq.

Colin Powell began his address by discussing the UN Resolution 1441. On November 8, 2002 the UN Security Council voted unanimously to disarm Iraq. **"Iraq had already been found guilty of material breach of its obligations, stretching back over 16 previous resolutions and 12 years."** Resolution 1441 was Iraq's last chance to unilaterally disarm. This meant that *all* of its biological, chemical, and nuclear weapons must be destroyed and programs halted. At that point Iraq had to comply or face serious consequences.

Concealment of Weapons of Mass Destruction

On the concealment of WMDs, Colin Powell said "This council placed the burden on Iraq to comply and disarm and not on the inspectors to find that which Iraq has gone out of its way to conceal for so long. Inspectors are inspectors; they are not detectives.... The facts on ...Iraq's behavior demonstrate that Saddam Hussein and his regime have made no effort--no effort--to disarm as required by the international community. Indeed, the facts and Iraq's behavior show that Saddam Hussein and his regime are concealing their efforts to produce more weapons of mass destruction.... This effort to hide things from the inspectors is not one or two isolated events, quite the contrary. This is part and parcel of a policy of evasion and deception that goes back 12 years, a policy set at the highest levels of the Iraqi regime." This pattern of concealment is exposed in the Pentagon report on Saddam. In one memo it states **"some targets are mobile, and Iraq has proven that it moved throughout the country very expansive equipment and data to evade United Nations' weapons inspection teams."** (Appendix, Figure 66)

The fact that Iraq continued to conceal its weapons and programs is clearly seen in memo ISGQ-2005-00034061. This memo is dated October 22, 2000 and is addressed to the Deputy Director of Intelligence Service regarding scientific ideas and is from the General Security Section Director. The General Security Section Director asks that the biologist named Uday Salim Mahdi destroy all documents he has in regards to his biological weapons research. The memo states that Mahdi should **"destroy all of the documents related to his**

research to avoid any inconvenience with the inspection groups or the possibility of it reaching the country's enemies." (See Appendix, Figure 63) The response letter from the Deputy Director of Intelligence Service to the General Security Section Director explains that the biologist has been working on the "**production of viruses and bacteria that could be used to contaminate enemy water supplies in American military bases in Kuwait and Saudi Arabia.**" (see Appendix, Figures 63-64)   Apparently the biologist, Mahdi sent a suggestion in that was forwarded to the *nuclear energy organization*. This provides new evidence that Saddam was continuing his nuclear energy program long after he said the program had been halted. The Deputy Director was concerned that this research would be found out by the inspectors, so he asked the biologist stop working on these viruses and bacteria and to destroy all documentation related to this research and development. At the end of the memo it says "**if a decision was made to carry out an operation of this kind, the material required can be found in the local markets.**" It is not as if they are destroying the documentation and biological agents to comply with the UN, but to conceal the research and agents from the UN inspectors. From these two letters we see clearly that as of October 22, 2000 Saddam was still researching and developing biological weapons and continuing his nuclear program.   Concerned about the UN inspectors finding out about this research and development, they are asking the biologist to stop working on these biological agents and to destroy all related documentation.

Committee of Concealment

Colin Powell goes on to talk about an Iraqi committee of concealment whose job is to mislead and evade the UN inspectors. Colin Powell says "**Iraq has a high-level committee to monitor the inspectors who were sent in to monitor Iraq's disarmament. Not to cooperate with them, not to assist them, but to spy on them and keep them from doing their jobs. The committee reports directly to Saddam Hussein.... [Their] job is not to cooperate, it is to deceive; not to disarm, but to undermine the inspectors; not to support them, but to frustrate them and to make sure they learn nothing.**"[286]

Saddam's pattern of deceit is clearly seen in the transcript ISGQ-2003-M0006443 (Appendix, Figure 15). Saddam's method of evading inspectors is described. In this transcript, Saddam is discussing with his command members the visit of Rolf Ekeus and the UN inspectors. Tarik Aziz tells the other command members that he is handling the UN inspectors as follows: When the inspectors ask, what amounts of biological weapons have been produced and what the goals of these weapons were, we "**told the technical comrades that when they ask, tell them this is not our job.**" The researchers and developers of the chemical, biological, and nuclear weapons were supposed to say to the inspectors simply that: "**We have the duty of implementation. Ask us in the implementation matters.**" The researchers and developers were further told if these types of political or security questions were asked, then they should defer the UN inspector to the appropriate Iraqi political official. Likewise questions regarding the quantities transformed into weapons, timing of production, and timing of destruction should be handled by the appropriate political official.

Mobile WMDs Units

Another concern raised during Colin Powell's address to the UN was that Iraq had mobile WMD units. Colin Powell said that Iraq had **"mobile production facilities used to make biological agents. The trucks and train cars are easily moved and are designed to evade detection by inspectors."** These mobile units allowed Saddam to quickly move the weapons when the UN inspectors arrived. Even more importantly is that these mobile units were highly sophisticated production units. They were capable of actually producing both chemical and biological weapons.

Transcript ISGQ-2003-00003598 is dated January 4, 2001, so its just eight months before the September 11, 2001 attacks. Saddam was concerned that the U.S. might bomb Iraq. This transcript describes that the Iraqi leadership was concerned that Iraq's chemical and biological weapons sites may be bombed. The Iraqi Intelligence Service had learned that the American weapons manufacturers were developing bombs that were able to **"penetrate deeply into the ground or concrete."**[287] The transcript says that if one of these sites was hit and not completely annihilated by the blast, then the chemical and biological weapons could **"be detected from the air by some**

hazardous airborne substances." The transcript goes on to boast that **"some targets are mobile, and Iraq has proven that it moved throughout the country very expansive equipment and data to evade United Nations' weapons inspection teams.** Still, precision is essential and fundamental to the Americans if they want to strike vital targets while minimizing civilian losses simultaneously." (Appendix, Figure 66) Clearly Saddam still had both chemical and biological weapons as of the writing of this memo, January 4, 2001. The memo proves that Saddam used mobile units to produce biological and chemical weapons and to evade UN weapons inspectors.

Rolf Ekeus, the leader of the first UN Inspections Team to go into Iraq, warned that these production facilities were the biggest threat. The reason is that chemical and biological weapons can lose their potency over time, but having production facilities that can quickly produce the agent and move them to where they are needed is the most serious threat. Rolf Ekeus warned in 2003 that "This combination of researchers, engineers, know-how, precursors, batch production techniques and testing is what constituted Iraq's chemical threat -- its chemical weapon. **The rather bizarre political focus on the search for rusting drums and pieces of munitions containing low-quality chemicals has tended to distort the important question of WMD in Iraq and exposed the American and British administrations to unjustified criticism. The real chemical warfare threat from Iraq ... is the chance that Iraqi chemical weapons specialists would sign up with terrorist networks such as al Qaida.... While biological weapons are not easily adapted for battlefield use, they are**

potentially ... more devastating as a means for massive terrorist onslaught on civilian targets."[288]

What biological weapons were being produced? Well Colin Powell said that anthrax and botulinum toxins had been produced. We know from the attacks on the Kurds that Saddam also had typhoid spores and cholera. Colin Powell goes on to warn, "In fact, they can produce enough dry biological agent in a single month to kill thousands upon thousands of people. And [a] dry agent of this type is the most lethal form for human beings." Another more chilling fact is that Iraq was producing weaponized anthrax. When Iraq finally admitted to having biological weapons in 1995 the quantities were large. Colin Powell continued by explaining that less than a teaspoon of dry anthrax could cause catastrophic results. He gave the example of when the United States Senate was shutdown in the fall of 2001 because of an envelope with less than a teaspoon of anthrax. Several hundred people had to receive emergency medical care, and the two postal workers who handled the envelope were killed.

Ties to al Qaida

Colin Powell warned that Saddam had direct operational ties to terrorism and explained that al Qaida had a camp in the Northern part of Iraq. In the Pentagon Report on Saddam there are numerous memos, transcripts, and documents that prove Saddam's alliance with terrorists. Here in 2003, Colin Powell said that **"Our concern is not just about**

these elicit weapons. It's the way that these elicit weapons can be connected to terrorists and terrorist organizations that have no compunction about using such devices against innocent people around the world. Iraq and terrorism go back decades. Baghdad trains Palestine Liberation Front members in small arms and explosives. Saddam uses the Arab Liberation Front to funnel money to the families of Palestinian suicide bombers in order to prolong the Intifada. And it's no secret that Saddam's own intelligence service was involved in dozens of attacks or attempted assassinations in the 1990s."

In the Pentagon report on Saddam, all of Saddam's terrorist ties are illustrated. These connections have been illustrated throughout this book. In addition, Saddam's Fedayeen recruited martyrs to carry out suicide attacks. In Appendix, Figure 67 is a letter from an individual who is volunteering to carry out a suicide mission. The letter says "I ask your Excellency to allow me to participate in carrying out the martyrs missions to prove to the full world that we are with our brothers in the occupied territory by soul too."

Saddam was also financing terrorists in large sums. Figures 68 and 69 in the Appendix illustrate this financing. In the Figure 68 memo, it states that 4 million dinars were paid to the families of Palestinian martyrs. Figure 69 includes a memo that describes that one of Saddam's commandos is being paid 1.5 million dinars in order to execute a hostile agent who resides in London, England.

In addition to all of the above, Saddam was creating jihadist propaganda for the Islamic terrorists. In the Appendix, Figure 70, there is a memo that describes this jihadist propaganda created by Iraq titled

"Lessons in 'Secret Organization and Jihad Work'. These lessons were authorized, directed, reviewed, updated and margin-notated as well as signed by Saddam Hussein himself. The Minister of Culture, the Press Secretary and members of a select committee were directed to write and re-write all of these lessons. These activities were from 1992 through 2000." These lessons in jihad were distributed in multiple formats including cassette tapes, internet, radio, newspapers, television, videos, booklets, and e-mails.

Colin Powell stressed the danger of Iraq having a connection to al Qaida. Powell continued by saying **"But what I want to bring to your attention today is the potentially much more sinister nexus between Iraq and the Al Qaida terrorist network, a nexus that combines classic terrorist organizations and modern methods of murder.** Iraq today harbors a deadly terrorist network headed by Abu Musab Al-Zarqawi, an [associate and] collaborator of Usama Bin Laden and his Al Qaida lieutenants. Zarqawi, a Palestinian born in Jordan, fought in the Afghan war more than a decade ago. Returning to Afghanistan in 2000, he oversaw a terrorist training camp. One of his specialties and one of the specialties of this camp is poisons. When our coalition [forces] ousted the Taliban, the Zarqawi network helped establish another poison and explosive training center camp. And this camp is located in northeastern Iraq."

"The network is teaching its operatives how to produce ricin and other poisons. Let me remind you how ricin works. Less than a pinch— [imagine] a pinch of salt--less than a pinch of ricin, eating just this amount in your food, would cause shock followed by circulatory failure. Death comes within 72 hours and there is no antidote, there is no cure. It is fatal. Those helping to run this camp are Zarqawi lieutenants operating in northern Kurdish areas outside Saddam Hussein's controlled Iraq. But Baghdad has an agent in the most senior levels of the radical organization, Ansar al-Islam, that controls this corner of Iraq. In 2000 this agent offered Al Qaida safe haven in the region. After we swept Al Qaida from Afghanistan, some of its members accepted this safe haven. They remain their today."

There is a memo not included in the Pentagon report but is included in the Harmony database at West Point. This letter dated July 9, 2005 is titled "Zawahiri's Letter to Zarqawi." The letter was written by Ayman al-Zawahiri who was in Afghanistan at the time. The letter was addressed to Abu Musam al-Zarqawi who was the leader of al Qaida in Iraq. Zawahiri explains that al Qaida had four main goals:

1. "Expel the Americans from Iraq.
2. Establish an Islamic authority and develop it into a caliphate, extending influence over as much Iraqi territory as possible.
3. Extend the jihad to Iraq's secular neighbors.
4. Extend the jihad to Israel."

From the Pentagon report on Saddam, we know al Qaida was in Iraq as early as 1995. As discussed previously, in transcript ISGQ-2003-M0006443 (Appendix, Figures 80-84) which is a conversation that was made in 1995 as part of a discussion about the United Nations (UN) weapons inspection after the Gulf War. Keep in mind, that this transcript is dated six years prior to the 2001 WTC bombing.

Saddam's command member wants al Qaida to be recognized for their efforts.

Apparently some of the Arab mujahideen from Afghanistan were relocated to Iraq to aid Saddam after the Gulf War. Previously in the memo presented in chapter 1 describing Iraq renewing its relationship with the IG, it says "**To make use of the Arab Islamic elements that were fighting in Afghanistan and do not have current operating bases. They are dispersed in Sudan, Somalia and Egypt.**" (Appendix, Figure 7 2B) Part of the agreement that was made between Iraq and the IG was that Iraq would make use of the Arab mujahideen forces that originated in Afghanistan.

In memo ISGQ-2003-M0006443 these mujahideen forces are discussed again. By 1995, some of al Qaida and the Arab mujahideen have relocated to Iraq and are helping Saddam rebuild broken airplanes, equipment, and weapons. The conversation begins with a discussion of al Qaida described as the "believers" and how they operate. Saddam says "I mean the determination of *believers* and how they work. The idea of military manufacturing began with the idea of utilizing all the other militarization capabilities to repair the equipment that was repairable. I mean whether in service or not. The idea of using air power was born and [the] air force and the engineering of electrical equipment along [with] the military manufacturing capacities. They created a campaign [and] they called it the call of the leader for two months." Saddam continues describing this campaign led by al Qaida in Iraq to fix massive amounts of military equipment for

Saddam. A large number of al Qaida members must have been in Iraq working on this project because the list of fixed equipment is long. "In the two months [al Qaida] repaired tools that were beyond usage." Saddam continues by saying that they were working at an airport. He says the following items were repaired by al Qaida and the Arab mujahideen.

"
- 250 Armored Personnel Carriers
- 40 Tanks
- 40 Transporters
- 15 Mobile Canons 155 millimeters
- 30 Transporters of a different kind
- 9 "Chifton" tanks
- 35 T-55 Tanks
- 5 T-72 Tanks
- 9 Rescue Tanks
- 10 improvised rocket launchers/tubes
- 90 Various vehicles/trucks
- 9 guns (155 mm)
- 20 guns (155 mm)
- 17 Canons (152 mm)
- 1 gun (150 mm)
- 9 Tanks (55 mm) attached with a 160 mm mortar
- 4 guns (120 mm) B-30
- 57 guns (105 mm)
- 2 guns (240mm)
- 8 guns (120mm)
- 151 mortars (83mm)
- 305 mortars (60mm)
- 30,000 Kalashnikov Rifles
- 1,212 RPK machine guns
- 852 PKC machine guns
- 1,912 RPG-7 bombers
- 63 SPG-9

- 80 Sniper Rifles
- 1 Single machine gun
- 1 gun (106mm)
- 50 various guns
- 10,000 Simanov Rifles
- Surface to surface missile equipment
- 7 Ar-Ra'd Missile Launchers
- 22 Ar-Ra'd Missile Transporters
- 13 At-Tareq Missile Launchers
- 10 At-Tareq Missile Transporters
- 6 Missile Command Sites
- 4 Ababil Missile launchers
- 7 Surveying wheels
- 452 Various Radio Tools
- 659 Field Phone Equipment
- 125 generator engines
- 1,050 Anti-air bases
- 50 coaxial machine guns
- 2 bilateral machine guns
- 7 grenade Launchers (30mm)
- 123 helicopters Aircraft:s
- 18 Fixed Wing Fighter Plane
- 11 Training Planes"

Saddam continues by saying that all of these items have been repaired in "two months". Obviously a large number of al Qaida members and Arab mujahideen have been relocated to Iraq to aid Saddam after the Gulf War. An unidentified person replies to Saddam, "Can I make a suggestion, sir? ...These big efforts regarding the Mujahideen, I suggest that the Council of ministers takes a look at these big and good efforts conducted by these Mujahideen ... [and we should] present them with thanks and high appreciation for these good efforts in the service of Iraq." Saddam continues by saying "These are young men. ...They are all professionals and effective in their duties." The unidentified person replies, "**In this time it is difficult sir and they present Iraq with this big present I see they deserve all appreciation and respect from our part and the thing is left to al Qaida God preserves it.**" Saddam replies, "**They [al Qaida] suggested an exterior I doubled the proposal that's why they are happy that I am aware of their efforts to the details and every time they present a finding we tell them to do to this person this thing etc I mean and they take the initiative.**" Here we clearly see that Saddam was directly working with al Qaida in Iraq in 1995. Al Qaida forces had relocated to Iraq and were actively working to help Iraq in any way they could. In this case they were repairing equipment and aircraft for Iraq.

Conclusion

Saddam was not only financing and supporting terrorism, but he was giving al Qaida a safe haven in Iraq. From creating and distributing Islamic terrorist propaganda to ordering the execution of dissidents, Saddam was in alliance with terrorists. Colin Powell was correct in saying that there existed a sinister nexus with Saddam, al Qaida, and weapons of mass destruction. Everything that Colin Powell said in his 2003 address to the United Nations was true. The Pentagon report on Saddam bears out all of Powell's assertions. As a result, the U.S. invasion of Iraq was fully justified according to UN Resolution 1441.

The War on Terror began under the Clinton Administration. Because al Qaida was not properly dealt with, it formed more alliances and increased it stronghold until 9/11. Finally America woke up and realized we were in a War on Terror. Once Saddam Hussein who was a partner with terror formed an alliance with al Qaida, he had to be dealt with in the War on Terror.

The United States was completely justified in invading Iraq due to Saddam's state support of al Qaida and worldwide terrorism in general. As Rolf Ekeus, the lead UN inspector, said the U.S. and Britain were fully justified in the "international military intervention" to overthrow Saddam Hussein. "To accept the alternative -- letting Hussein remain in power with his chemical and biological weapons capability -- would have been to tolerate a continuing destabilizing arms race in the gulf, including future nuclearization of the region, threats to the world's energy supplies, leakage of WMD technology and expertise to terrorist networks, systematic sabotage of efforts to create and sustain a process of peace between the Israelis and the Palestinians and the continued terrorizing of the Iraqi people."[289] Operation Iraqi Freedom destroyed Iraq's state support of terrorism as follows:

1. No longer can the Iraqi Government issue passports to known terrorists;
2. No longer can Iraq train known terrorists at Iraqi Fedayeen training camps;

3. No longer can Iraq finance and give support to terrorists; and
4. No longer can Iraq give a safe haven to al Qaida.

The U.S. and its allies had to take Saddam Hussein out before the unimaginable occurred with al Qaida getting access to nuclear, chemical, or biological weapons.

Appendix

1.1 Terrorist Organizations affiliated with Iraq

```
                                          Memo No: 110/2/43
                                          Date: 25 Jan 1993
Republic of Iraq Presidency of
the Republic IIS

Top Secret Personal
Very Urgent

              Subject: Execution of Directive

     In reference to your memo Top Secret Personal and Very Urgent
425/K dated 18 Jan 1993. Below are the groups with whom our agency
has relations, and who have elements dispersed on the Arab land
and have the expertise to carry out the aforementioned mission.

1. Palestinian Organization:
     A. Fatih Organization - Revolutionary Council (Abu Nidal
        Organization.)
        This movement was established after October War of
        1973 following its separation from the Fatih
        Organization. It is under the leadership of Sabri Al-
        Banna

        (Abu Nidal) who was the head of the Fatih office in
        Baghdad. This movement believes in political aggression
        and it practices assassination operations. We have had
        relations with this organization since 1973 and they
        currently have a representative in Iraq, whom we
        financially subsidize in the amount of 20,000 I.D. (TC:
        Iraqi dinar) in addition to the other forms of aid like
        vehicles. They have elements dispersed in the Arab world.

     B. Palestinian Liberation Front
        This front was established in 1983 after the secession
        led by Abu Al-Abbas, at the time when he held the
        position of deputy chairman of the front. They currently
        have an office in Baghdad. We had previously assigned
        them to carry out Fedayeen operations against American
        interests during the Mother of All Battles (TC: The First
        Gulf War),
```

Figure 4 – Terrorist organizations affiliated with Iraq – second translation (part 1 of 5)

which they were successful.

C. Forces 17 (Abu Al-Tayyib Group)
A Security Service which specializes with operations inside the occupied territories and is responsible for the security of its leadership and particularly Abu 'Ammar. We have good relations with their Baghdad office. They were not assigned to carry out Fedayeen operations during the Mother of All Battles, but were assigned to gather intelligence, and they supplied us with good information.

D. Organization of Al-Jihad and Al-Tajdid (TC: Struggle and Renewal)
A secret Muslim Palestinian organization which was formed after the Mother of All Battles, it believes in Jihad armament (TC: Military Jihad) against American and Western interests. It also believes that Saddam Hussein is the leader of the believer group against infidels. Two of Its leaders, who live in Jordan,

Are Nasif Nasir Ahmad (Abu-Ayyub) and Sabir Tawfiq Al-Muqbil (Abu-Sharaf). Abu-Sharaf heads the organization and visited Iraq two months ago and voiced his organization's willingness to perform operations against American interests at any time.

E. Al-Murabitun Organization (TC: The binding or the Positioned Organization)
A Palestinian organization that specializes in operating inside the occupied territories, and it was supervised by Salah Khalaf (Abu Ayyad). After his death, the organization's relationship declined with Yasser Arafat and financial aid was cut off. They have elements dispersed in the occupied territories and Palestinian camps. Our apparatus has ties with its military organizer, Mustafa Mir'i and his aide, Lutfi Abd-al-Rahman. We have previously

Figure 5 - Terrorist organizations affiliated with Iraq second translation (part 2 of 5)

> met with them in Baghdad in Dec 1992. They have voiced their willingness to carry out assignment given to them.
>
> F. The Palestinian Abd-al-Bari Al-Duwayk (Abu Dawud)
> He was the representative for the organized group Hamid Abu Muhammad (The National Front - The Foreign field). His relationship with them was severed some time ago. He currently resides in Cyprus, and was previously assigned to carry out Fedayeen operations during the Mother of All Battles. He carried out some of these operations.
>
> G. Abd-al-Fattah Abd-al-Latif Fakhuri (Abu Yihya)
> Deputy Manager of the office of Farouq Qaddumi (Abu Al-Lutuf) in Amman, Jordan. He was one of the leaders in the Western Sector Apparatus. He is considered an operations man of a certain type and he has elements
>
> > attached to him directly to carry out his orders. We have good relationship with him and he could be utilized in Fedayeen operations.
>
> 2. Our apparatus recently met with Sheik Ali 'Uthman Taha, Deputy of the National Islamic Front in Sudan. We have come to the following agreements:
>   A. To reinstate our relationship with the Organized Islamic Group, known in Egypt as (The Islamic Groups Organization) that was founded in 1979 by Egyptian Muhammad Abd-al-Salam Faraj. It is currently led by Dr. 'Umar Adb-al-Rahman. It is considered one of the most radical and violent Egyptian organizations. It has executed both the assassinations of Sadat and the president of the National Egyptian Council, Rif'at Almahjub. We've previously met with the Organization's representative

Figure 6 - Terrorist organizations affiliated with Iraq second translation (part 3 of 5)

> On December 14, 1990, and we agreed on a plan to move against the Egyptian regime through Fedayeen operations, provided that we guarantee them (TC: Financial) aid, training and whatever they need.
> B. To make use of the Arab Islamic elements that were fighting in Afghanistan and do not have current operating bases. They are dispersed in Sudan, Somalia and Egypt.
> C. What was aforementioned in 2.A and 2.B will be discussed during the anticipated visit of Sheik Ali 'Uthman to Iraq. Hopefully this will be soon and we will see their capabilities and evaluate the results based upon that.
>
> 3. Asian Organizations:
>   A. Jam'iyyat 'Ulama' Al-Islam (J.U.I.), (TC: The Society of Islamic Scholars)
>   1. It was established in 1948 and is considered one of the political parties that influence
>
>   the Pakistani arena and in particular the northern region Bolujistan and Punjab. It is headed by Mulana (TC: or Mawlana) Fadil Al-Rahman.
>   2. It depends on its financing on its organizations in Pakistan and foreign aid from Iraq and Libya.
>   3. Secretary of the Party, Mulana Jawid Ahmad Nu'mati, has a close relationship with our apparatus since 1981 and is willing to perform any mission that he would be assigned.
>
>   B. The Islamic Afghani Party:
>   1. It was established in 1974 when its founder escaped from Afghanistan to Pakistan.
>   2. It is considered one of the radical religious and political movements that are very intransigent towards the West.

Figure 7– Terrorist organizations affiliated with Iraq second translation (part 4 of 5)

> It is also the strongest among the seven Afghani parties from the stand point of its political and military organizational skills.
> 3. It opposes the current president of Afghanistan and has influence on the Pashtun tribes that comprise more than 70% of the Afghani population.
> 4. Depends financially on contributions from its organizations and aid from Iraq and Libya.
> 5. Our apparatus has had a relationship with the Party since 1989 and this relationship developed into a direct relationship between our country (Iraq) and the leader of the Party, Hikmatyar, or through his representative (his cousin and son-in-law) Dr. Ghirat (TC: or Ghayrat) Bahir.
>
> C. Pakistani Scholars Society (J.U.P.)
> 1. It was established in 1970, its objectives are religious and political reform.
> 2. It has huge popularity all over Pakistan, especially in Karachi and Lahore and expands into India. It has offices in Holland and England.
> 3. Our apparatus has had ties with this party since 1987. It is considered one of the founding members of the Popular or People's Islamic Conference, its headquarters being in Baghdad.
>
> D. The aforementioned organizations were not assigned to carry out Fedayeen operations during the Mother of All Battles, with the exception of the Secretary of the JUI, Mulana Jawid Ahmad Nu'mati. He was assigned at the time

Figure 8 - Terrorist organizations affiliated with Iraq second translation (part 5 of 5)[290]

Page 2

The Republic of Iraq
The President Office
Intelligence Service

Top-Secret, Personal
and Urgent

The Republic of Iraq
The President Office
Intelligence Service

Top Secret, Personal and Urgent
Date: / /

To: the Secretary of the office of the president of the Republic of Iraq
Subject: Carrying out directive

With refernce to your letter classified top-secret and personal and Urgent directive number 425/K dated 18/01/1993, we list herein below the organizations that our agency cooperates with and have relations with various elements in many parts of the Arab world and also have the expertise to carry out assignments indicated in the above directive number [425/K]:

1- Palestinian Organizations

   A- Fatah   Revolutionary Council (Abu-Nidal's organization)

Established after the November war in 1973; split from the Fatah organization lead by Sabri al-Bana (Abu-Nidal) who used to be the head the Fatah office in Baghdad. The Organization's political belief is based on violence and assassinations. We [IIS] have been in contact with this organization since 1973 and currently they have contacts with

* First Translation *

Figure 9 - Terrorist organizations affiliated with Iraq - first translation (part 1 of 5)

our representative in Iraq who gave them financial aid in the amount of (20) thousand Dinars in addition to other logistic support, such as vehicles. They [Abu-Nidal's Org] have members in many Arab countries that participated in Umm-al-Ma'arik [first Gulf war/Desert Storm] but had no vital role in carrying out any operations.

Page 3

    B- Palestine Liberation Front

It was established in 1983 after the split by Abu-al-Abbas who was the deputy general secretary of the front which currently has an office in Baghdad. They were assigned to carry out commando operations against American interests abroad during Umm-al-Ma'arik war. They carried out a number of successful operations.

    C- The 17 Forces of (Abu-al-Tayyib)

Security agency specialized in operations inside the occupied territories whose responsibility is to provide security to the president and specifically to protect the chairman, Abu-Ammar. We [IIS] have good relations with them and they [force 17] have an office in Baghdad. They were not assigned any commando operations during Umm-al-Ma'arik war. Nevertheless, they were assigned to collect intelligence information and they provided us with valuable information.

Page 4

    D- Renewal and Jihad Organization

Secret Islamic Palestinian Organization was established after Umm-al-Ma'ark [the first Gulf war]; it believes in armed Jihad against the Americans and Western interests. They also believe that our leader, the president, may God protect him, is a leader who is against the infidels' camp. The organization's leaders live in Jordan; some of its prominent figures are: (Nasif Nasir Ahmad aka Abu-Ayub; Var: Ayoub; Ayyoub), Sabir Tawfiq al-Muqbil aka Abu-Ashraf). The Organization's chief, visited the region [Iraq] two month ago. The organization showed willingness to carry out operations against American interests at any time.

    E- Al-Wathiqun [the confidants]   Al-Murabitun [those on guard]

This is a Palestinian organization whose main objective is to carry out operations inside the occupied territories. It is supervised by Salah Khalaf aka Abu-Iyad.

Page 5

After his [Salah Khalf] death, the Organization's relations with Chairman Yasir Araft worsened, and all financial support was halted. They have members spread within the territories and in the Palestinian camps. We [IIS] have relation with the organization's

Figure 10 - Terrorist organizations affiliated with Iraq- first translation (part 2 of 5)

military advisor (Mustafa Mur'i) whose assistant is Lutfi Abd al-Rahman. We have previously met with them in Baghdad in January 1992. They were willing to carry out any assignment we tasked them with, but we did not assign them any task during the first Gulf war since our relationship with them was fairly new.

F- The Palestinian Abd al-Bari al-Duwaik aka (Abu Dawoud)

The above-mentioned individual was the representative of the organization to the group of Hamid Abu-Muhammad (Popular Front abroad operations). His relations with this group discontinued for a long time. He currently lives in Cyprus, and he was assigned to carry out a number of commando operations during Umm al-Ma'arik which he did. Our relationship with him is still outstanding and we can benefit from him in carrying out operations.

Page 6

G- Abd al-Fatah Abd al-Latif Fakhuri (Abu_Yahya)

He is the deputy of the director's office, Farouq Qadumi (Abu-al-Lutuf) in Amman. He was one of the leaders of the western-sector agency. He is known as the special operation man, and he has members directly connected to him that can carry out operation. Our relationship with him is good and we can benefit from him in commando operations. He was not assigned to carry out any operation in the Umm al-ma'arik since our relations with him was fairly new.

2- During our recent meeting with al-Sheikh Ali 'Uthman Taha, deputy chairman of the Islamic National Front in Sudan, we agreed to:

a- Renew our relations with the Islamic Jihad Organization in Egypt which is aka Islamic Group Organization. Our information on this organization is as follows:

Page 7

First: It was established year 1979 by the Egyptian Muhammad Abd al-Salam Faraj, lead by Dr. Umar Abd al-Rahman

Second: Its goal is to apply the Islamic shari'a's law and establish Islamic rule.

Third: It is considered to be one of the most brutal Egyptian organizations. It carried numerous successful commando operations against the Egyptian regime, and it assassinated Sadat and Rif'at Mahjoub, the head of the people' council.

Fourth: The group's council headed by Dr. 'Umar Abd al-Rahman includes leaders of the organization. This group has branches in provinces, and organized units in universities, mosques and villages.

* First Translation *

Figure 11 - Terrorist organizations affiliated with Iraq- first translation (part 3 of 5)

Page 8

Fifth: We have previously met with one of the organization's representative on 14/12/1990, and we agreed on a plan to carry out commando operations against the Egyptian regime, meanwhile we [IIS] will provide it with support, financial help and training.

- b- Arab Islamic members who fought in Afghanistan and have no place to go to [to live in], are spread in (Sudan, Egypt and Somalia).
- c- According to the above-mentioned paragraphs (a and b), it will be discussed during the proposed visit by the above mentioned person to Iraq which we hope that it will take place soon. At this visit we will know their potential and evaluate the results in view of that

Page 9

3-Asian Organizations

      a. Islamic 'Ulama Group (J.U.I) Islamic Scholars Group

First: Established in 1948, considered on of the influential parties in Pakistan especially in the Northern district, Balushistan and Bunjab, chaired by Maulana Fadl al-Rahman

Second: They rely on their financial support from their organizations from Pakistan and foreign assistance that they receive from Iraq and Libya.

Third: The party's secretary is Maulana Jawid [Javid] Ahmad Nu'mani. He has strong relations with our agency since 1981, and he is ready to carry out any assignment we task him with

      b. The Afhani Islamic Party [Hizb Islami]

Page 10

First: established in 1974 when its founder escaped from Afghanistan to Pakistan

Second: It is considered one of the extreme political religious movements against the west, and one of the strongest seven Sunni parties in Afghanistan with respect to political and military organizations

Third: He is one of the current opponents of the president of Afghanistan and has strong influence among the Afghan Pashtu tribes which constitute more than 70% of the population

Fourth: He relies on the organizations' financial support as well as foreign assistance from Iraq and Libya

* First Translation *

Figure 12 - Terrorist organizations affiliated with Iraq- first translation (part 4 of 5)

* First Translation *

The classification markings are original to the Iraqi documents and do not reflect current U.S classification.

Fifth: Our agency has relations with the above-mentioned party since 1989, and this became direct relation between the country, which is Iraq, and the head of the party, Hikmatyar or via his representative, his cousin and son-in-law, Dr. Ghayrat Bahir

Page 11

    c. Jam'iyat 'Ulama Pakistan (J.U.P) Pakistan Scholars Group

First: established 1970, its goals are religious, political and reform

Second: It is well known in Pakistan especially in Karachi and Lahore all the way to India, has office, in Holland and England

Third: Our Intel agency has relations with the above mentioned party since 1987, knowing that the party in considered to be one of the founding members of the Islamic people's conference who's HQs is in Baghdad

    d. We would like to point out that the above mentioned Asian Organizations have not been tasked with any commando operations and Umm-al-Ma'arik except the secretary of Islamic Ulama' Group, Maulana Jawid [Javid]Ahmad Nu'mani who was tasked at the time to carry out commando operations. He did carry out several successful commando operations. As for the other organizations, they were tasked to go on undertake protest demonstrations against the American aggression. They did undertake several activities for this purpose.

Please be advised and you may appoint the above mentioned parties to carry out this task.

Regards

[Page 13 is a duplicate of page 12 except for the names:]

Director of the intelligence service

Cc: Farouq [Var: Faruq; Farooq]
1/24

Page 14

Top-Secret - personal
Republic of Iraq
Secretary
Number 425/K
Date: 1/18/1993

Figure 13 - Terrorist organizations affiliated with Iraq - first translation (part 5 of 5)[291]

1.2 Origins of al Qaida – 1989 Founders Meeting

1.2.1 From US.vs Usama Bin Laden (day two) p. 192

7   A.   He said we going to make group and this is group that

8   under Farook, and it's going to be one man for the group and

9   it's going to be focussed in jihad and we going to use the

10   group to do another thing out of Afghanistan.

11   Q.   And did Abu Ayoub al Iraqi tell you what the name of this

12   group was?

13   A.   Yes.

14   Q.   Can you tell the jury what the name of the group was?

15   A.   Al Qaeda.

16   Q.   When you were there did anyone tell you why you were one

17   of the people invited to this meeting?

18   A.   Yes.

19   Q.   What were you told?

20   A.   They say we love if you join the group and if you continue

21   about jihad.

1.2.2 From US.vs Usama Bin Laden (day two) p. 193-194

6   Q. You said you were before with them. Can you tell us who

7   "them" was?

8   A. The people who want to establish a group, I work with them

9   in Afghanistan.

10 Q. Can you tell us who those people were that wished to

11 establish the group?

12 A. Abu Ayoub al Iraqi and Abu Ubaidah al Banshiri.

13 Q. Will you stop there. We'll put that on the screen.

14 Why don't we continue and give us the name and we'll

15 discuss each name.

16 A. Abu Faraj al Yemeni.

17 Q. Is it fair to say a person has the name "al Yemeni," they

18 are of the background that comes from Yemen?

19 A. Yes. And Dr. Abdel Moez and Ayman al Zawahiri.

20 Q. Would you stop there. Dr. Abdel Moez, you also mentioned

21 the name Ayman al Zawahiri. If you make two things clear:

22 Are Abu Moez and Ayman al Zawahiri, are they the same or

23   different people?

24   A.   Same person.

25   Q.   And you mentioned the word "doctor," is he in fact a

1   doctor?

2   A.   Yes, he's general doctor.

1.2.3 From US.vs Usama Bin Laden (day two) p. 196

11   Q.   Will you tell us what Abu Ubaidah al Banshiri explained to

12   you about the papers he said he handed out to you?

13   A.   The papers about the agenda of the al Qaeda group and

14   about the rule, about what your duty, what emir duty and about

15   the shura council.

16   Q.   Why don't we stop there. First, you said "the papers."

17   Explain what the al Qaeda agenda was. Can you tell us what

18   those papers said about the al Qaeda agenda?

19   A.   The al Qaeda, it's established for focus in jihad, to do

20   the jihad.

1.2.4 From US.vs Usama Bin Laden (day two) p. 197-198

2   Q. You mentioned that it talked about the rules. Explain

3   briefly what type of rules there were in those papers that he

4   gave you about al Qaeda?

5   A. The rules you have to make if you agree about everything

6   in the paper, you have to make bayat.

7   Q. And can you explain to the jury what bayat is?

8   MR. SCHMIDT: Objection.

9   THE COURT: How he knows.

10   BY MR. FITZGERALD:

11   Q. Did you yourself make bayat?

12   A. Yes.

13   Q. And did you think about it before you made bayat?

14   A. Yes, because he explain for you and he give you papers

15   about if you agree, you make bayat.

16   Q. Can you tell the jury what your understanding of bayat

17   was?

18   A. What mean?

19   Q. What it meant. What does "bayat" mean?

20   MR. SCHMIDT: Objection.

21   THE COURT: Overruled.

        22   You may answer.

        23   BY MR. FITZGERALD:

        24   Q. Can you tell us what bayat means?

        25   A. "Bayat" means you swear you going to agree about the

         1   agenda and about jihad, listen to the emir, outstanding from

         2   any order and do -- whatever work they ask you in group, you

         3   have to do it.

1.2.5   From US.vs Usama Bin Laden (day two) p. 200

        15   Q. Can you explain what it is that you understood at that

        16   meeting they might ask you to do if you made bayat to al

        17   Qaeda?

        18   A. If they ask me to go anywhere in the world for specific

        19   mission or target, I have to listen.

        20   Q. Did they tell you other things they might ask you to do?

        21   A. They say when you make bayat and you agree about the al

        22   Qaeda and about the war, anything we can ask you -- if you are

        23   a doctor, maybe we ask you to wash car or anything. So you,

24   whatever special you have, we can use for your special or we

25   can use for something different.

1.2.6   From US.vs Usama Bin Laden (day two) p. 201

12   Q. If a person in al Qaeda gave you an order to do something

13   that you knew to be haram, or forbidden, would you have to do

14   it?

15   A. Yes, because the scholars in al Qaeda -- the scholars in

16   the group, they discuss that and they make the fatwah and they

17   say it's OK.

18   Q. During that meeting did you make a decision whether to

19   make a pledge of bayat?

20   A. Yes.

21   Q. Did you pledge bayat?

22   A. Yes, I swear and I sign.

23   Q. Can you tell the jury what it is that you signed.

24   A. He give me three paper, I read it, and after that I swear

25   in front of him and I sign the papers.

1.2.7 From US.vs Usama Bin Laden (day two) p. 202-205

1   Q. Can you tell us who it was that gave you the papers that

2   you signed?

3   A. Three guys. Abu Ayoub al Iraqi, Abu Ubaidah al Banshiri,

4   and Abu Hafs el Masry.

5   Q. Did you have an understanding of who the emir of al Qaeda

6   was at that time?

7   A. At that time Abu Ayoub al Iraqi.

8   Q. Did you understand whether or not Abu Ayoub al Iraqi had

9   anyone that he reported to?

10 A. At that time our general emir, Usama Muhammad al Wahal Bin

11 Laden.

12 Q. After you joined al Qaeda -- what year was it that you

13 joined al Qaeda?

14 A. It's end of '89 and area of '90.

15 Q. When you signed the contract, did you have an

16 understanding of how many persons had previously signed the

17 contract that you did?

18   MR. SCHMIDT: Objection, your Honor.

Appendix

19   A.   In the same meeting --

20   THE COURT: No. First does he know, then how does he

21   know it, and then what the answer is.

22   Q. Just answer my specific question yes or no. At the time

23   you signed the al Qaeda contract, did you know how many people

24   had signed the contract before you? Yes or no.

25   A. Yes.

203

1   Q. Can you tell us, without telling us how many people there

2   were before you, how you knew how many people had signed the

3   contract before you?

4   A. Because we were in the same meeting.

5   Q. But did you know whether or not people had signed the

6   contract earlier? Yes or no.

7   MR. SCHMIDT: Objection.

8   A. Yes.

9   Q. How did you know whether or not other people had signed

10   the contract at other meetings?

11   A. No, in the same meeting, he bring all the papers, and I

12   signed, and other people near me, they signed too and they

13   sweared.

14   Q.   Let's focus on this meeting. How many people signed the

15   contract at the meeting that you attended?

16   A.   It's a lot. I don't know the exact number.

17   Q.   In terms of that meeting, do you remember how many people

18   signed the contract before you?

19   A.   Two. I'm the third one.

20   Q.   Simply answer this question yes or no. Were you told at
21   that meeting whether or not anyone had signed a contract at

22   any earlier meetings?

23   A.   Would you repeat it.

24   Q.   Did you know at the meeting that you attended where you

25   signed the al Qaeda contract whether or not there had been

204
1   meetings in other places with other people beforehand, where

2   they signed contracts? Yes or no.

3   A.   No, that's first meeting.

4   Q.   How do you know that that was the first meeting?

5   A.   Because Abu Ubaidah says that.

6   Q.   Were you told at that time what the structure of al Qaeda

7   was, in other words, who belonged and what positions they were

8   in?

9   A.   Could you repeat that.

10   Q.   Was he told what the structure of al Qaeda was?

11   (Interpreted)

12   A.   Yes.

13   Q.   Can you explain to the jury what the structure of al Qaeda

14   was?

15   A.   It got emir and different committee.

16   Q.   Besides the emir, can you tell us what the committees were

17   in al Qaeda?

18   A.   Under the emir it's something called shura council.

19   Q.   S-H-U-R-A, shura?

20   A.   Yes.

21   Q.   Can you tell us what the function of the shura council

22   was.

23   A.   Shura council, it's discuss in a group and the people --

24   and some people, they got more experience about Jihad.

```
25   Q.  Can you tell us, did the membership of the
shura council

1    stay the same or did it change over time?

2    A.  Sometimes change.

3    Q.  Do you know, at various times, who the
different members

4    of the shura council was?

5    A.  The names?

6    Q.  Yes. Do you know any of the people who served
in the

7    shura council at one time or another?

8    A.  Yes.

9    Q.  Can you tell us some of the names of the
leading members

10   of the shura council?

11   A.  Abu Hafs el Khabir and **Dr. Abdel Moez [Ayman
     al Zawahiri]**.  Abu   Ibrahim al

12   Iraqi.  Dr. Fadhl.  Abu Faraj al Yemeni.  Abu
Fadhl al Makkee.
```

1.3   Origins of al Qaida – IG Relationship

From US.vs Usama Bin Laden (day two) p. 294-295

```
11   Q.  During the time that al Qaeda was in the
Sudan, did al
```

12   Qaeda have a relationship with a group by the name of al Gamaa

13   al Islamiya?

14   A.   Yes.

15   Q.   Can you tell the jury what the group al Gamaa al Islamiya

16   is.

17   A.   It's called Gamaa al Islamiya Masria.

18   Q.   What does that mean, that word?

19   A.   From Egypt.

20   Q.   Can you tell us what the relationship was between al Qaeda

21   and Gamaa al Islamiya?

22   A.   The Gamaa al Islamiya help al Qaeda for their agenda, and

23   at the same time al Qaeda help Gamaa al Islamiya for their

24   agenda.

25   Q.   Can you explain, who was the leader of Gamaa al Islamiya?

1   A.   That time it's Sheik Omar Abdel Rahman.

2   MR. SCHMIDT: What time are we talking about?

3   Q.   When you said at that time, what year are you discussing?

4   A.   I talk about when we establish the group. That's in early

5   '90.

6   Q.   Did there come a time when there was a different leader

7   for Gamaa al Islamiya?

8   A.   Yes. His name Abu Talal el Masry. But if you want me

9   explain more, I can explain more.

10 Q.   What was the purpose of Gamaa al Islamiya, as you

11 understood it?

12   MR. SCHMIDT: Objection.

13 A.   They try to --

14   THE COURT: You have to wait for the judge to rule.

15   What did you understand this group -- how did you

16 learn about this group? This group that you are talking

17 about, how did you learn about it?

18   THE WITNESS: I learn about it because we are in the

19 guesthouse and I am in al Qaeda membership and I make bayat to

20 al Qaeda, and I know about the agenda and I know about the

21 relationship between al Qaeda and other groups.

22 Q.   **The members of the Gamaa al Islamiya, did some of them**

23 **also belong to al Qaeda?**

24   A.   Yes.

1.4   Origins of al Qaida – IG and EIJ in Sudan with al Qaida
1.4.1   United States of America vs. Osama bin Laden (day ten), p. 1364-1374

23   Q.   It was your understanding that the Sudanese were keeping

24   close track of the activities and Mr. Bin Laden and the people

25   who worked for Mr. Bin Laden, is that right?

1   A.   Sudanese, their role is to take you from your guesthouse

2   in the morning to the airport and just to make sure you cross

3   the immigration in the airport. They don't know what you are

4   carrying.

5   Q.   You knew also many Egyptians who were members, you met

6   many Egyptians who were members of jihad organizations from

7   Egypt, is that right?

8   A.   Yes.

9   Q.   **Was there more than one jihad organization of Egypt that**

10   **were in the Sudan when you were there?**

11   A.   Yes.

12   Q.   **What were those organizations' names?**

13   A. There is Gamaa Al Jihad. It means Al Jihad group. And

14   Gamaa Islamiya.

15   Q. One is often called Egyptian -- EIJ. Egyptian Islamic

16   Jihad.

17   A. I said Gamaa Jihad and al Gamaa al Islamiya, it means

18   Egyptian Jihad of Sheik Omar Abdel Rahman.

19   Q. When we refer to the Egyptian Islamic Jihad, who is the

20   leader of the group, of that particular group? Who was the

21   leader back then?

22   A. The leader was Sheik Omar Abdel Rahman.

23   Q. When we talk about, what was the other one, Gamaa?

24   A. I am talking about Gamaa Islamiya.

25   Q. Is there another group simply called shortly like the

1   Islamic Group?

2   A. I don't know.

3   Q. **Have you heard of a person named Zawahiri?**

4   A. **Yes.**

5   Q. Was he a leader of a particular group?

6   A. Yes.

7 Q. What particular group was he a leader of?

8 A. Al Jihad group.

9 Q. Is that the same group that Abdel Rahman was a leader of?

10 A. No.

11 Q. Two different groups?

12 A. Yes.

13 Q. Just so we can understand it and use English initials, if

14 I say IG, which group would that be referring to, with who as

15 the leader?

16 A. Islamic jihad?

17 Q. Yes, Islamic Group.

18 A. They are all Islamic groups.

19 Q. So if I say Gamaat, which group are we talking about?

20 A. Gamaa?

21 Q. Yes.

22 A. It is Sheik Omar Abdel Rahman group.

23 Q. That's Gamaa?

24 A. Gamaa.

25 Q. I think that has been referred to at times as IG. So the

1 Sheik Rahman group we refer to as IG?

2 A. Yes.

3   Q. **The Zawahiri group we will refer to as Egyptian Islamic**

4   **Jihad.** Is that sometimes referred to as that?

5   A. The translation I don't know.

6   Q. It would be Islamic Jihad, is that correct, from Egypt?

7   A. We call it Gamaa Jihad, it means Al Jihad Group of Egypt.

8   Q. Al Jihad Group of Egypt.

9   A. OK.

10 Q. These two groups obviously were not, the leadership was

11 not able to stay in Egypt, is that right?

12 A. Excuse me.

13 Q. That leadership was wanted in Egypt. They would be

14 arrested and imprisoned and tortured and maybe executed,

15 right?

16 A. Yes.

17   MR. FITZGERALD: Objection, again to competence and

18 401.

19   THE COURT: Sustained. The answer is stricken.

20 Q. Did you know any members of either the Islamic Jihad of

21   Egypt or the, what we call the IG, Sheik Rahman's group, in

22   Khartoum?

23   A.   Yes.

24   Q.   Could you tell us the names of some of the people that you

25   knew who belonged to that group, either one of those groups.

1   A.   For example, Sheik Faraj el Masry, he is one of the Al

2   Jihad Group of Himan Zawahiri.

3   Q.   Was he one of the early people in Afghanistan 1234?

4   A.   Yes, he went to Afghanistan long time before me.

5   **Q.   Was there a lot of people from the Egyptian groups that**

6   **went to Afghanistan early on?**

7   **A.   Yes.**

8   Q.   Who else did you know from Islamic Jihad?

9   A.   I don't remember their names.

10   Q.   There were some people that you dealt with that it was

11   your belief they were not Al Qaeda members, is that correct?

12   A.   From which country?

13   Q.   When you were in Sudan, there were a number of people that

14   you dealt with -- withdrawn.

15   When you were in the Sudan and sometimes in Nairobi,

16   there were people that you dealt with that it was your belief

17   that they were not Al Qaeda members, is that correct?

18   A.   Yes.

19   Q.   Sometimes these people worked for companies owned by Bin

20   Laden, is that correct?

21   A.   Yes.

22   Q.   Sometimes these people might have assisted people who were

23   Al Qaeda members, is that correct?

24   A.   Yes.

25   Q.   Some of them might have been borrowed from groups like the

1   Egyptian jihad of Egypt.

2   MR. FITZGERALD: Objection to the form, the word

3   borrow.

4   THE COURT: Yes.

5   Q.   Sometimes people who were not Al Qaeda but were members of

6   Egyptian Jihad of Egypt do some training of members of Al

7   Qaeda.

8   A.   In Sudan?

9   Q.   In Sudan and even in Afghanistan and Pakistan.

10 A.   In Sudan I have never seen some trainings.

11 Q.   In Afghanistan or Pakistan where sometimes the trainer was

12 a person who was Egyptian jihad, not Al Qaeda, but was used as

13 a trainer.

14 A.   Sometimes, yes.

15 Q.   There were also some people that you knew who you had no

16 idea whether they were or were not Al Qaeda, is that right?

17 A.   Yes.

18 Q.   For example, Abu Hajer, he was one of what we call old

19 timers from Afghanistan, who went to Afghanistan early on, is

20 that right?

21 A.   Yes.

22 Q.   You saw him being involved in Mr. Bin Laden's businesses

23 in the Sudan, is that correct?

24 A.   Yes.

25 Q.   You never saw him do any training or anything like that,

1   did you?

2   A.   No.

3   Q.   He was a person who had great respect of Mr. Bin Laden and

4   others who were in Al Qaeda, is that correct?

5   A.   Yes.

6   Q.   But you could not say that he actually was a bayat member

7   of Al Qaeda, could you?

8   A.   No.

9   Q.   There were people like Ahmed Sheikh in Nairobi.

10   A.   Yes.

11   Q.   He was somebody who was friends with a number of people

12   that were Al Qaeda, is that right?

13   A.   Yes.

14   Q.   He was somebody that helped in some ways, assisted some of

15   those people in Nairobi, is that right?

16   A.   Yes.

17   Q.   You described on direct examination because he lived in

18   Nairobi for a long time, he was able to assist with the legal

19   problems of members of Al Qaeda, is that right?

20   A.   Yes.

21   Q.   You are fairly confident that he is not a member of Al

Appendix

22   Qaeda, is that correct?

23   A.   Yes.

24   Q.   Abu Ibrahim is a person that you knew in the Sudan, is

25   that correct?

1   A.   Which Abu Ibrahim?

2   Q.   Abu Ibrahim al Iraqi?

3   A.   Yes.

4   Q.   Did you know him in Afghanistan?

5   A.   I had heard of him, yes.

6   Q.   But you didn't meet him until you went to Sudan, is that

7   right?

8   A.   Yes.

9   Q.   He was running al Hijra company for a while, is that

10   correct?

11   A.   Yes.

12   Q.   That is the construction company?

13   A.   Yes.

14   Q.   The road building company?

15   A.   Yes.

16   Q.   In the road building company, most of the engineers that

17   worked in that company were Iraqis, weren't they?

18   A.   Yes.

19   Q.   They were not Al Qaeda, they were just al Iraqis?

20   A.   Yes.

21   Q.   There were a lot of Sudanese that worked in al Hijra as

22   well, doing a lot of the menial jobs, is that correct?

23   A.   Yes.

24   Q.   In fact, it is your understanding that the Sudanese

25   government and the Sudanese people were very happy about the

1   jobs that Mr. Bin Laden brought in to the Sudan with all of

2   his companies, is that right?

3   A.   Yes.

1.5   Chemical and Biological Weapons Admission

Tarik Aziz	والله سيدي عندنا زيارة اكيوس	Sir, we have the visit of Ekeus
Saddam	السيد اكيوس	Mr. Ekeus
Tarik Aziz	اكيوس جاي الى بغداد بعد ان سمع قبل ما يجي بموقفنا المعلن. لما وصل الى بغداد باللقاء الاول التقى بالسيد وزير النفط الرفيق عامر لقاء منفرد وخلال هذا اللقاء وضعه بصورة الموقف بشكل كامل.	Ekeus came to Baghdad after he heard, before his arrival, about our outspoken position. When he arrived in Baghdad for his first visit, he met with Mr. Minister of Oil, comrade Amer in a secluded meeting. And during this meeting, he showed him the complete picture of the position.
	ثم بعد ذلك جرى لقاءات عمل فنية لمتابعة استكمال الملف البيولوجي. كان عندهم الفريق السابق اللي جاء، فريق التفتيش ابدى ملاحظات على التقرير اللي قدمناله اياه وصار استكمال للمعلومات وفي هذا الجانب جرى عمل جيّد.	Then after this he had technical work meetings to continue compiling the biological file. They had the former team that came. The inspection team gave notes on the report that we submitted to them and a compilation of information was done. And in this matter there was good work.
	يعني هما اقرّوا بانه هناك عدد مهم من النقاط التي كانت موضع تساؤل من قبلهم تمّ التعامل وياها بشكل الانطباع الاول اللي أعطوه.	So they stated that there were important numbers of points that had raised inquiries from their side which was taken care of in the first impression they gave.
	ثم جرى اللقاء السياسي انا شفته بحضور السيد وزير الخارجية والسيد وزير النفط واعضاء وفده. يعني هذه المرّة ما اتّبعت وياه اسلوب اللقاء المنفرد.	Then there was the political meeting, which I attended in the presence of the Minister of Exterior and the Minister of Oil and members of his delegation. So this time I did not adopt the isolated meeting style with him.
	والقصد من ذلك هو ان الكلام اللي نحكيه وياه ما يدور ويصل للاخرين. الوفد اللي يرافقه المستشار القانوني للجنة الخاصة وفي الناطق الرسمي اللي هو بريطاني وفي هذا الروسي	And the reason for this is that what we speak with him about not going around and reaching others. The delegation accompanying him includes the legal

Figure 14 – UN Inspections of Iraq's Biological and Chemical Weapons (1 of 16)

	المتآمرك، فمحضر يتسجّل فيصل الى جميع الاطراف.	counsel to the special committee and there is also the official spokesperson, that is British, and there is also that Americanized Russian, thus a recorded proceeding to reach all parties.
	اللقاء السياسي كان احنا من ناحيتنا ردت على مستوايا ومستوى الرفاق الحاضرين ان نبلغه بشكل قاطع وواضح ما فيه اي لبس وهو في نفس الوقت كان عنده استفسارات كانت تخرج عن دائرة الاجابات الفنية. لما سأل انه انتم انتجتوا هذه الكميات من البيولوجي فشنو كان الهدف منها يعني شنو المفهوم السياسي او الامني من انتاجها.	The political meeting, was from our point of view, I wanted from my side and from the side of the comrades in attendance was to inform him in a clear and a concise way without any discrepancies and he, at the same time, had inquiries which were outside the circle of technical responses. When he asked that you have produced such amounts of the biological, so what was the goal of it, meaning what is the political or security meaning for its production.
	طبعاً نحن كنا قابليهم للرفاق الفنيين لما يسألوكم قولولهم هذا مو شغلنا احنا علينا واجب للتنفيذ. اسألونا في الامور التنفيذية ولما عندكم اسئلة من هذا النوع من يجي اكيوس هو يطرحها ويا المسؤول السياسي اللي رح يلتقي به.	Of course we had told the technical comrades that when they ask, tell them this is not our job. We have the duty of implementation. Ask us in the implementation matters and when you do have questions of this kind, when Ekeus comes he will present them to the political official with whom he will meet.
	وانه هل تحوّل هذا الخزين الى سلاح ام لم يتحوّل. وكذلك بالنسبة لتوقيتات الانتاج وتوقيتات التدمير. فهو جاب هذه الاسئلة ويعني عوقها حتى يطرحها امامنا.	And that if this quantity was transformed into weapons or not. Also in regards to the timing of production and timing of destruction. He brought these questions and I mean he delayed them so he could address them to us.
	فانا قلت له، قلت له احنا خطة التسليح اللي عندنا هي اصلاً تطوّرت اثناء الحرب مع ايران يعني احنا قبل ان ندخل الحرب مع ايران ما كان عندنا	I told him, I told him that the strategy or armament that we have was originally developed during the war with Iran, I mean, before entering the war with Iran we did not have
MV: Saddam?	كيماوي	Chemical
Tarik Aziz	لا كيماوي ولا صواريخ. ما كان عندنا صناعة عسكرية متطورة، كان عندنا صناعة عسكرية بسيطة جداً وهذه الصناعة تطوّرت خلال فترة	Neither chemical [weapons] nor missiles. We did not have a developed armament industry, we had a very

Figure 15 - UN Inspections of Iraq's Biological and Chemical Weapons (2 of 16)

	الحرب مع ايران وبسبب التهديد اللي كان يواجهنا.	simple armament industry and this industry was developed during the period of war with Iran due to the threat facing us.
	فاول شي شفت انت لاحظت من عملك خلال الاربع سنوات والنصف الماضية انه كان هناك مجهود كبير ولكن تاريخ هذا المجهود لما ترجع له تجده كله خلال فترة الحرب.	So, first of all you saw, you noticed from your work during the last four and a half years that there was a big effort, but the history of that effort, when you go back to it, you find it entirely during the period of war.
	اثنين هم كانوا يسألوني عن بعض الامور، سيدي، كثير لحّوا عليها خاصة في الفترة الاخيرة انه مو معقولة انتو تاخذون هيك قرار وتحطون هلقد اموال الا عندكم اهداف زين، وين الاوليات وين الاوامر وين الوثائق الخ؟ هذه النقطة ضلت من النقاط اللي يثيرها فانا شرحت له قلت له شوف احنا التهديد اللي تعرضنا له من قبل ايران كان تهديد استثنائي.	Two were asking me about some issues, sir, they insisted a lot on them especially during the last period, that it is unconceivable that you take such decisions and you pour out this much funds unless you have good objectives. Where are the beginnings, where are the orders, where are the documents etc? This point remained as one of the points they raised so I explained to him, look, I said, the threat we faced from Iran was an exceptional threat.
	بعدين احنا دولة مستقلة احنا ما كان بيننا وبين ايران اكو جهة تقول لهنا قف، يعني الايرانيين يصلون الى حد معين اكو جهة دولية تقول لهنا كافي.	Moreover, we are an independent country. There was no such party between Iran and us to say "stop here", meaning the Iranians would reach a certain limit and there would be an international party that would say it is enough up to here.
	قلت له الحروب اللي صارت في المنطقة	I told him the wars that occurred in the region
Saddam	؟؟	[inaudible]
Tarik Aziz	الصراع العربي الاسرائيلي: يعني الاسرائيليين وصلوا الى قناة السويس قالوا لهم قف، بعد قناة السويس ما تفوتوا. وصلوا للجولان قالوا لهم بعد الجولان هاي هي، يعني اكو ناس تقول لهم سواء امريكا حليفتهم او الاتحاد السوفيتي اللي هو حليف للعرب وفي بعض الاحيان بصير انذارات وتتعبأ الجيوش وتنحط الاسلحة الاستراتيجية بالانذار في سبيل ايقاف صراع معين عند حدود معينة القوى الكبرى كانت تتحكم بيها.	The Arab-Israeli conflict: I mean the Israelis reached the Suez Canal they told them "stop". After the Suez Canal do not enter. They arrived to the Golan they told them after the Golan this is it, I mean there are people who tell them, whether it is America (their ally) or the Soviet Union which is the ally of the Arabs, and in some instances there are some alerts and armies become

Figure 16 - UN Inspections of Iraq's Biological and Chemical Weapons (3 of 16)

			mobilized and the strategic weapons are placed in the alert in order to stop a particular conflict to particular limits. The larger powers were controlling it. As to our conflict with Iran, no one came to tell us, tell them Basra or Baghdad or I mean any spot in Iraq is a red line you cannot cross.
MV		اما في صراعنا مع ايران ما حد جاء قال لنا قال لهم للإيرانيين ترى انتو البصرة او بغداد او يعني اي بقعة بالعراق هي خط احمر ما ممكن تتجاوزه. ؟؟	[inaudible]
Tarik Aziz		اثنين الناس اللي كنا بدنا نقاتلهم هو مو ناس لا ما عايشين بهذا الكوكب اللي احنا عايشين به. انتو خضتم حروب في اوروبا واحنا خضنا حروب. كل انسان يروح للحرب هو مشروع لكي يقتل في الحرب معروف هذا ولكن الفرد يريد يقتل ويبقى حي يبذل مجهود والا اذا قتل يعني هذا موضوع آخر. احنا كانوا ييجونا مئات الوف من المتعصبين العميان بعقولهم وبقلوبهم يريدون يموتون هو ينقهر من ما يموت. فاذا تهديد من هذا النوع. تهديد من هذا النوع يتطلب مواجهة يعني مواجهة خاصة ما ممكن انت تيجي تجيبلي سياقات اوروبية وانت سويدي وخبرائك يجيؤون من اوروبا ومن اميركا يريدون سياقات نظامية في التعامل في ال...	Second, the people we wanted to fight are not people, they do not live on this planet on which we live [under the same circumstances]. You conducted wars in Europe and we conducted wars. Every person going to war is expected to be killed in the war but an individual who wants to kill and stay alive makes an effort, otherwise if he is killed, that is another story. Hundreds of thousands of fanatics blind in their minds and in their hearts used to come to us who wanted to die. He would get upset when he does not die. Thus, a threat of this kind. [laughing] A threat of this kind requires confrontation, I mean special confrontation. You cannot come [whispering] and bring me European contexts, you are a Swede and your experts come from Europe and from America who want disciplinary contexts in the interaction with the…
8:04		نعم، نعم	[Inaudible Whispering] yes, yes
Tarik Aziz		فتيجي انت تفتش عن سياقات اوروبية او سياقات كلاسيكية في التصرف وتريد تطبقها على حالة مو كانت حالة مو كلاسيكية. هاي اولا. ثانيا احنا لما تواجهنا واجهنا هذا النوع من العدوان وهذا الخطر الذي هدد وجود شعبنا	So you come and search for European contexts or classical contexts in the behavior and you want to apply it on a case that is not a classical case. That is the first thing. Second, when we were confronted we faced this type of aggression and this

Figure 17– UN Inspections of Iraq's Biological and Chemical Weapons (4 of 16)

وبلادنا يعني احنا اخذنا قرار كقيادة سياسية وان جزء من القيادة السياسية انه كلما نستطيع ان نوفره لمواجهة هذا العدوان نوفره.	danger that threatened the existence of our people and our land, we I mean, took a decision as a political leadership, and I am a part of the political leadership, that whatever we can save to face this aggression, we saved.
اولا في المال. قلت له نحن دولة منظمة، انتو تجون تسألون انه زين هذا الموضوع انتوا صرفتوا عليه كذا مليون دولار ووين الوثائق مالتو ووين الحسابات حتى نعرف بالضبط.	First in money. I told him we are an organized state, you come ask us that, okay you spent several million dollars. Where are its documents and where are the accounts so we could know exactly?
قلت له نعم نحن دولة منظمة عندنا وزارة تخطيط كفوءة ووزاراتنا كلها تشتغل على ميزانيات وعليها حساب بس اكو ميدانين أطلق فيهم التصرف والصرف بسبب هذا النوع من التهديد. الاول في بداية الحرب بشكل خاص هو شراء الاسلحة والاعتدة. تفوقنا احنا، الاتحاد السوفيتي قاطعنا بواخرهكانت متوجهة من الخليج الى ميناء القصر رجعوا ونحن دخلنا حرب ما عندنا مصدر للتسليح.	I told him yes we are an organized state we have an efficient ministry of planning that works entirely on budgets and has an account but there are two areas given the disposition and spending because of this type of threat. The first at the beginning of the war especially was the purchase of weapons and military supplies. We became isolated. The Soviet Union cut us off. The ships heading from the Gulf to the port of Al-Qasr were turned back and we entered a war without a source of armament.
نحن نعم كنا نعطي جنط. جنطاط نجيب نحط له جنطة بيده ونقول له هاي عشر ملايين، عشرين، خمسين مليون، روح ايش تقدر تحصل دبابات او مدفعية او عتاد روح جيبها، سويناها. مو كلها هذه هي نظامية ولا كل الدولة العراقية تشتغل بهذا الشكل ولا كل الجيش العراقي يشتغل بهذا الشكل. لكن لهذه الفعالية بالذات اللي هي كانت مطلوبة لمواجهة العدوان الخاص اللي تعرضنا له، كنا نساويها.	We, yes used to give bags, bags we would bring and put a bag in his hand and tell him here are ten million, twenty, fifty million, go get whatever you can, find tanks or artillery or equipment, go bring it, we did this. Not all of this is orderly nor does the Iraqi state work this way, nor all the Iraqi army works this way. But for this performance especially it was required to face the exceptional aggression we encountered, we used to do it.
بيها رسك؟ بيها رسك. بيها خسائر؟ بيها خسائر. لكنه لما تقيصها ازاء الظرف القائم نحن نعتبرها كانت جيدة وضرورية ولسنا نادمين عليها. هذا من جانب.	Is it risky? It is risky. Are there losses? There are losses. But when you measure it with the current situation we consider that it was good and necessary and we do not regret it. That is on one side.
الجانب الاخر هو التسلح. قلت له احنا كقيادة سياسية انت الان تحكيلي عن المواثيق الدولية،	The other side is armament. I told him that, as a political leadership you now tell me about international charters,

Figure 18 - UN Inspections Of Iraq's Chemical and Biological Weapons (part 5 of 16)

	المواثيق الدولية نعم احنا دولة احترمت المواثيق الدولية. بس خوميني ما كان يحترم اي ميثاق دولي. فمو مفروض انا احترم الميثاق الدولي حتى خوميني بيجي يستبيح بلادي، ويبيد شعبي. المواثيق الدولية تُحترم لما الاطراف المتعاقبنة تحترمها. اما لما طرف ما يحترمها الطرف الاخر يجد نفسه مضطر الى ان يتصرف لحماية النفس. قلت له فاحنا اطلقنا العنان للعاملين بالتصنيع العسكري انه اي سلاح يقدرون ينتجوه ينتجوه. قالوا نقدر نطور الصاروخ؟ قلنا لهم طوروه. قالوا نقدر ننتج كيماوي؟ قلنا لهم انتجوا الكيماوي. قالوا ممكن ننتج بيولوجي؟ قلنا لهم انتجوا بيولوجي. كل شي يستطيعون الفنيين والخبراء يجون يقولولنا انه نحنا نقدر ننتجه ونقول لهم نعم انتجوه. ونستخدم ما نستخدمه من عند الضرورة. قرار الاستخدام هو قرار سياسي، ولكن العمل مطلق	international charters, yes, we are a state that respected international treaties. But Khomeini was not respecting any international treaty. So I am not supposed to respect international treaties so that Khomeini can come violate my country, and exterminate my people. International treaties are respected when warring parties respect them. But when a party does not respect it the other party finds itself obliged to behave to protect itself. I told him so we authorized the workers for the military production that any weapon they could produce let them produce it. They asked, can we improve the missile? We told them to improve it. They said, can we produce chemical weapons? We told them to produce chemical weapons. They said can we produce biological weapons? We told them to produce biological weapons. Everything that the technicians and experts came and told us that they can produce, we told them, yes, produce it. And we use whatever we use when necessary. The decision for use is a political decision, but the work is absolute.
Saddam	حتى الصواريخ ما استخدمناها الا بعدما وجّهنا انذار لايران واستخفوا به واعتقدوا انه واحدة من كذباتهم	Even the missiles we did not use until after we sent an ultimatum to Iran and they undermined it, thinking it was one of their lies
Tariq Aziz (11.50)	فقلت له احنا ما كان عندنا ؟ سياسية نعم يقوللك انا اتحمل المسؤولية يعني انه احنا قرارنا كان هو انه ننتج اي سلاح ممكن لخبراءنا وفنيينا يتوصلون الى انتاجه. محرم دوليا ما محرم دوليا، مخالف للاتفاقيات ما مخالف، هذا موضوع اخر لانه الطرف اللي كنا نواجهه هو طرف خارج عن القانون، خارج عن الاتفاقيات، خارج عن العصر، خارج عن هذا الكوكب.	So I told them we did not have [inaudible] politics? Yes, he tells you that I will take the responsibility, I mean; our decision was that we produce any weapon which our experts and technicians can reach its production. Forbidden internationally, not forbidden internationally, a breach to international treaties or not, this is another subject because the party we were facing was an outlawed party, out of the treaties, out of the epoch, out of this planet. We, until the war ended between us and

Figure 19 - UN Inspections Of Iraq's Chemical and Biological Weapons (part 6 of 16)

	احنا، الى ان انتهت الحرب بيننا وبين ايران، ما كنا منتجين البيولوجي، ما متوصلين الى الانتاج واستمر الانتاج. خُزِن انت تقول لي حطيتوه بعبوات لغرض، عبوات، يعني تسليحية بقنابل وصواريخ، نقول لك لا. ما احتجنا. يعني ما كان الخطر اكو خطر دائم علينا. ايران ما عادت تشكل خطر دائم وكان عندنا قوة ردع ممكن كافية لاحتمالات تجدد النزاع بيننا وبين ايران. فما احتجنا للتسليح.	Iran, were not producing biological weapons, had not reached the production stage, and the production continued. A reservoir, you tell me, you put in propellers for a reason to, propellers, meaning armed with bombs and missiles, we tell you no, we did not need to. I mean the danger was not a permanent one on us. Iran was no longer a permanent danger on us and we had a retaliatory force sufficient for the possibilities of renewing the conflict between us and Iran. So we did not need armament.
	انت في بالك اسرائيل. قلت له نعم احنا في كل البلدان العربية: مصر ولبنان وسورية والأردن والعراق، هذه تاريخياً من عام 48 حتى يعني مؤتمر مدريد هذه البلدان هي بلدان تتحوّط ازاء اسرائيل. وتبني قدراتها العسكرية والردعية آخذةً بعين الاعتبار اسرائيل. هذه معروفة، تاريخ هذا، الجيش العراقي حارب بال 48 ويّا الجيوش العربية بال 67 ما لحّق بس كان متجه، يعني كانت قطاعات عسكرية متجّهه للاردن صار وقت اطلاق النار. بال 73 اشتركنا	You think of Israel, I told him yes, in all the Arab countries: Egypt and Lebanon and Syria and Jordan and Iraq, this is historical since the year '48 until, like, the Madrid conference, these countries are countries that take precautions against Israel. And build their military and retaliatory capabilities taking Israel into account. This is well-known, this is history, the Iraqi army fought in '48 with the Arab armies, in '67 it did not reach it but it was heading towards it, I mean there were military sectors heading to Jordan during the first launch. In '73 we participated
Saddam	على الجبهتين	On both fronts.
14:08	على الجبهتين وشرحت له، قلت له نحن في الجبهة المصرية كان عندنا ترتيب مسبق ودزينا طيارات والطيارات موجودة واستخدمت. لكن على الجبهة السورية قلت انا كنت في مكتب الرئيس البكري حينها بالليل خابر حافظ الاسد قال ساعدوني. ما قال حتى كم دبابة يريد وكم طيارة، قال ساعدوني. قلت له دبابات مالتنا على ال؟ مشيت على الجبهة السورية، ما أحد يمشي الدبابات على ال؟ بس احنا مشيناها. فاذا انت تشوف اشياء غير قياسية، هذه هي ظروف المنطقة.	On both fronts and I explained to him, I told him, on the Egyptian front, we had a pre-arrangement and we sent planes and the planes we presented and were used. But on the Syrian front, I told him, I was in the office of president al-Bakr at that time at night he phoned Hafez al-Assad saying "help me". He did not even say how many tanks and planes he wanted, he said help me. I told him our tanks moved in the [inaudible] on the Syrian front, no one moves tanks in the [inaudible] but we moved them. So if you see things non-standard, these are the conditions of the region. Israel yes was always present on our

Figure 20 - UN Inspections Of Iraq's Chemical and Biological Weapons (part 7 of 16)

minds and any weapon we produce after and along the defense against Iran we were thinking that Israel could attack us thus we would have the retaliatory weapon.
And Israel attacked us in '81. It is well-known that it hit the nuclear power plant that was known that... so we, any deterrent weapon that could be used to deter which we could produce, we produced, you see.
And we do not apologize for that and during my meetings when I was minister of foreign affairs during the war with "Klovchefson" and with Germany's foreign minister when they raised these issues I was frank and clear with them and I told them we have the right to possess what will enable us to retaliate against an [inaudible] aggression.
Also Israel has nuclear weapons and this is against international laws and treaties and you cannot tell me that Israel has no biological or bacterial weapons therefore, I..., so if you would like to search for the political thought or for the philosophy behind the Iraqi military industry, this is it.
But for us, you know, we entered the war in '91, we did not use it, except for the missiles which are considered conventional weapons, so it is not considered non-conventional weapons. We did not need to change the biological stockpile into weapons because the war with Iran was not over. When the war and its possibilities with America came, we destroyed them. Your group said that you destroyed them in September and October and you did not have a security council resolution for a war against you. I told him why, we, what are you, these people are ignorant. Directly after the events of August a theory called the surgical operation came into existence, meaning

اسرائيل نعم كانت دائماً حاضرة في تفكيرنا وانه اي سلاح ننتجه بعد والى جانب الدفاع ضد ايران كنا نحسب به ان اسرائيل تعتدي علينا وبالتالي يكون عندنا سلاح ردع.
واسرائيل ضربتنا عام 81 – معروف انه ضربت المفاعل النووي اللي معروف انه ... فاحنا اي سلاح ردع ممكن يستخدم للردع عندنا امكانية ننتجه انتجناه ترى.

وما، يعني ما ما نعتذر على ذلك وانا في لقاءاتي لما كنت وزير خارجية اثناء الحرب مع **كلوفتشيفسون** ومع وزير خارجية المانيا لما اثاروا هذه الموضوعات كنت وياهم صريح وواضح وقلت لهم نحن من حقنا ان نمتلك ما يمكننا من الرد على عدوان ؟؟

وبعدين اسرائيل هي عندها سلاح نووي وهذا مخالف للقوانين والمواثيق الدولية وما تقدر تقول لي ان اسرائيل ما عندها كيماوي وما عندها جرثومي لذلك انا... فاذا تريد انت ان تبحث عن الفكر السياسي او على الفلسفة للصناعة العسكرية العراقية هي هذه.

لكن لاستخدام، تعرف انت، احنا دخلنا الحرب عام 91، ما استخدمناه، عدا الصواريخ التي هي تعتبر من الاسلحة التقليدية يعني ما تعتبر من الاسلحة غير التقليدية. ما احتجنا نحول ال ال الخزين البيولوجي الى سلاح لانه ما كان اكو الحرب مع ايران منتهية.

لما اجت الحرب واحتمالات الحرب ويا اميركا دمرناها. جماعتك قالوا انه انتم دمرتوها بايلول وبتشرين الاول وما كان عندكم قرار من مجلس الامن من اجل الحرب عليكم. قلت له ليش احنا شنو انت، هؤلاء غشمة. مباشرة بعد احداث آب طلعت نظرية التي سموها ال surgical operation يعني العملية الجراحية وهذه العملية او هذه الفكرة كانت رائجة لعدة اشهر انه اميركا تقوم بضربة سميت جراحية لمنشأتنا العسكرية

Figure 21 - UN Inspections Of Iraq's Chemical and Biological Weapons (part 8 of 16)

	والصناعية.	the surgical operation and this surgery or this idea was preponderant for several months that America will conduct a strike called surgical against our military and industrial establishments. This was a known truth I mean another thing Margaret Thatcher and George Bush were talking about article 50 of the United Nations Charter that permits them to launch a war without the approval of the security council. I said later, later, did they go to the security council when Gorbachev wanted a cover to go to the security council and after that Gorbachev accepted four billion dollars and went to the security council. He benefited from the cover of the security council in order to accept a bribe. And Mitterrand needed the cover, Bush forced him to go to the security council and made a resolution.
	هذا كان حقيقة معروفة يعني شي آخر مارغريت ثاتشر وجورج بوش كانوا يتحدثون عن المادة 50 من ميثاق الأمم المتحدة اللي يجيزوهم ان يشنون الحرب دون العودة الى مجلس الامن. قلت هاي بعدين بعدين راحوا على مجلس الامن لما غورباتشوف راد له غطاء حتى يروح لمجلس الامن وبعدين غورباتشوف قبل اربع مليارات دولار وراح الى مجلس الامن. استفاد من غطاء مجلس الامن حتى يقبل رشوة. وميتران كان يحتاج الى غطاء اجبره بوش على ان يروح الى مجلس الامن وياخذ قرار.	
	قلت له هذه سياسة نعرفها نحن كنا عايشين \ تفاصيلها فاذا كان اكو خطر علينا. نحن كنا نعرف وكنا نقدر كقيادة سياسية ان هذا الخزين او هذا السلاح ما ممكن يستخدم في نزاع من هذا النوع لان الطرف المقابل عنده سلاح نووي وبالتالي اذا استخدم هذا السلاح، الطرف الاخر رح يتخذه ذريعة لاستخدام السلاح النووي ضدك. بقاءه كخزين يعرضنا الى خطر لما يُضرب. فالامر الطبيعي والمنطقي هو انه يُتلف. كمان قال انتو الكيماوي بقيتوه بس البيولوجي ما.	I told him we know this policy. We were living its details; therefore there was danger on us. We knew and we estimated, as a political leadership, that this stockpile or this weapon cannot be used in this type of conflict because the opposing party possessed a nuclear weapon therefore if you use this weapon, the other party will use it as an excuse to use nuclear weapons against you. Its remainder as a stockpile puts us in danger when it would be hit. So the natural and the rational thinking is that it should be destroyed. He also said you kept the chemical weapons but not the biological ones.
	قلت له الكيماوي موجود. الكيماوي سلاح موجود معبئ جاهز انا ليش اتلفه، ما استخدمه بعدين لما يعني	I told him the chemical weapons are present. Chemical weapons are present, loaded, ready, why should I destroy it. I do not use it. Also, when, I mean
Saddam	وحتى خطره اقل	Even its danger is less
Tariq Aziz	خطره اقل	Its danger is less
Saddam	من خطر الجرثومة	From the danger of bacterial

Figure 22 - UN Inspections Of Iraq's Chemical and Biological Weapons (part 9 of 16)

Tariq Aziz	قلت له كردع. كردع. في المواجهة التي كانت تبدو معالمها في عام 90 كردع احنا اعلنا	I told him as a deterrent, as a deterrent. In the confrontation whose features appeared in the year 90 as a deterrent we announced
Saddam	لما -- البيولوجي	When [inaudible] biological weapons
Tariq Aziz	نعم	Yes
Saddam	لكن قلنا صراحة اذا اسرائيل تضربنا او تفكر باستخدام النووي، احنا نستخدم عليها	We honestly said that if Israel hits us or thinks of using the nuclear weapons, we shall use on it
Tariq Aziz	المزدوج	The dual
Saddam	وسمّينا سمّينا حتى نوع ال... نوع الكيماوي	And we named, named even the type... the type of chemical
Tariq Aziz	قلت له قلت له هذا ليش السيد الرئيس اطلق تصريح في اول نيسان عام 90 احنا احنا ما كنا بالكويت في ذاك الوقت. ليش؟ لانه كان اكو احتمالات ان اسرائيل تضرب العراق. السيد الرئيس قال ترى اذا ضربت اسرائيل العراق بالسلاح النووي سنستخدم الكيماوي المزدوج وجاء بوب دول ووفد الكونجرس الامريكي وشرح لهم السيد الرئيس افكارنا واستعداداتنا في هذا الموضوع. اذا ضربتنا اسرائيل بسلاح تقليدي نضربها كرد بالمثل بالسلاح التقليدي اذا استخدمت سلاح غير تقليدي فاحنا عندنا الكيماوي.

اذا البيولوجي ما فكرنا يعني في تلك الفكرة باستخدامه لا قبل احداث آب ولا بعد احداث آب. وبعدين لقينا انو ندمرّه.

قلت له الان لا تحكي تقولي حولتوه الى قنابل او ما حولتوه الى قنابل. قلت له يعني هو بالنهاية شو اللي تريد تتوصل له شو الفرق اذا حولناه او ما حولناه ؟ احنا ما حولناه لكن شو اللي تريد تتوصل له انت؟ هل يوجد لدى العراق في قناعتك الان اسلحة بيولوجية مخفية؟ انت بقناعتك كخبير نزع سلاح كرئيس لجنة خاصة صار لك اربع سنوات ونصف تشتغل | I told him, I told him this why Mr. president made a statement on the first of April of the year '90 we were, we were not in Kuwait at that time. Why? Because there were possibilities that Israel would hit Iraq. Mr. president said, look, if Israel hits Iraq with nuclear weapons we will use the dual biological weapon. And Bob Dole and a delegation from the Congress came and Mr. president explained to them our ideas and our preparations regarding this matter. If Israel hits us with conventional weapons we will retaliate with conventional weapons. If it used non-conventional weapons we have the chemical.

Thus, we did not think of the idea of biological weapons neither before the August events nor after the August events. Then we found it fit that we destroy it.

I told him now not to talk and tell me you altered it into bombs or you did not alter it into bombs. I told him I mean in the end what do you want to reach what is the difference if we altered it or if we did not alter it? Does Iraq have in your belief hidden biological weapons? You in your belief as an expert in dismantling weapons as a chair of a special committee you have been |

Figure 23 - UN Inspections Of Iraq's Chemical and Biological Weapons (part 10 of 16)

تلوج بالعراق	working for four years and a half Roding in Iraq
اذا اكو واحد يثير هذا التساؤل او هذا الشك فهذا إهانة لذكانك وإهانة لكفائتك. مو تشكيك بالعراق. تشكيك بالعراق احنا سمعنا هوايا تشكيك بالعراق. بس إهانة لذكانك وإهانة لكفائتك كرئيس اللجنة الخاصة. انو يجي واحد يقولك لا العراقيين خافيين يعني أسلحة بيولوجية. انت صارلك اربع سنوات ونصف تشتغل في كل انحاء العراق، ماكو مكان ما حفرتوا وسبق ان جانت الدعايات من هذا النوع. انت بال 93 مو جنت علينا قلتلنا انواكو تقارير تقول انو هناك صواريخ مخفية؟ دزيت هذا الروسي، هذا سميدوفيتش، شو قال هذيش انت بقيت في الصحراء الغربية، قال ستة اسابيع.	If one would raise this question or this doubt thus this would be humiliating to your intelligence and a humiliation to your competence. Not distrusting Iraq. Suspecting Iraq? We have heard plenty of distrust toward Iraq. But a humiliation to your intelligence and a humiliation to your competency as head of the special committee when someone comes and tells you "no" Iraqis are hiding, like, biological weapons. You have, for four and a half years, been working all over Iraq, with no place that you haven't dug and this type of propaganda has appeared previously. In '93 didn't you come telling us that there are reports saying that there are hidden missiles? You sent this Russian, this "Smidovich", what did he say, how long have you spent in the western desert, he said six weeks.
قلت له ست اسابيع، اكو مكان ما حفرتوا؟ بعدين انتو من شون تتحفرون على الصواريخ اذا لقيتو شي كيمياوي تقولون هذا مو شغلنا؟ مهو كله شغلكم.	I told him six weeks, is there a place you haven't dug? Also while you dig for missiles if you find something chemical would you say this is none of our business? This is all your business.
تلقون بيولوجي مو شغلكم، كله شغلكم؟ الرفيق ابو زياد قال لهم انتم حتى دوّرتوا على الطيار الامريكي المفقود. ما وجدتوا ؟؟ فاذا انت صارلك اربع، جانتك شيء تقارير على الصواريخ وما لقيت وجانتك تقارير اخرى وما لقيت وجانتك تقارير اخرى وما لقيت فشو معنى هذا الشكوك حول البيولوجي قد تكون صحيحة بالوقت اللي كل سابقاتها من التقارير اثبتت انها غير صحيحة. اكو منطق يعني، يعني هسع العراق يجي يخفي فذ عشرين او خمسين او الف قنبلة بيولوجية ويعرض نفسه الى استمرار الحصار بعدين على من يستخدمه؟ على من؟ انتو حبايبكم حبايب امريكا: الكويت واسرائيل.	You find biological not your business, it's all your business? Comrade Abu Ziyad told them you even searched for the missing American pilot. You did not find [Inaudible] So if you have been for four- you received reports on the missiles and you did not find any and you received other reports and did not find any and you received other reports and did not find any so why would those suspicions regarding biological weapons might be true in a time when all the precedent reports proved to be wrong. I mean it is common sense, so now Iraq comes and hides, like, twenty or fifty thousand biological weapons and exposes itself to a continuation of the

Figure 24 - UN Inspections Of Iraq's Chemical and Biological Weapons (part 11 of 16)

		embargo, besides, on whom would it use it? On who? Your loved ones are America's loved ones: Kuwait and Israel
	اذا نستخدمها على الكويت، الكويت مو محمية من قبل...	If we use it against Kuwait, isn't Kuwait a protectorate of...
Saddam	وما تحتاج نستخدمها، على ايش يعني فوقها مدرعات ؟؟	And it is not necessary for us to use it, why, I mean, there are on top of it [inaudible] infantries.
Tariq Aziz	نعم، واذا نستخدمها على اسرائيل، اسرائيل عندها قنبلة نووية تقدر تضربنا وتضرب عاصمتنا وتدمر عاصمتنا. يعني هو سلاح مو لازم يكون بيه منطق؟ يعني هذا واحد يخفي سلاح شو ؟؟ . قلت له الاتهامات مال السيدة اولبرايت ان العراق يستخدم يستخدم ممكن يستخدمه للارهاب. قلت له تاريخ العراق هم العراق ما ثبت عليه انه مشترك في عملية ارهابية.	Yes, if we use it against Israel, Israel has a nuclear bomb that can hit us and hit our capital and destroy our capital. I mean isn't it a weapon that should have rationality with it? Like, one could hide a weapon what [inaudible]. I told him Mrs Albright's allegations that Iraq uses, could use it for terrorism. I told him the history of Iraq. It was never proven that Iraq has participated in a terrorist operation.
Saddam	احنا فرد يوم نبهناهم الى خطورة ان ياتي اليوم تستخدم به اسلحة غير تقليدية للارهاب.	We even warned them of the danger that one day non-conventional weapons could be used for terrorism.
Tariq	نعم	Yes
Saddam	في وقت مبكر وبمحضر، يمكن حامد يتذكره يعني ويا يا احد الاطراف الغربية والفرنسية والانجليزية يعني اتذكر بوقت مبكر	At an early stage and in a meeting, maybe Hamed remembers it, I mean this was with one of the Western: French or English parties, I mean, I remember at an early stage

Figure 25 - UN Inspections Of Iraq's Chemical and Biological Weapons (part 12 of 16)

Tariq	نعم، قلت له في عام 82 قلنالهم ما تستغربوا ما فرد يوم تتطور الشعوب والدول والعالم الى انه تجيجيكم شاحنة وفي احدى العواصم الغربية هاي الشاحنة تنفجر وبيها سلاح غير تقليدي، مو قنابل. فيعني لازم علاقتكم وويا الشعوب والامم وطريقة التعامل يُعاد النظر بيها على اساس واحدة من العوامل الخطرة حالة من هذا النوع قد تحصل.	Yes, I told him in the year '82 we told them not to be surprised that one day peoples, states, and the world would evolve that you receive a truck in one of the western capitals and this truck would explode with a non-conventional weapon, not bombs. So your relations with people and nations and the manner of conduct have to be revisited on the basis of one of the dangerous elements; a situation of this sort could take place.
	قلت له في عام 82 احنا ما طلبنا من الاميركان انهم يشيلون اسم العراق من لائحة الدول اللي تساند الارهاب، ما طلبنا. هم اخذوا قرار وسمعناه وكان جيّد، احنا قلنالهم يعني هذا شي جيد. هم رفعوا اسم العراق من اللائحة اللي يدعون انها دول اللي تساند الارهاب، بدليل ان هم توصلوا الى استنتاج ان العراق ما يمارس الارهاب.	I told him in the year '82 we did not ask the Americans to take Iraq's name off the list of states that sponsor terrorism; we did not ask. They took a decision and we heard it and it was good. We told them, like, this is a good thing. They removed Iraq's name from the list of states which they claim support terrorism, which proves they reached a conclusion that Iraq does not practice terrorism.
Saddam	اي سنة؟	What year?
Tariq	82 قبل ما نعيد علاقاتنا الدبلوماسية وياهم. قلت له لسبب واضح، قلت له العراق بلد قوي قوي قوي يعني العراق بلد قوي وبلد غني وبلد عنده دور كبير بالمنطقة. ؟؟ القوي والغني واللي عنده دور كبير ما يستخدم وسائل. هاي يستخدموها الدول اللي تريد تخلق لها دور، تريد تستخدم نوع من الابتزاز كوسيلة لتقوية دورها، قلت العراق طبيعيا يعني هو يتكوينه ما يميل الى هذا النوع من السلوك.	'82 before we renewed our diplomatic relations with them. I told him for a clear reason, I told him Iraq is a strong country, I mean strong, strong. Iraq is a strong country, and a rich country and a country that has a big role in the region. The strong and rich [inaudible] who has a big role does not use means... these are used by states that want to create a role for themselves. They want to utilize a form of intimidation as a method to strengthen its role. I said Iraq naturally in its formation does not lean towards this type of conduct.
	اذاً هذا كلام فارغ، المهم احنا مقتنعين وانت مقتنع انت تعرف جيداً انو احنا لا نمتلك الان ما هو محظور من قرارات مجلس الامن.	So this is non-sense, the important thing is that we are convinced and you are convinced. You know well that we do not possess now what is forbidden by the security council resolutions.
	وليس لدينا القدرة على اعادة انتاجه بدون معرفتك لانو نظام الرقابة مالتك نظام كفوء ويشتغل بشكل كامل. انت عندك قصص، اكو تفاصيل معينة لا تزال تبحث عنها، ابحث عنها	And we do not have the capability to renew its production without your knowledge because the monitoring system that you have is an effective

Figure 26 - UN Inspections Of Iraq's Chemical and Biological Weapons (part 13 of 16)

ولكن انت عليك ان تروح الان الى مجلس الامن وتقول لهم الهدف الاساسي من قراركم 687 فيما يخص الاسلحة قد تحقق	system and works at full capacity. You have stories, there are specific details you are still looking for, look for it but now you have to go to the security council and tell them the main objective of your resolution 687 pertaining to the weapons has succeeded. And I do have
وانا عندي متابعات ويا العراقيين على امور ذات طبيعة ثانوية ما تأثر على هذا الاستنتاج. قلت له انت قلت هذا في تقريرك في حزيران حول الصواريخ والكيماوي والوكالة الدولية للطاقة ايضا تقريرها واضح، نريد نقول شيء في نهاية آب في المجال البيولوجي. قلت له هذا الموضوع ما يخصك، رح اقولك شيء، اذا هذا الشيء ما تساويه في نهاية آب ما تساويه هذا يعني ان إما انت اذا كنت المسؤول شخصيا او اللجنة الخاصة او من يكون وراء مثل هذا القرار من جانبك فسيكون هذا الموقف مغرض وعدائي.	follow-ups with Iraqis regarding issues of secondary nature that will not be affected by this deduction. I told him you mentioned this in your June report regarding the missiles and the chemical weapons. And the International Atomic Energy Agency's report is also clear; we want to say something at the end of August in the biological domain. I told him this is none of your business; I will tell you something, if you do not do this thing at the end of August, you do not do it, this means unless you were personally responsible or the special committee or whoever is behind such a resolution from your part, this stance will be biased and hostile.
واول من سيفسر ذلك على انه مغرض وعدائي هو المتكلم. قلت له انتو نسمع من قصص تتحاكون فيما بينكم تكتبون انو اكو بالقيادة العراقية حمائم وصقور وواصفيني على اساس انا يعني في مقدمة المعتدلين والحمائم. قلت له نعم انا في مقدمة المعتدلين والحمائم بس هذا يعني شيخ الحمائم رح هو اول واحد يستنتج بانو موقفكم مغرض وعدائي، وبالتالي هذا يستدعي التصرف وانا سبق ان قلت لك في السابق انو ماكو جدوى انه نستمر نعمل وياك وويّا مجلس الامن اذا ما تنطونا حقنا.	And the first thing to explain this to be prejudiced and hostile is the speaker. I told him, you, we hear stories that are going on between you writing that there are in the Iraqi leadership doves and falcons and I was described as being at the forefront of the moderates and doves. I told him yes I am at the forefront of moderates and doves but this means that the leader of the doves will be the first one to infer that your position is biased and hostile, which will necessitate action and I previously told you in the past that there is no point in continuing to work with you and the Security Council if you do not give us our right.
تريد تسميه تهديد، قلت له انا الكلمات ما ما رح ادخل في جدل وياك. عندنا حق، نحن انتو طلبتوا من عندنا اشياء ننفذها، نفذناها عندنا حق في ان ترفعون عنا الحظر الاقتصادي، حصار	You want to call it threat? I told him that I will not enter into an argument with you over words. We have the right, we, you asked us to do things which we

Figure 27 - UN Inspections Of Iraq's Chemical and Biological Weapons (part 14 of 16)

executed. We have a right that you lift the economic embargo, economic siege [inaudible]. Give us our right and we will continue to work with you to the end. You don't give us our right, we will not continue with you. And this is clear, I made it clear to you last time and I am now, without doubt so that it is understood to you. And go tell the Security Council, tell them this is what Tariq Aziz told me.

He told me this is how things are with the Security Council. I told him even your friends; I told him send my greetings to the enemies and friends alike. We respect the friends and want all of them to be our friends. And we want - I am very cautious in having a majority in the Security Council that understands and supports our cause. But you see we will not give up our cause because even our friends consider it when they are not too busy with something else, then, they will get busy themselves with.

See this Bosnia, what does it mean? All the countries are busy with it while the number of people who are dying in Bosnia does not exceed 10% of the people who die daily in the Iraqi hospitals and no one cares about us.

And we will not let go of our cause even our friends when they remember us barely continue to follow this issue. We have a right. The Security Council whether it was America or the entire Security Council has to make a decision in this regard. It has to give us our right. We want a majority in the Security Council, we do not have a majority, this another topic, so no, I mean I will not take into account your analysis that there are people who will be upset and others who won't or that there will be

Figure 28 - UN Inspections Of Iraq's Chemical and Biological Weapons (part 15 of 16)

	أنو هذه شغلة بعد ما تخوّف العراقيين.	people who will take advantage of this issue and others who won't. And I told you last time I told you, you see, the worst thing you could do is to hit us, the Americans, and I told you this at that time, two months ago, that this is something that does not scare the Iraqis.
	واحنا هم خلي نعرف لأنه نضلّ ننفذ ننفذ ننفذ على أمل رح يرفع الحصار ورح نصدّر النفط. اذا ما رح نصدّر النفط ماكو خلي نقول لشعبنا اخي ماكو نفط. احنا بس أكو نفط لاستهلاكنا. نفط ماكو، نرجع نعيش كأمّة وكشعب وكان شعب عظيم ودولة عظيمة في قرون سابقة في عروض سابقة ما كان يكون ؟ شعبنا يتعوّد وكل واحد يشوف طريقه. قلت له هذا كلام واضح وبسيط وصريح. هذا هو موقفنا.	And we would like to know that we keep complying complying complying in the hope that the embargo is lifted and we could export oil. If we will not export oil, then we will tell our people that we do not have any oil. We only have oil for our own consumption. There is no oil; we go back and live as a nation and people and we were a great people and state in previous centuries and settings there weren't? Our people will get used to and everyone will look after himself. I told him this is a clear, simple, and honest statement. This is our position.
	انطباعنا انا والرفيق محمد والرفيق عامر وممكن ايضاً يتكلمون. اولا هو كل هذا الكلام الذي حكيناه اللي في الجلسة وقبله ويّا الفريق عامر ما جاوبنا بانفعال اولاً. ما قال اطلاقاً	The impression I and comrade Mohamed and comrades Amer got, and they can also speak. First, all this talk we made in the session and before it with comrade Amer he did not answer us with anger, firstly. He said absolutely...
Saddam	جيب سيجار شهير جيب سيجار	Get a cigar Shaheer, get a cigar

Figure 29 - UN Inspections Of Iraq's Chemical and Biological Weapons (part 16 of 16)[292]

1.6 Saddam meets with Arafat

ISGQ-2003-M0006248
This file is a Video Tape that contains the following:

The Full Translation:
Saddam Hussein: they said that they wanted to state that to Iraq before the American Congress Delegation meets me, but, as long as the American Congress Delegation met me and couldn't deliver these points to me, they want to deliver them now, one of these points is that your emplaced missiles are threaten our American bases. As you said, (Talking to Yasir Arafat), when you were in Beirut, and you said "it is time to die, and now I can smell the breeze of heavens", it is the same for us, as long as the small players are gone, and it is the time for America to play Directly, we are ready for it, we will fight America, and with God's well we will defeat it and kick it out of the whole region. Because, it is not about the fight itself, we know that America has Air Force more than us while we have few, America has rockets more than us, but I think that when the Arab people see real action of war is real not only a talk, they will do the same and fight America everywhere, so we have to get ready to fight America, we are ready to fight when they do, when they strike, we strike, we will strike any American troops in the Arab Gulf with our Air Force, and then we will state it saying that our Air Force has assaulted the American bases on that day. Therefore, when the battle is on, you do not say how much did you lose and do not make expectations, or even to make some expectations for the end of the battle. It is what happened for us during the war with Iran, we made a lot of expectations for that war and we wrote a lot of letters, even the Ministry of Foreign Affairs and Comrade Tariq, no it wasn't Comrade Tariq, it was Doctor Sa'dun Hammadi, I didn't ask him to write a letter, I did it by myself saying "My brothers: what you are doing is war, please ask the old specialists in the Ministry of Justice, because you are new to the system, also ask the specialists in the Ministry of Interior sorry in the Ministry of Foreign Affairs, maybe they will guide you and show you from legal point of view that what are you doing, striking cities, and occupying lands is a war . In other letter, ask the old specialists in the Ministry of Interior, Ask the old specialists Zayn Al-Qaws and Sayf Sa'd are Iraqi properties, you occupied Iraqi Lands and then you emplaced your cannons in it to hit the rest of Iraqi lands. We tried, but when the war occurred, we did not make expectations about how much we are going to lose, because it is something that must happen. So be ready for this level of battle, in your land (talking to Yasir Arafat) you don't have a state, you don't have oil or factory to be stroked, unlike us, we got out of 8 years of war, frankly, let me tell you something, if America strikes us, we will hit back. We said that before, you know us, we are not that talkative type of people that holds the microphone to say things only, we do what we say. Maybe we cannot reach Washington but we can send someone who has explosive belt to reach Washington. Our missiles do not reach America, but I swear if it does! I would strike it. We can't keep silent like this, while the Americans are hitting Arabs or Iraqis and say we can do nothing, yes we can, we can send a lot people to Washington just like the old days, for instance; the person with explosives' belt around him would throw himself on Bush's car. However, the American Bases, which are all over the world, in Turkey... etc, we can sweep them. We have to be ready for that level. Meaning, we shouldn't get fanned by talking only because we have to do what we say, it is a matter of decision and commitment, all the words that we said came through chain of meetings with the military officers, it didn't go like that, what the missiles can do, what the Air Force can do, we check our defenses and their requirements, we check our bases, what are the commands to be sent for these bases, when Baghdad is stroke by the Atomic bombs how we are going to react, we got all these expectations. It is not our

Figure 30 – command members discuss Kuwait invasion (1 of 4) choice I swear, but it is a must, when the enemy comes and there is no heavy foot that would stop it, the Palestinian issue and Arab situation won't be a good, so it Is not our timing, if it our choice we would chose the right time, but it is a matter of necessity, and we have to be obliged to the necessity which says that we have a strong attitude, conspiracy comes from flexibility, this is an assumption that would never happen because we never done it before, you make a decision, so make the right one ,(Yasir Arafat Says: As always), am sure that all Arabs wish me good thing , what do they want from us, we got out of the war on that day , meaning either you forget the matter of Arab Union and the hope to restore Palestine ,or you let us do something , we will move to war , yes to war, the hope's gate towards Palestine and the gate of development for any nation can't be closed by anyone , meaning, Palestine has been occupied for along time and they say we are the invaders!, they let the war on for eight years and blood shed all over and they call us invaders!! We know their conspiracies, those Americans and Israelis. Maybe we stop for 20 days, and then we hit back once upon time with rockets and Air Forces hitting Tel Aviv, we don't have to strike them daily; we will chose times so they will never now meaning of sleeping, we are a disaster, good and flexible people but once, if someone is stuck with us, we will not let him go unless he got on his knees, or crawl on the ground, we don't have something in the middle, we don't want to negotiate, we don't want any mediators, (looking at Yasir Arafat and Saying : Right Abu-'Ammar?, Yasir Arafat Replies saying: yes 100%). Today, one of my Arab brothers stood by my side and said that someone says hi to you, he is on your side. I told him tell him hi back to him and tells him that I know his attitude. We don't know the mediators; we don't know how to work with it, this war we had with the Iranians, we don't know how to mediate with them, (Yasir Arafat interrupts saying, despite of my efforts in the Islamic, Nonalignment and Eastern Countries), we don't know this way, you either have an enemy or friend, you can't have something in the middle , they are two , to be a brother and friend on Arab level, or a friend on the world wide level, or enemy on world level. Because we cannot hang these things, we used to be on that way and thanks God, we like it that way. So Sab'awi (talking to one of the Iraqi delegation members), get all of you old books , coordinate with the Intelligence System Director and our Palestinian brothers to check every single place that the Americans exist in, within the Middle East area, even if some American man came to Greek for trade, we have to know about him also . This is the battle; we have to be beasts in the battles, to remain beasts to the next, (Yasir Arafat Says: Yes …Beast.).

(Sheikh 'Abd-al-Hamid Al-Sa'ih from the Palestinian delegation speaks to Saddam and says according to this, we have to get ready for the battle) Saddam says: and the battle develops, for me, I do my own expectations according to nation's quantities and requirements, let say how many cannons do we have, how many Air crafts we have, but the most important is, what we have seen in the war. (Translator Comments: The tape stops and Saddam resumes talking starting with information) Information for Israel, they would get in and strike us, so we have to be ready for that level of war. (Yasir Arafat Interrupts and says: almost like what they have done in Panama) Saddam says no, not like panama, (Yasir Arafat says I mean the way that they got in) I wish maybe USA needs to get a hard lesson. I wish they occupy Iraq; I want them to get in, so we sweep all of them. (Unidentified person talks to Saddam saying What about the Oil, they would think that we would burn it) Saddam says , I will give them guarantees that I am not going to burn the oil , let them in, let them get their army and to start from Al-Faw borders, I will demolish them all, (Unidentified person talks to Saddam saying: but they won't take a risk on that). Panama! Panama is nothing while

Figure 31 - command members discuss Kuwait invasion (2 of 4)

comparing to us, I swear Abu 'Ammar we are something different, they will roast them and eat them. (Unidentified person talks to Saddam saying his talk, which is more effective than works). Abu 'Ammar ,it is about the timing , if we have the right timing and the situation of Arab countries and Palestinians are fine , we would see this talk applied on real, but as long as we are on this way, we will never make it and the enemy wont give us the chance for it , when the enemy saw a rocket , he said that Iraq owns missiles that would reach Tel Aviv, well Tel Aviv has missiles that reach all Arab countries , Iraq has Chemical weapon and successfully used it on Iranians, and Iraq won't think twice about Striking Israel with Chemical weapons, when you ask Israel , why would the Iraqis use the Chemical weapon against you ? The answer is to restore Palestine for the Arabs, and do not assault Arabs and that is it! Therefore, you do not have to be afraid of the Iraqi Chemical weapon anymore. But Israel owns the Atomic Bomb, this is not a big deal, it is a right for it, (Yasir Arafat says: also the atomic, chemical and germ bomb, it has 240 nuclear warhead for Arab countries, 12 nuclear war head for every Arab country, these things wont threat the Arab security) Saddam continues saying: I am saying these words and am completely calmed wearing my civilian suit, (Yasir Arafat says unclear words for joking), (another unidentified person says it is a matter of diplomacy). Saddam resumes saying: so, I am saying these words because we have to be ready for that level, maybe we say some words that could make people happy and make us happy too, and we don't know what these words mean, today also, I insured that thing in front of the parliament, I said we are Arabs, since we were kids, we learned that in the school by Abu-Khaldun (Sati' Al-Husari) who is not Iraqi, he taught us that we are Arabs, from Najd to Yemen and from Egypt to Tatwan (Arab Poem), so, it is not a political theory so they say we made that theory and violated the rules of the International Law, meaning that being Arabs is old thing , so the word Arabs means; that we have duties and rights ,among these duties, is to defend Arabs ,we can't change the fact of being Arabs after we learned it since we were kids! In addition, Arab nations exist since we were kids. We say, "We are Arabs, and we are one nation, and we don't defend Arabs! We can't make it make it that way, in order not to have dualism, especially, God gave us fortune and gave us the ability to do so, we say we are Arabs and we defend our Arab rights, (Saddam looking to one of the Palestinian delegation saying: Right Sheikh?) Saddam resumes talking: so what we can do. (Yasir Arafat interrupts him saying until victory.) Saddam resumes talking: do you call this assault? We did not forget Palestine and our Palestinian brothers, they call us the invaders while Israel occupied Palestine, rape the Palestinian women and kill the kids daily and they are not invaders! .we know this reason before, the diplomatic language , no one has talked about Palestine since long time ago and the Arab union as if it is shame to talk about it , it is like when someone is talking about the Arab union and Palestinian issue his head down because of being shame of talking about that thing, Israel did it because no one talked about it and if someone talks about it he is not Palestinian , he is invader, it is the same for us , have you ever seen someone who has been in war for 8 years and at last you call him invader? Even if he is invader from the start, is there any invader, who can keep in war for 8 years? So do you want to step on Arabs' dignity daily and everybody has to keep silent, so you did not call anyone invader? That's it, when we get mad, we get mad for while but we get real mad. (Yasir Arafat interrupts saying: Be aware of the silent when he gets mad.) Saddam resumes talking: put God in front of your eyes always, (Yasir Arafat says together until victory.), Saddam resumes talking: with God's power, I can see the victory in front of my eyes.

Figure 32 – command members discuss Kuwait invasion (3 of 4)

(Sheikh 'Abd-al-Hamid, One of the Palestinian delegations says: God has his own people, if they want something, He will achieve it for them, so when they have determination and well to do so he will achieve it for them) Saddam resumes talking to one of the delegation member saying: Right 'Abdallah? Before, when we were in Cairo, and we sentenced to death, why did we call 'Abdallah Al-Hurani to come for us from Gaza, as long as the Palestinian issue is new one? What for? Now they call us the presidents, we are not presidents we are fighters. (One of the Palestinian delegation members says: you know something Mr. President, your high spirit is not a new thing for you since I met you in Cairo, and it is the same for the Iraqi people.

Figure 33 - command members discuss Kuwait invasion (4 of 4)[293]

November 28, 1990 - Fedayeen Dispatched to Saudi Arabia

General Manager Military Intelligence
Second Support

Sir:

RE: Sending Assistants

Reference your letter of deploying supporters who already completed their training to some of the areas of interest, the committee discussed on November 28th 1990, their names and requirements for deployment. Below are details:-

Al-Ihsa' area:

1. They will deploy all from Conscript soldier Hakem Ghayedh Thajeb and Conscript soldier Rayssan Rayed Haty participating in unit (999), because the brother of the first name and his cousin are located in the area. Previously, second person repetitively visited the area bearing in mind that both were smugglers before.

2. The assigned goal for both agents is to sabotage famous oil establishment American company in Saudi (ARAMCO) where the cousin of the first agent works.

3. They both can be contacted via: -

    a) The phone of one of our outside agencies using a special (code).
    b) The repetitive visit of the brother of the first agent to the area as he works there and able to get a Saudi active residency permit.
    c) Both agents will be provided with sufficient amount of explosives enough to cause required sabotage. This will be coordinated with Department 3 and division 8.
    d) Both agents need a good vehicle to use for deployment when they settle in the target place.
    e) It is important to pay 5000 SR (FIVE THOUSAND) Riyals to each of them plus continue paying their monthly salaries to their families as usual.
    f) It is possible we can provide them with required papers and coordinate that with division 8.

Hafr Al-Baten:

1. The volunteer Fedayee, police commissioner (Abed Al-Satar Jassem Ali Attia) was prepared to get deployed to area mentioned above and to settle there.
2. The goal of settling the agent mentioned above is to provide (a secure base) to Unit (999) members planned to be deployed to that area for the reason mentioned below:

    a) Eliminate any of Al- Sabbah when found in the area as soon as you receive accurate information from above agent.

Figure 34 – Fedayeen dispatched to Saudi Arabia (1 of 4)

b) Execute sabotage operations in Kuwaiti Military Command or other countries' command located in Hafr Al-Baten and near Khaled Military base.

3. The agent would be contacted through using one of our agency's telephones and through some other sources constantly visiting the area.
4. The agent needs a suitable vehicle to facilitate sending him there to accomplish our mission and later use it for (transportation, booby trap).
5. It is important to provide him with a personal suitable weapon. (pistol)
6. The source needs an amount of 5000 SR (FIVE THOUSAND RIYALS) to facilitate his stay for some time. His salary should be paid monthly to his family.

Al-Riyadh Area

1. Members who are prepared to settle in the area mentioned above are:

2. Special Forces, Lieutenant Waleed Sabri Atyia Abed Al-Aziz Al-Saadoun working at unit (999); for the following reasons:

   a) His relatives are in Saudi Arabia.
   b) His sister married to one of the Saudis from an Iraqi descent, and is settled with her husband in Riyadh, bearing in mind that her husband's brother is one of our sources personal friend; he visited the country several times and volunteered in the Popular Army during the war against Iran.

3. The reason for our agent settling in Riyadh is:-

   a) For him to get a secure base for our other members that will be deployed later.
   b) Collect information on Al Sabbah activities and Saudi and American targets in the area (Central commands), officers /soldiers/ foreigners housings, essential weapon areas, military installations …etc.)
   c) Eliminate any of Al Sabbah clan when opportunity arises and to coordinate with us.

4. Secure communication with him via phones or through our sources that can reach Riyadh.
5. His best cover-up is having his sister and relatives there; he can keep alleging that he escaped military because authorities were vexing him about the marriage of his sister in Saudi Arabia. We will try to arrange this cover-up and choose a name and location of the unit he belonged to before (his desertion).
6. It is necessary to pay 5000 SR (FIVE THOUSAND RIYALS) to cover his expenses in Saudi Arabia.

Figure 35 - Fedayeen dispatched to Saudi Arabia (2 of 4)

> 7) It is possible to arrange for the process of (his escape) through one of our sources.
>
> <u>United Arab Emirates</u>:
>
> 1) We will send the Fedayee (Sahib Mahdi Saleh Malbous) to the area above mentioned reasons:-
>
> > a) Worked with his brother there for a period of three years (restaurant owner).
> > b) Some of his relatives are present there (Abu Dubi) married to agent's cousin.
> > c) He has other friends and acquaintances. He gave us their names and numbers and mentioned that some of them were supporting him during our war with Iran. Among some of them are sons of some (Sheikhs).
>
> His reason for settling over there:-
>
> a) To establish a safe base for members that will be deployed later.
> b) Gathering information on vital targets for the Emeritus and enemy nations there.
>
> > 8) It is possible to connect with him via a phone or through another supporter assigned by the South command to go there.
> > 9) He was not supplied with ammunition for sabotage at this stage until he settles.
> > 10) It is important that he travels to Jordan to contact his relatives and friends in the Emirates and ask them to get an affidavit from their Embassy in Amman to ensure his entrance to the Emirates, bearing in mind that the documents in his hand prove that he work there and will help him to enter to targeted area.
> > 11) It is necessary that (3000) dollars (THREE THOUSAND DOLLARS) be given to him to cover expenses of his travel and for him to settle there. On our part, we will do what necessary to pay suggested monthly salary family.

Figure 36 - Fedayeen dispatched to Saudi Arabia (3 of 4)

> COMMITTEE SUGGESTIONS AND OBSERVATIONS:
>
> 1) All those deployed to above mentioned areas are not from our Command or unit.
>
> 2) It is possible to send other groups to same targets or to other important targets. This will be done depending on secrecy of mission.
>
> 3) It is possible to send individuals voted upon above within this week or coming week as soon as we receive approval.
>
>   5)   The committee will perform final (exams) on any member to be sent for final approval and inspect any week points that might arise last minute.
>   6)   The committee suggests the following:-
>
>   a) Inform authorities with what mentioned above.
>   b) Approval, Sir, of final and execution of plan.
>
> For your consideration… what you see fit…with respect
>
> Signatures:
> Major Mahmoud Ibrahim Hamadi (Member)
> Sarhan Hafez Fahd (Member)
> Taha Abbas Ahmad, Committee Chair
>
> Date: November 28, 1990

Figure 37 – Fedayeen dispatched to Saudi Arabia (4 of 4)[294]

1.7   11/29/1990 Fedayeen Dispatched to Arab Nations

>   IN THE NAME OF GOD THE MERCIFUL THE COMPASSIONATE
>
> PRESIDENTIAL PALACE
> Secretary
> IIS Military Headquarter
> Date: November 29, 1990   TOP SECRET & PERSONAL
>
> Vice Chairman
> Headquarter Revolutionary Council
>
>   RE: Commando (Fedayee) Work
> Sir:
>
> Following our correspondence (Top Secret & Personal), M 2/, Place 15257, dated September 30, 1990, below are commando (Fedayeen) names who had been trained and are ready to go to certain cities, i.e. (Najd ,Al-Hijaz and Emarites) for commando operations.

Figure 38 – 11/29/1990 Fedayeen dispatched to Arab Nations (1 of 3)

Targets shown are as follow:

Target Places:

a) Target chosen is Saudi oil company (**ARAMCO**).

b) Commando (Fedayee), Hakim Ghayad Thajeb, and Fedayee Raysan Ra'id Hati, both in our Unit (999) Headquarter, to accomplish above mission.

    3)   Hifr Albaten Area:

          i. Goals targeted in this area:

FIRST   Military Headquarter for Al-Sabbah clan.

SECOND   Military Headquarters: (Egyptian, Syrian, foreign and Gulf areas in Khaled military city.

    (P.36 of 57)   SEAL OF MILITARY HEADQUARTER

                                    TOP SECRET & PERSONAL

4)   Commando (Fedayee), Commissioner Police, Abdul Al-Sattar Jasem Ali, had been set to settle in (Hadr Albaten). We are preparing to send other groups from the Unit (999).

5)   Riyadh City:

        i. 1st Lieut. Special Forces, Walid Sabri Al-Saadoun, to stay in this city for following purposes:

FIRST: Monitor (Al-Sabbah) clan and take chance by eliminating some of them.

SECOND: Collect information on vital American and Saudi targets.

        ii. As soon as these officers settle down more groups will be sent to the area.

6)   Arab Emirate:

        i. We prepared commando (Fedayee) (Sahib Mahdi Saleh) to be in (Abu Dabi) for the following missions:

Figure 39 - 11/29/1990 Fedayeen dispatched to Arab Nations (2 of 3)

> FIRST: To collect vital information on the Emirates and other enemy nations in the area.
>
> SECOND: To monitor (Zayid and his son) and to collect information on them.
>
> ii. Later, other groups will be sent to the area.
>
> 7) Previously, we sent Palestinian (Jamal Hussein Jawhar) to Riyadh so he can eliminate some of (Al-Sabbah) clan. He is still there.
>
> For your information, please acknowledge ... with appreciation and respect, Sir.
>
> Signed: Staff Lieutenant General
>
> IIS Head, Intelligence Military Headquarter, DATE: November 29, 1990

Figure 40 - 11/29/1990 Fedayeen dispatched to Arab Nations (3 of 3)

1.8 December 1990 – Unit (999) Training

> TOP SECRET & PERSONAL
>
> **REPRESENTATIVE TRAINING REPORT**
>
> 1. **Name of PersonTrained**: Commissioner Sattar
> 2. Training Duration: Nine days, from (1) to (9) December, 1990.
> 3. **Training Forum**:
> a) Introduction to explosives and other elements pertaining to terrorism.
> b) Connect terrorist training period used in quick missions by using dough and plastic explosives.
> c) Practical training on use of explosives and connecting terrorist mission by using time electronic devices
> d) Ways to destroy buildings, Oil refineries, Pipes and planting car explosives.
> 4. Training Place: Unit (999)
>
> 5. Capabilities of Trainer's for these missions: Good
> 6. Opinion on their possibility of using training technique: There is a good trainer's agreement about the use and the ways trained on.
>
> Signed: Major Fawaz Abboud Hamad
>
> Date: December 20, 1990

Figure 41 – Fedayeen Training Report Unit (999)[295]

1.9 9/14/1990 Sri Lankan Socialist Student federation

> ISGP-2003-00011487
>
> Page 14,
> Report from the Iraqi intelligence office in Bangkok, Thailand to base in Iraq (D-4/4), on Sep 14, 1990. Reporting that on Sep 9, they met with
> - Mr. Mahindra Amanayel, and
> - Mrs. Kamina Wastawenkon, representatives of the Sri Lankan Socialist Student federation (30 members) whom are ready to carry out suicidal activities against American targets In Thailand, or as per instructions of the Iraqi command. Their relations with Iraq go back to 1982, when their leader met with Saddam Hussein.

Figure 42 – Terrorist connection in Thailand

1.10   1) Iraq working with OIG to attack coalition forces (1-2)
   2) only financial aid be given to EIJ

```
Memo #: 140/D1/4/1  Date: 18 March
1993

To the office of the Presidency—The Secretary      Subject:
                Execution of Directive

The esteemed Presidency Memo Top Secret and Personal 1576/ K on 16
March 1993

1. On 24 December 1990, we agreed with the representative of the
   Islamic Organized Group in Egypt on a plan to move against the
   Egyptian Regime through conducting Fedayeen operations provided
   we secure for them financial aid, training, and other things,
   based upon orders from the esteemed Presidency to execute
   Fedayeen operations against the coalition countries that are
   against us. We stopped targeting Egypt Promptly after the cease
   fire.

                         (1 - 2)
                  Top Secret and Personal


2. Our Apparatus' recommendation to bring over the Islamic Group
   representative in Egypt to Iraq, as per our Memo Top Secret and
   Personal, and very urgent 4/533 on 11 March 1993, was based on
   the order of his Excellency the President may God keep him (no
   way now except for financial aid, because he is not convinced
   now, and that the Iraqi Intelligence should gage the situation
   in the Arab world), and as per the Presidency Memo Top Secret
   and Personal 1681/K on 25 March 1992.

       Please review ---with respect

       Signature
       Director of IIS
       18 March 1993

                         (2)
                  Top Secret and Personal
```

Figure 43 – Admission of working with OIG to attack coalition countries[296]

Note: Although number 2 says Islamic Group (OIG) representative, this is actually referring to the EIJ. We know this is the EIJ because memo 4/533 is the memo discussing the EIJ member flying to Baghdad on a meat cargo plane. (see chapter 1, Figure 2)

Appendix   273

1.11 11/29/1990 Fedayeen Dispatched to Arab Nations

```
Number 140/D/4/1
Date: 25 Ramadan
March 18, 1993

Office of the president of the Republic    Secretary
Subject: Carrying out a directive

The reference is made to the letter of the president 1576/K dated March 16, 1993
classified top secret and personal

        1. There has been an agreement on 12/24/1990 with the representative of the
           Islamic Group organization in Egypt on a plan to move against the
           Egyptian regime by carrying out commando operations provided that we
           guarantee them financing and training and providing them with the
           requirements in accordance with the honorable order of the president
           which calls for carrying out commando operation against hostile alliance
           governments. Afterwards, the operation targeting Egypt will cease
           immediately after the cease fire.

                                       (1-2)

Page 31
        2. With respect to the proposal of our special agency [IIS] regarding calling a
           representative of the Islamic group in Egypt to Iraq as specified in our top
           secret, immediate and personal and letter 4/533 dated March 11, 1993.
           This letter was in response to the president (Only financial support is
           possible as of now. Intelligence should be present in any movement in the
           Arab homeland), as indicated by the president letter classified top secret
           and personal number 1681/K dated March 25,1992

                                       (2-2)

For Review
Sincerely
[Signature]
Director of the Intelligence agency
March 18, 1993

[Copy to]
Khudayr
3/18
```

Figure 44 – Saddam meets with EIJ

1.12 12/18/93 Iraq and OIG to attack coalition forces

```
Memo #: 140/D1/4/1  Date: 18 March
1993

To the office of the Presidency—The Secretary      Subject:
            Execution of Directive

The esteemed Presidency Memo Top Secret and Personal 1576/ K on 16
March 1993

1. On 24 December 1990, we agreed with the representative of the
   Islamic Organized Group in Egypt on a plan to move against the
   Egyptian Regime through conducting Fedayeen operations provided
   we secure for them financial aid, training, and other things,
   based upon orders from the esteemed Presidency to execute
   Fedayeen operations against the coalition countries that are
   against us. We stopped targeting Egypt Promptly after the cease
   fire.

                           (1 - 2)
                    Top Secret and Personal
```

Figure 45 – Admission of working with OIG to attack coalition forces[297]

1.13 After Gulf War

MV4:	...	In regards to the opposition sir...
SADDAM:		I would like to make a clear statement, and in proper Arabic language. In the event America and its allies object to the Soviet Union initiation, Iraq will cooperate with the Kuwaiti political and religious organizations in order to erect a national democratic rule.
MV5:	[Minutes 03:15-33:53 blank]	Sir, with this step, the world is going to look at us in a completely different way. [Minutes 03:15-33:53 blank]
SADDAM:		...Kuwait will last...However, this is an international revolution, which if occurred, no one would survive on earth, including Qarun and Tauj. God to Whom be ascribed all perfection and majesty, might wish to cancel that day, do you think Qarun will still exist? Qarun will still exist, if...For instance, if we were in Kuwait and they destroyed the Americans...
MV6:		We would vanish as well.
SADDAM:		This is an international revolution, with prophets, not with human beings, could that ever happen? Even the prophets were...he died long time ago...I mean, I noticed in all of you, how you worry about people; we will deal with it through careful instructions and awareness...
MV1:		It will be best, if we have instructions.
ABU USAMA:		Besides that Mr. President, you must issue instructions and orders to our party members and to our organizations, that for the upcoming days, starting today, we need to launch a celebration and a victory

Figure 46 – After Gulf War (1 of 10)

		campaign, in a positive method, in order to execute the enemy traces, which affected our people. I mean launching campaigns to remove the traces as fast as possible, for example, just like the Qamuss effort in World War II, to erase the war effect on the Armenian women's' behaviors.
SADDAM:		We must first erase the negativity, sins and then the other issues.
ABU USAMA:		This way, our people will observe positive and constructive formations.
SADDAM:		When the people notice our party members following this method, they will then follow. Just find a comfortable and rapid method. The party method is usually very effective.
ABU-AHMAD		I swear to Allah, that the enemy had a major impact on the party's spirit. I mentioned that to you before, I did not submit it in a letter; I considered it an irrelevant issue. I just wanted to identify what project, which he wrote regarding the morale of the party members. He mentioned only the morale of the party members, in the south, not including the north, Baghdad, The Palace Center, Al-Hillah, the effect on bridges, Al-Amarah, Al- Nasiriyah, and Al-Basra.
SADDAM:		Not to mention the hateful and childish attack on Al-Nasiriyah, this would never have crossed our mind.
ABU-USAMA:		By the name of Allah sir, you should engrave at every city entrance, and on every rock, how many attacks were launched on it by the enemy…
SADDAM:		Wow Abu- Usama! I am impressed with your way of thinking. You are

Figure 47 – After Gulf War (2 of 10)

		right. Why do you think we trusted the prophets? It is because they recorded every incident.
ABU-USAMA:		Every city keeps its record, in order to record the martyrs, numbers of the children and the numbers of the women. Every city will obtain photos of the destroyed buildings, in the event we build a museum, in the future.
SADDAM:		As well as improving negativity among them. Let the Arabs, when they come to visit the first time, to observe what the betrayer Americans have done.
ABU-USAMA:		We should generate a long movie on what occurred, and show it to the visitors in the future.
SADDAM:		We generate videotapes on what occurred in Al-'Amria, Al-Fallujah and in Al-Nasiriyah...
MV9:		We need to generate more than just a movie...
ABU-USAMA:		Yes, yes you are right. It should contain comments for the future...
SADDAM:		It should be a very rare movie in its nature, which no one has ever seen before, in order to be remembered... I mean in regards to its party organizations and for the Arabs to witness it themselves...
MV10:		Sir, God willing, the road opens, I have 35 videotapes, which I would like to record our events on them, in 'Arafat, France and in Algiers, in order to prevent any exposure of our army sites.

Figure 48 – After Gulf War (3 of 10)

SADDAM:	...	Ask the Army personnel and the ambassadors, to record all the events, which will show the world...to show how an Algerian speaks for us and answers. You record 35 videotapes, from all over the world, and through different nationalities, to prove it. We need to evaluate their quality first, otherwise, it might be better for us...I mean not better, but more beneficial for us, to use our newspapers and radio stations for that purpose, instead of spending millions of Dinars.
ABU-USAMA:		We also need sir, to stress our gratitude to those who supported Iraq, including the non-Arabs, such as the Peace group...
MV10:		By the name of Allah, those peace group people are not good!
SADDAM:		We do not need to mention details about it. We should just say, "This is special thanks, with respect, appreciation and love, to those who stood by us and supported us in a way that proved their sincerity, nationalism or their true humanitarian support." Just like that, we do not mention names or...
MV10:		Sir, we met and talked to those people in Al-Rashid City, they said to us, "We are neutral group and we only support peace."
SADDAM:		They support the lawful side and the unlawful side.
MV10:		If we acknowledge this group, the public will criticize us, because they are neutral.
ABU-AHMAD		We should mention special thanks to the patriotism of the Muslims and the Christians, especially to Al-Jamahir group who are the main base for Islam.

Figure 49 After Gulf War (4 of 10)

SADDAM:		Where is the Islamic base? I do not know it, I swear to Allah!
ABU-AHMAD		All the people in the city included special gratitude to the 99%
		religious Egyptian groups, who are some of them, are prominent respectable Egyptians, and they are never influenced by even 5% of the Islamic movements.
SADDAM:		The officials will try to buy them for information; however, they will never be able to buy them.
ABU-AHMAD		They tried to buy whomever they could from their leaders, such as Al-Ma'diyah and especially the poor individuals however, they could not buy the Al-Jamahir leader. 'Abass is a very good man...
SADDAM:		See if 'Abass could arrange it.
ABU-AHMAD		When the uprising occurred, he sent his representative, who attended our meeting and provided assistance, since 'Abbas was busy.
SADDAM:		Even his representative is good...
ABU-AHMAD		Yes, I agree. I mean Al-Jamahir... however, the Al-Ma'diyah movement...
ABU-USAMA:		Ben Bella told me, "The representative of 'Abass is untrustworthy and do not be misled by him." That is what he stated to me.
ABU-AHMAD		What do you think of his talk with us?
SADDAM:		Abu-Ahmad Listen! I do not care much for Al-Sheik, based on my first impression of him, which is the most important, in regards to how he speaks and handles situations. I noticed that he is a good politician and religious leader; however, he does not speak the truth.
ABU-AHMAD		After 'Abass arrived from Saudi Arabia and met with you, he returned and prevented every uprising, including Al-Muqadra, Al-Murtadin, Al-Tahrir, and other party members...
SADDAM:		I believe he realized that politically

Figure 50 – After Gulf War (5 of 10)

		he was secluded, and wanted to return to politics.
MV10:		I believe Mr. President that he is following his father's, Ahmad Sa'id Al-Deen, footsteps, He was…
SADDAM:		He is a fake and I even consider Al-Khomeini better than him. I mean he is a fake from the Al-Faliq family. This is his pattern.
MV10:		Saudi Arabia does not like Algiers or the Algerians; there is a possibility that they might change their opinion in the future…
SADDAM:		Algiers is under nationalism and Islamic pressure, which did not exist before.
MV11:		It is great country, especially the Algerians sir!
MV12:	[UNINTELLIGIBLE]	[UNINTELLIGIBLE] I heard a statement from Ahmad, and from that other person, Ghanimi, they all are young men. They have a new political office here, and the one in charge of the students, is a young intelligent man.
ABU-USAMA:		There is one important issue, sir, which I believe we must achieve. We must establish from now on, a radio station, which will be heard easily accessibly and widely all over the world, as Saudi Arabia and Egypt, and you instruct them to broadcast Baghdad. We need to establish a research center, as well, connected to this radio station, its main task is to search for numbers, facts and documents in regards to the Gulf corruptions. Moreover, it will broadcast to the region regularly, in connection to their budget, their money, their scandals and their Western investments, not in general, we should broadcast information and numbers…then we

Figure 51 – After Gulf War (6 of 10)

		end the truce period. Lately, when the Gulf was granted truce, his corruption and his money were in peace, and everything else.
SADDAM:		On a political and diplomatic level, it is considered inappropriate; however, we may wait for a while, a year or six months. I suggest that we think this over.
ABU-USAMA:		That is fine.
SADDAM:		No, I am asking your opinion on the matter.
MV10:		You mean I will say no to you! That will indicate you are wrong and that is a lie.
SADDAM:		What was the outcome of the truce?
MV10:		It caused public interference.
SADDAM:		You mean it caused interference, and the majority of public security was lost, which means that some people established relations with Saudi Arabia! However, we are not opposed to that.
ABU-USAMA:		We will expose them to the Arab Nation and to the whole world, in order for the world to hear…
MV11:		Even the Shiite countries, we created banners asking them to listen to our station.
SADDAM:		Okay, then we must concentrate on our Arab nation. Am I right? In addition, to our party and all the good people, I mean not just our party. Whoever is following the same path; we must support him and help him.

Figure 52 – After Gulf War (7 of 10)

MV16:		Sir we thank Allah for our good life. What are your expectations toward the Americans' situation, in the upcoming days? Do you believe they might try to…?
SADDAM:		I do not believe that the Americans will accept this project easily as it is, they might try to agitate the situation, through other tricks, and this is the first aspect. The other aspect is I am not comfortable with the Kuwaiti's restraint in the first four days, in Qazim City. It is a very devastating situation, since Kuwait is located by the ocean, if we withdraw in the first four days, the opening area will be inside our region. Kuwait or the American army could enter through it; therefore, we are not sure of what they might use as an excuse, in the event we withdraw.
MV14:		In those four days, we shall concentrate on the open field towards them…
SADDAM:		This is a controlled revolution; they send you a letter today to implement it in the morning.
MV16:		Sir, in regards to your pictures for the banners, would like us to remove it before they would…
SADDAM:		Yes, I swear to Allah, from the first day, I thought it was inappropriate to…
MV16:		Yes, sir that is right, however, as soon as we hear anything regarding when they start…
MV17:	.	They will start in the beginning of the month.
MV16:		What do you mean?
MV17:		They are going to start at the beginning of the month…
SADDAM:		Even the buildings do not…

Figure 53 – After Gulf War (8 of 10)

MV16:		We will protect the buildings and would not even let them touch it. That is what I would like to express...
ABU-AHMAD		It is going to be a very difficult sight to watch, when our army and the troops are withdrawing...
MV16:		It is going to take place at night.
SADDAM:		It is better to withdraw the troops yourself, instead of the enemy doing it for you!
ABU-AHMAD		I mean not at the beginning, I am just concerned they might record it as two weeks from the last day of the last week.
SADDAM:		Please record it! What do you mean by the withdrawal takes three to four days?
MV17:		I mean four days from the fourth day.
SADDAM:		They will withdraw from Kuwait City, on the fourth day.
ABU-USAMA		Why should they wait to the last day? They should remove it at night... Sir, could we assassinate the Prince of Kuwait upon his entrance to Kuwait?
ALL THE COMRADES:	]	[LAUGH]
ABU-USAMA		I understand that it is a daring task; however, it is for a good cause. The Palestinians have not done anything courageous regarding our situation. How could they call themselves Palestinians? They have not performed anything.
SADDAM:		If they could just help the Iraqi Intelligence, it would be great.
ABU AHMAD		No, they did help us, and the Intelligence carried out operations based on this situation, including Lebanon. We have received

Figure 54 – After Gulf War (9 of 10)

			documents from their Intelligence, stating that our organization carried out such and such operations in your honor.
ABU-USAMA			The commander Taha's idea is not 100% considerable.
SADDAM:			Why should we not consider it?
ABU-USAMA			Well, sir they must be depressed for the attack, we should try to imagine how its legendary loss, its tumult, its fun, and the celebrations in Kuwait…
MV18:			The 25th is a national holiday in America, and the Americans want to be in Kuwait on the 25th…
MV19:			How could they arrive on the 25th?
MV18:			Yes, they are trying…
MV20:			They stated in America, that within two days…

Figure 55 – After Gulf War (10 of 10)[298]

1.14 1/4/2001 Chemical and Biological Weapons in Iraq

> ISGQ-2003-00003598
>
> [Page 45:]
>
> -18-
>
> As a matter of fact, developing weapons that can penetrate deeply into the ground or concrete is one of the foremost priorities of American weapon manufacturers. Some targets may contain chemical and biological weapons. Unless these are annihilated to the highest degree, they can be detected from the air by some hazardous airborne substances. No matter how precise these weapons are, it is necessary for the attacking force to know exactly what its aim in the attack is: some targets are mobile, and Iraq has proven that it moved throughout the country very expansive equipment and data to evade United Nations' weapons inspection teams. Still, precision is essential and fundamental to the Americans if they want to strike vital targets while minimizing civilian losses simultaneously.
>
> Signature: Sa'ad Najim 'Abdullah, translator, 1/4/2001.

Figure 56 – Chemical and Biological Admission[299]

1.15 1/7/1991 Terrorist Training in Iraq

> **TOP SECRET & PERSONAL**
>
> Defense Plan (private) pertaining to Feda'aye, Police Commissioner,
>
> **Abdul Sattar Jassem Ali**
>
> 1) Areas of Interest: Saudi Arabia/ Hafr Al-Batin
> 2) Entrance Date: Night of December 25/26, 1990
> 3) Duration & Approximate Date of Return: (Blank)
> 4) Place of Entrance: Police prescient, Tammouz 17 (Iraq)
> 5) Ways of Crossing Borders: Infiltrating at night
> 6) Unit Supervised Enforcing Plan: Committee Headquarter (Private) with Unit (999) help.

Figure 57 – Terrorist training in Iraq (part 1 of 3)

7) Documents in hand:

    a) An introduction document in the name of (Atwi Khaidan Jousha), issued by so called Sami Azara Aal Ma'ajoun, Assistant of Saudi's authority.

    b) Personal I.D. (citizen) Iraqi, in the above name (forged).

8) Equipments delivered:

    a) A hidden code in his shoes
    b) A pistol "bed awing" 9 mm.

TOP SECRET & PERSONAL

(P.18 of 57)   TOP SECRET & PERSONAL

9. Amount paid to him: (5000) Saudi riyals with receipt that he received (enclosed)

10. Way to Contact Him:

a) Phone contact via our embassy in Jordan (639-818) or (639-331), Abu Yassir, Athens: 672-1688 Abou Hassan Al-Khourtoum 43747, or 480-47 Abou Ahmad.

b) The Meditator: Hola Maaiji Jabbar Al-Zalimi (Iraqi).

11.) Pressure Agency Type:

    a)   Volunteering personally for Feda'ay work
    b)   Signed a personal commitment
    c)   His father and the rest of his family are in Iraq.

12. Training Received:

    a) Physical exercise (Saaqa Exercise)
    b) Using all kind of weapons
    c) Explosives (use of all kinds and ways)
    d) Planting Car bombs

Dated: January 7, 1991

Figure 58 - Terrorist training in Iraq (part 2 of 3)

TOP SECRET & PERSONAL

13. Cover-up he will use in his mission: He ran away to Saudi Arabia because he has relatives over there and because they called him for military service being born (1960).

14. Purpose of Operation:

   a) Settling in (Hafr Al-Batin) to establish a safe base for other individuals coming to the area.
   b) Collect information on enemy military forces from other nations present in the region.
   c) Monitor movements of Al-Sabbah family (those important) and get rid of them when possible and when they are in the area.

15. Other issues regarding the operation:

   a) Had Vice President's approval. Revolutionary Council, sent him to Saudi Arabia, in reference to a letter that came from Vice President, dated, 12/1/1990 (enclosed herewith).

Signed: Major Mahmoud Ibrahim Hamadi (member) and Brigadier Sarhan Hafiz Fahd (member)

TOP SECRET & PERSONAL

Figure 59– Terrorist training in Iraq (part 3 of 3)[300]

1.16 7/28/1998 Abu al-Abbas Terrorist Operations

IISP-2003-00027918

From: The Republic of Iraq
       Presidential Office
       Office of the Arab Liberation Organizations in Iraq
Date: July 28, 1998

To: The Vice Director of the Office

Subject: Abu al-'Abbas

1- On April 25, 1998, Abu al-'Abbas left Iraq to the occupied territories (TC: West Bank) to meet with Yasir 'Arafat and other Palestinian leaders and discuss the Palestinian issues; he came back to Baghdad on July 17, 1998.
2- On July 22, 1998, the meeting with Abu al-'Abbas took place (TC: it appears to be meeting with the writer of this letter) and he discussed, in details, the Palestinian conditions in the occupied territories. He stayed in Gaza for two and a half months and met with most of the prominent Palestinian personalities and in particular Mahmwd 'Abbas (Abu Mazen), Fisal al-Husaini, Sa'ib 'Uraikqat, Shikh Ahmad Yassin, and the leaders of all the Palestinian political parties. In addition, Abu al-'Abbas meet with the leaders of the Arab political parties of the pre 1948 Palestine and with various Palestinian security organizations.
3- Abu al-'Abbas stated that he is willing to fully work, in any area, which will serve Iraq's objectives towards the Zionist enemy. We believe that Abu al'Abbas has the capabilities to conduct several assignments that are in the interest of the Service (TC: the Iraqi Intelligence Service- IIS) towards the Zionist regime. After reviewing and discussing many suggestions and ideas in this regard, Abu al-'Abbas has proved, throughout all the previous period, his good intentions towards Iraq especially during the first Gulf war when his organization conducted several military operations as follows:
    a- Burning of the Japanese embassy in Manilla- Philippine.
    b- Burning of the American Airlines office in the Philippine.
    c- Placing an explosive device in near an American army base in Azmiir.
    d- Placing an explosive device on the pipe lines that carry oil to an American base in Southern Spain.
    e- Placing gliding airplanes (including their pilots) under the command of the Service (TC: IIS) and an agreement was reached with the Iraqi Special Work Team to use these planes.
    f- Abu al-'Abbas has provided a team of his organization to carry out some of the operations in the Saudi territories; this team has is now under the command of the Iraqi Special Work Team.
This stand of the Organization (TC: probably Abu al-'Abbas' organization) was submitted to the Secretary of the Presidential Office in our letter No. 159, and dated August 19, 1998.

Figure 60 – Abu al-Abbas terrorist attacks (part 1 of 2)

4- Abu al-'Abbas has provided personal IDs and summaries of the political life of the members of the current Israeli Knesset, in accordance with the attached forms. The forms start with 'Azra Wizman (1), the president, and end with Benjamin Alwn (122). This information and the forms were given to M4 in the Israel Directorate (TC: an Iraqi diroctarate that is deals with Israeli issues)
5- Abu al-'Abbas has requested a meeting with your Excellency to greet you and update you with the Palestinian situation.

Please review and direct as you see fit.

Signed by Akram 'Umar Salih   Office Director.

There is a hand written note at the end of the document stating: "very welcomed, Comrad Akram, we should set the date for the meeting either by the calling each other or by personal meeting with you." (TC: Signature could not be recognized.). Date July 28.

Figure 61 - Abu al-Abbas terrorist attacks (part 2 of 2) [301]

```
                Republic of Iraq Office of the
                Presidency IIS

                              Very urgent Memo #: M4/7/3/586

                                      Dated: 18 March 1993

                     To the Director of M14

    Please supply us with a detailed inventory or audit of the Arab
    Fedayeen that were trained in Iraq during the Mother of all
    Battles, in the Fedayeen Operation.

    With respect

    Signed

    On behalf of the Director of M4

    18 March 1993

                              (1 - 1)
                       Personal and top secret
                              Promptly
```

Figure 62 – Memo asking for a list of non-Iraqi's trained in Iraq

1.17 10/22/2000 Chemical and Biological Weapons in Iraq

ISGQ-2005-00034061

[Page 2:]

In the Name of God, the Compassionate, the Merciful

The Republic of Iraq
Intelligence Service

To: Honorable Deputy Director of Intelligence Service for Operations
Subject: Scientific ideas

In reference to the report prepared by the biologist Uday Salim Mahdi (Part 1) and in response to your directive to discuss with the concerned section in Directorate 4 the possibility of including the ideas and information that came in the report in a letter to the President of the republic or the military industry commission, the section has indicated the following:

1. Refer the information related to the encryption method to D18 since it is the directorate concerned with the creation of algorithms for encryption for our service and all state establishments.
2. There is no scientific material that makes it necessary to refer to the President of the Republic or the military industry commission.
3. The concerned section recommends that the staff member above to destroy all of the documents related to his research to avoid any inconvenience with the inspection groups or the possibility of it reaching the country's enemies.

Please review. Respectfully,

[Signature]
General Security Section Director
22 October 2000

Figure 63 – Destruction of Documents Related to Production of Biological Weapons[302]

ISGQ-2005-00034061

[Page 3:]

The Republic of Iraq
The Presidency of the Republic
Intelligence Service
Secret and Confidential

Memorandum

Date: 10/14/2000
Number: D4/4/5/1631

To: Honorable Director of the General Security Section

Your secret communication number 125 in 10/8/2000.

The report by Mr. Uday Salim Mahdi sent to us with your communication above was reviewed and we decided the following:

1. The first idea in the report submitted last August by the individual mentioned above and its details were reviewed and they were referred to the nuclear energy organization for further study. The initial report indicated that the idea was unrealistic and cannot be practically implemented.
2. Regarding the second idea regarding a new method of encryption, we propose referring it to D17/2 since it is the directorate concerned with implementing encryption algorithms for the service and for all centers of the Iraqi government for evaluation and recommendation regarding its content.
3. The third idea regarding the production of viruses and bacteria that could be used to contaminate enemy water supplies in American military bases in Kuwait and Saudi Arabia, we say the following:
    a. This is not a new idea. Furthermore, the preparation of viruses and bacteria in limited quantities is easy and can be replaced with various other poisons available in large quantities. The execution of the operation is difficult from a security, practical, and logistic aspect [continue on next page]

1-2
Secret and confidential

Figure 64 – Biological Weapons in Iraq (part 1 of 2)

ISGQ-2005-00034061

[Page 4:]

<u>Secret and Confidential</u>

The Republic of Iraq
The Presidency of the Republic
Intelligence Service

[continue from previous page] which has to do with how to store the viruses and bacteria and keep it alive and effective until it is used; and also how to carry it to water and food supplies in the military bases of the enemy and ensuring it is not detected or killed with decontaminants and disinfectants used; in addition to the very dangerous repercussions both political and military.

b. Producing these viruses and bacteria and using is considered a biological weapon banned by the Security Council resolutions. The current directives from the political leadership does not allow handling it because if found it would cause a grave political problem for Iraq. For this reason, we see that it is important that Mr. Uday must stop the research and production of this material and destroy everything that have to do with this topic including material and documents, because the enemies might get hold of it and present it to the United Nations which would cause the country and our intelligence service problems and give the director of the special commission a reason to put the area where the research was done under continuous surveillance. Furthermore, if a decision was made to carry out an operation of this kind, the material required can be found in the local markets.

Please review. Respectfully,

[Signature]
[Illegible]
12 November 2000

Figure 65 - Biological Weapons in Iraq (part 2 of 2)[303]

ISGQ-2003-00003598

[Page 45:]

-18-

As a matter of fact, developing weapons that can penetrate deeply into the ground or concrete is one of the foremost priorities of American weapon manufacturers.
Some targets may contain chemical and biological weapons. Unless these are annihilated to the highest degree, they can be detected from the air by some hazardous airborne substances. No matter how precise these weapons are, it is necessary for the attacking force to know exactly what its aim in the attack is: some targets are mobile, and Iraq has proven that it moved throughout the country very expansive equipment and data to evade United Nations' weapons inspection teams. Still, precision is essential and fundamental to the Americans if they want to strike vital targets while minimizing civilian losses simultaneously.
Signature: Sa'ad Najim 'Abdullah, translator, 1/4/2001.

Figure 66 – Mobile WMD units[304]

Appendix 295

In the Name Of God, Most Gracious, Most Merciful

Ba'th Party
Secretariat office

Subject / Martyrdom Project

To his Highness Commander Activist Saddam, may God save you and bless you…

I am Comrade/Zahir Muhammad Tahir Majid Al-Barzanji, a member of Fedayeen Saddam and volunteer for the sake of Al-Quds…

My Commander Sir,
We can see on the TV all martyrs' missions inside the occupied territory… Moreover, we can see your Excellency how you encourage all the Muslims and Arab Countries, to volunteer and fight to liberate Al-Quds and holy sites. As I am one of the volunteers to liberate our Quds from Jews, I ask your Excellency to allow me to participate in carrying out the martyrs' missions to prove to the full world that we are with our brothers in the occupied territory by soul too… Moreover, with your holly hand we will liberate our Quds with the help of God.

Party Organization
Diyala Branch Command
'Adnan Section Command
Halabjah Party Division Command

Zahir Muhammad Tahir
Dayalli-Ba'qubah-Al-Yarmuk village
Mayor-'Ali 'Abbas Windi
8 Jun 2001

Figure 67 – Volunteer for Fedayeen Martyr Operation[305]

Thirteenth. Coordination with the Directorate of Delegations and reserving cards for delegations as guests of the Office numbered 3 instances.

G. In the Area of Joint Issues with Other Departments as a Work Team:

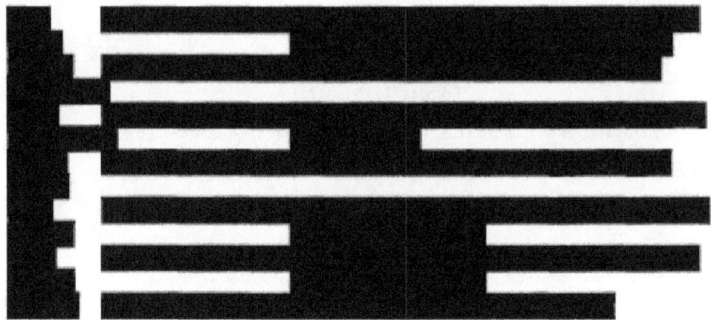

H. Financial Payments the Services Allocated as follows:

First. Financial allotments to Palestinian groups 4,000,000, four million Iraqi dinars.
Second. Financial allotments to the Arab Front for the Liberation of Ahwaz 10,000,000, ten million Iraqi dinars.
Third. Financial allotments to the Organization of Arabs Expelled from Kuwait 1000000 one million Iraqi dinars.
Fourth Financial allotments to equip the Al-Quds Special Military Base in the amount of 65,000,000 sixty five million Iraqi dinars, 25,000,000 twenty five million dinars have been paid, the rest is maintained by the Office to complete the requests to equip the base.

Figure 68 – Payments made to Terrorists[306]

Appendix 297

> In the Name of God, the Merciful, the Compassionate
> Logo: God, the Nation, the Commander
> Those who pledge allegiance to you, they pledge their allegiance to God
> Proverb: Be fair and swords against oppression with the truthfulness of men
> Republic of Iraq
> Presidential Directorate
> (Saddam Commandoes)
> General Secretariat
>
> [TC: Hand written comment on top of the main correspondence]
> The Decision: I agree and our reliance is on God
>
> Signed
> Director of Saddam Commandoes
> 2/10/1999
>
> Mr. the Honorable Director of Saddam Commandoes
> Greetings and Salutations
>
> Subject: Special Duty
> This is in reference to your Excellency's directives regarding the meeting with General Secretariat on the evening of the 27th of September 1999 regarding the dispatching of Commando 'Alaa Nuri Ibrahim to carryout the special duty, we advise that we have taken the following steps:
>
> 1. Commando 'Alaa Nuri Ibrahim was told and briefed about his special duty of eliminating the hostile agent Ahmad al-Chalabi and the method of eliminating.
> 2. He was presented with a new passport from Intelligence Service
> 3. He was presented with the sum of (1,500,000) one million five hundred thousand dinar for the purpose of conducting the mission and the return from London

Figure 69 – Execution of Iraqi Enemy[307]

"Lessons in "Secret Organization and Jihad Work". These lessons were authorized, directed, reviewed, updated and margin-notated as well as signed by Saddam Hussein himself. The Minister of Culture, the Press Secretary and members of a select committee were directed to write and re-write all of these lessons. These activities were from 1992 through 2000.

These lessons were directed at the people of Saudi Arabia to encourage and teach them how to organize to overthrow the Saudi Royal Family. These were lessons that show the individuals how to start from one, two and three people to forming larger group. It teaches and calls for destructions and damaging of variety of systems to gathering the vital secret data of the Saudi Administration so they can be given to the operatives to use against the Royal Family.

The correspondences in this document also show the communication from the majority of the Iraqi government leaders agreeing to write and broadcast these lessons to the Saudi population as well as to the "Al-Mujahiden" in other Arab countries or The Islamic World.

These lessons were corrected and retyped several times. The distribution of these lessons was planned through the use of some or all of the following:
1. Cassette Tapes
2. Internet
3. Radio Broadcasts
4. Friendly Newspapers
5. Friendly TV Stations
6. Recorded Videos (being smuggled into the country)
7. Small Booklets
8. Electronic Emails
9. Letters to the embassies

These are samples or titles of the teachings in these lessons:

Lessons in al-jihad and how to arrange it with several steps:
- Defeating and passing the security & military machines.
- How to start arranging in your area.
- How you can include women in the organization
- How to arrange a revolution.
- Democracy and how to control the system.
- How to face people and convince them.
- Najed & Hejaz Revolutionary Organizing Maintenance Recommendation
- Media and Press of Revolutionary Organization.
- Secret Press Requirements

Figure 70 – Lessons in Jihad[308]

Doc ID: - -
Length: 13 pages
Date: July 9, 2005 (Jumada al-Thani, 1426)
Title: Zawahiri's Letter to Zarqawi
Author: Ayman al-Zawahiri

Synopsis
A letter from Ayman al-Zawahiri, written in Afghanistan, to Abu Musam al-Zarqawi, head of al-Qai'da in Iraq, in which the author presents his strategy of winning the jihad in Iraq. Zawahiri emphasizes that achieving al-Qai'da's main goal in Iraq, establishing a caliphate and extending the jihad to the greater Middle East, is as much a political as a military struggle in which all actions, military or otherwise, have political significance. Therefore, more attention should be given to the political efforts of building unity with the Muslim people (umma), the Muslim scholars (ulema) and the mujahidin. Further, any actions, which cause disarray among these groups, should be avoided.

Key Themes
The letter addresses the political situation in Iraq and advocates measures, which will foster unity among al-Qai'da's supporters or attract new followers. Zawahiri presents his argument by first listing al-Qai'da's 4-point goal in Iraq:
1. Expel the Americans from Iraq.
2. Establish an Islamic authority and develop it into a caliphate, extending influence over as much Iraqi territory as possible.
3. Extend the jihad to Iraq's secular neighbors.
4. Extend the jihad to Israel.

He explains that the long-term goals (points 3 and 4) are impossible to attain without first achieving the short-term goals (points 1 and 2). Zawahiri then explains his conviction that in order to achieve the long-term goals al-Qai'da must immediately begin to address the political side of the conflict so as not to lose the short-term goals. Only by using their most powerful weapon, namely, the popular support of the umma in Iraq and neighboring countries will al-Qa'ida be ready for the inevitable withdrawal of American forces.

According to Zawahiri, the only way to garner popular support is to make every effort to avoid actions, which the umma does not understand or approve. In order to avoid such actions Zawahiri offers five main strategies:
1. Consult as many factions as possible in governance and decision making.
2. Create unity among the mujahidin.
3. Strive for unity with the ulema.
4. Do not attack the Shi'a.
5. Minimize excessive violence.

Strategy 1
Zawahiri advises Zarqawi to strive for unity with the people of Iraq because he believes the American forces may leave Iraq sooner than anticipated. In order not to be marginalized by other political elements Zarqawi is advised to begin laying the groundwork so that he may be ready. In order to accomplish this goal Zawahiri suggests including tribal and political leaders in al-Qa'ida decision making as much as possible. The letter invokes the example of the Taliban regime in

Figure 71 - Zawahiri's Letter to Zaraqawi (1 of 2)

Afghanistan as a negative example in order to illustrate this point by noting restrictions to participation in the government to students and the people of Kandahar. In the end, according to Zawahiri, when the Americans invaded, the Afghan people did not have a strong affiliation to the Taliban and did not defend the regime. Therefore, if they are to enjoy a broad base of support in Iraq al-Qa'ida must strive to include as many political groups as possible in a coalition.

Strategy 2
Zarqawi is instructed to foster unity among the mujahidin. Zawahiri argues that any division among the mujahidin will lead to divisions among the umma. Therefore, every effort should be made avoid conflict.

Strategy 3
The umma's perception of Al-Qa'ida's relationship to the ulema is also important. Zawahiri calls Zarqawi to avoid highlighting doctrinal differences or making disparaging remarks about specific scholars, which the general public does not understand. As the ulema are a symbol of Islam, people may come to believe that religion and its adherents are unimportant if public denunciations and doctrinal differences are highlighted. In Zawahiri's opinion, the loss of faith is a greater detriment to al-Qa'ida's cause than any benefit gained from criticizing a particular theologian.

The example of Mullah Muhammad Omar, Taliban leader in Afghanistan, is invoked to illustrate his point. He notes that Omar himself is a Hanafi adherent of the Matridi doctrine. Yet he did not draw attention to theological distinctions in the time of jihad. Zawahiri also argues that differences between religious doctrines will require generations to correct once the caliphate has been established. Therefore, the mujahidin should not concern themselves with solving these differences but concentrate on accomplishing the fundamental goals for Iraq.

Strategy 4
Al-Qa'ida's treatment of the Shi'a is another key element in fostering unity among the umma. According to the letter, Zarqawi is justified in attacking the Shi'a given the inevitability of a Sunni-Shi'a clash, the Shi'a's cooperation with America during the invasion of Afghanistan and the error of Shi'a beliefs. However, Zawahiri notes that the majority of Muslims do not understand these differences. Thus, the unity with the umma will be preserved by not attacking the Shi'a or highlighting doctrinal differences. Additionally, Zawahiri thinks that the threat of Iranian intervention on behalf of Iraqi Shi'a is a compelling reason to exercise restraint.

Strategy 5
Avoidance of unnecessary bloodshed is important for encouraging unity. Zarqawi is reminded that he is engaged in a struggle, which is being displayed in the news media and that the umma often does not comprehend the reasons for excessive violence seen in the media, though the actions are justified. Therefore, Zarqawi must refrain from excessive violence.

Figure 72 - Zawahiri's Letter to Zaraqawi (2 of 2)

Appendix   301

1.18 Details of the 1993 WTC Bombing Ignored

Note: The lines between the text are pauses in the speaking or page breaks in the original tape transcript.

Saddam	نعم – يعني الموضوع من الأوليات الأمامنا واضح اكو ترتيب معين فني لامريكا ليست بعيدة عنه وهيك شغلات وسخة ممكن المخابرات الامريكية تشتغلها اذا كان عندها غرض اكبر من يعني اكبر من الخسائر والتضحيات اللي تقدمها. لكن هذا الموضوع يخص مواطنين امريكا. تفجير المركز التجاري الامريكي رح (يتوقعون) بيه تضحيات, خسائر والخسائر وقعت فعلا يعني نشرتها الاعلام وانتم الان تستذكروها. فشلون ممكن للمخابرات ان تقدم على هيك عمل مع انه بيه مثل هذه الخسائر بالمواطنين الأمريكان؟	Yes, this issue from the preliminaries before us there has obviously been a special technical arrangement where the US seems to have a hand in. These dirty games are games that the American intelligence would play if it had a bigger purpose, which would be bigger than the losses and sacrifices it would have to suffer. But this issue concerns the American public- you would expect losses in the bombing of the World Trade Center. Losses. And they had losses; the media announced it and you remember it. So how could/would the American intelligence do such a thing even though they knew there would be American human losses?
Saddam	لانه العمل مو في طور التحضير حتى نقول مجرد عملية تكتيك فني يقصد بيها جهة معينة. لازم اكو جهة قلبها ما يوجعها على المواطنين الامريكان ولا	Because this is not in the prep stage for us to claim that it is just a technical tactic intended for a certain party. It must be done by a party whose heart
	أثرها سياسيا مباشرة تقع عليها. وهنا تيجي شكوكنا على اسرائيل. اسرائيل لما تسوي هيك عملية ممكن تقدم خسائر وهي عندها وسائلها اللي تقدر حتى لما تنكشف بعض الخطوط او الخيوط تقدر ترجم عليهم التراب وتضيع الشغلة, اللوبي الصهيوني موجود داخل امريكا وفعال. فهذا هم أحد الاحتمالات.	would not break over the loss of American lives and who would not suffer direct political consequences. Of course we immediately think of Israel. Israel, when it conducts such an operation is willing to suffer losses and it also has its methods by which even if some plans lead to it, it is able to cover the matter up and distract people from it. The Zionist Lobby is alive and effective in the US. So this is one of the options.

Figure 73 -1993 WTC bombing conversation (part 1 of 7)

Saddam	ولكن شنو الهي اغرى هاي الجهات كلها لان تبدي هذا التعاون خاصة اذا اتصالها بالسعودية صحيح. لان من يقول هذا اتصل فعلا متصل بالسعودية و [unintelligible] باسم عبدالله مثل ما قال [unintelligible] نوري - مثل ما قال عبد الرحمن يمكن تكون هذه القضية كلها مفتعلة من عبد الرحمن او قد يكون هو اتصل بغير جهة واشعره لعبد الرحمن ومن خططه والاعيب الناس اللي من هذا النوع انه هو ديتصل بالقنصلية السعودية بجوز اتصل بغير جهة. شون نوع العملية الاغرائية اللي تقدم للسعودية حتى تشارك بهيك عمل؟ او تدري بيه ما كو غير اذاء العراق. ولكن هذا يفترض الاطلاع الرسمي من امريكا.	But what tempted all these other factions to show such cooperation, especially if its contact with Saudi Arabia is correct. Because when he says he contacted then he really has contacted Saudi Arabia [unintelligible] in the name of Abdullah like [unintelligible] Nouri said. Like Abed al Rahman said, this whole matter could be thought up by Abed Al Rahman or he could have possibly contacted another faction and informed Abed al Rahman. One of the tricks and games of such people would be for him to pretend that he is contacting the Saudi consulate but maybe he is contacting a different party. What kind of temptation would they offer Saudi Arabia to participate in such an operation or know of it? Nothing would be as effective as bringing harm to Iraq. But we assume that we would need the official knowledge of the US.
Saddam	انه ممكن السعودية تدخل هيك مدخل الا باطلاع رسمي من امريكا. شنو ممكن يغري مصر؟ لانه هم ودت اشارات على مصر. يعني يغريها بالدرجة الاولى عملية توريط رجل الدين اللي دهو يحمل راية المقاومة ضدهم. اللي اسمه عمر عبد الرحمن. ويغريها بدرجة اذا تؤذي العراق. واعني بالنظام المصري. ولكن ايضا ما يمكن ان تخطو خطوات من هذا النوع الا باطلاع وبمعرفة بل وبطلب رسمي من امريكا. فيعني هذه كلها تشوف رح [unintelligible] انه باستمرار نطرح في هذه المرحلة عوامل متظاربة لانه مو كل الحقيقة مكشوفة امامنا كما هي. لانه المتهم اللي بايدينا انا اعتقد انه كل هذا الكلام اللي ديقوله يعني مرتب ويعني ديلعب ديلعب ويؤثر بالسناريو.	Is it possible for Saudi Arabia to enter into such an operation without the official knowledge of the US? What could tempt Egypt? Because it also sent signals to Egypt. Well, Egypt would primarily be tempted to involve the cleric who is carrying the banner of resistance against it. Whose name is Omar Abed al Rahman. And it also tempted to harm Iraq. And I mean by that the Egyptian government. But it also can not take steps of this nature with out the knowledge and even the official request of the US. So with all this you would see that [unintelligible] that constantly at this stage we offer conflicting factors because not the whole truth is revealed to us as it is. Because the suspect we have in our custody is too organized in what he is saying and is playing games, playing games and influencing scenario.

Figure 74 - 1993 WTC bombing conversation (part 2 of 7)

Saddam	الخلاصة من هذا الموضوع انا [unintelligible] ان نسوي صيغة اعلام مفاجئ ونقول احنا يعني اتطلعنا على معلومات خطيرة تتعلق التفجير اللي حصل في امريكا. وهناك جهات يعني كشفها التحقيق الاولي انها متورطة في هذا الموضوع وحتى الان لا نعلم اذا ما كان هناك جهات امريكية متفقة على هذا التكتيك ان لم نتوصل بعد اذا ما كانت هناك جهات امريكية ذات صيغة رسمية او شبه رسمية متفق على مثل هذا الترتيب ولكن نحن لدينا مثل هذه الدلائل ولدينا شكوك تدعمها بعض الادلة من انه هناك جهات عديدة مشتركة في هذا الموضوع ليس بالضرورة الواجهة الاولى التي اعلن عنها في التحقيقات الامريكية هي الصورة النهائية للموضوع.	The conclusion of this matter, I [unintelligible] to issue a surprise statement and say that we have become privy to dangerous information that concerns the attacks that occurred in the US. And that the initial investigation has uncovered factions involved in this matter and up to now we do not know if there are American parties in cooperation with this tactic. Because we have not yet found out if there are American official or semi official parties involved in this arrangement, however we have indication to that end and we have our suspicions that are supported by some evidence that there are several factions involved in this matter. The initial persons involved in this matter are not necessarily the complete picture of the situation.
Saddam	ونحن نكون قد اعلنا مسبقا ضيعنا على الامريكان فرصة الاعلان المستقل. لانه اذا سوى اعلان ونحن نيجي ندافع ما رح حد يسمع كلامنا. وانا اميل [unintelligible] لهذا [unintelligible] الاعلامي. يعني. نعم	By us announcing first we would preempt the Americans independent announcement. Because if they do announce and we try to defend ourselves no one will listen to us, and I favor [unintelligible] for this media [unintelligible].....yes?

Figure 75 – 1993 WTC bombing conversation (part 3 of 7)

Saddam	ولكن من يقرؤن اعلامنا ينطوي على شكل مسبق بأنه هذه اريد منها الاساءة الى العراق من غير ما نقول بيها الاساءة الى العراق. ما نجيب [inaudible] العراق. لانه من بصير -- هاي اساءة للعراق والى اخره يقصدت منه وما يقصد منه -- يفهم اعلامنا وكأنه دفاع عن النفس. بس يجي الاعلام بصيغة انه نحن اطلعنا على معلومات مهمة تتعلق بالتفجير اللي حصل ولدينا من الوثائق يعني ما يكفي لتشيير الاتجاه الاولي على الكيفيفة التي صار بيها العمل اللذي حصل ولا نعرف ولا نستطيع ان نجزم حتى الآن ما اي جهات اللي على علم باللذي نحن اطلعنا عليه في امريكا ولم تروج هذا الاطلاع او هذه المعلومات. يعني الى اخره -- يعني يصيغة من الصيغ الذكية لا تحوي كامل الصورة ولكن في نفس الوقت تموت اي اعلان دراماتيكي هم مخططين لان يقومون بيه ويعلنوه ويشووشون الراي العام.	But when they read our media which will previously show that the intention was to harm Iraq without stating that there was harm to Iraq. We don't want to bring in the [inaudible] of Iraq. Because once it is – this is an insult to Iraq etc, this implies and doesn't imply, then it will seem like we are trying to defend ourselves. But when we state in our media that important information was uncovered, which has to do with the attack that happened and we have documents that are sufficient to indicate the initial set up of the operation that occurred and that we do not know, nor are we able to determine if there were entities in the US who knew of this operation but did not advertise or announce this information etc. Put [Announce] it is a smart way that would not give the full picture but at the same time would kill any dramatic announcement they intended to make to confuse the public opinion.
Saddam	بالعكس الراي العام يقوم يسمع من عندنا. نحن صرنا نصير مصدر المعلومات ويوميا نصرح بشيء جديد بحلقة من الحلقات ونخلي المتابعة الاعلامية كلها تجري ومن خلال ال اه هي الشكوك رح تبدي تتجهه الى قصادها.	And the opposite will happen, the public will listen to us and we become the source of information and then we reveal something new daily in one of the episodes and let all the media follow up, go through the eh… the doubts will start being directed to the target.
Saddam	مثل هذا الاعلان لما يحكون اي شيء العراق -- والعراق ارهابي ويقول لك العراق عنده وثائق في هذا الموضوع وما عنده [inaudible] وصل للشيء اللي يتعلق بالارهاب والتخريب والعملية الاخيرة.	Well with this announcement, when they say anything about Iraq- that Iraq supports terrorism and then they have to say that Iraq has documents on this issue and they don't have [inaudible] it reaches the issues of terrorism, trouble making and the latest operation.

Figure 76 – 1993 WTC bombing conversation (part 4 of 7)

Saber	هم ينضبطون عليه لا يكون ينتحر هم احتمال [inaudible]	They need to watch him so that he doesn't commit suicide. There is a possibility [inaudible].
Saddam	ينتحر ويجوز اكو جهة هي تقتلك. فما يصير [inaudible] الحرس والخيزران وهناك يموتون	He could commit suicide and someone might kill him. They mustn't [inaudible] the guards, and whipping and then they die.
Saddam	ولكن اهم نقطة انه يكتمون والجهات اللي يشوفها [inaudible] ونسوي حذر شديد من احتمال قتله بالسجن بصيغة من الصيغ او انتحاره وما نخليه يسمع او يشوف جرائد ولا يسمع ولا حد [inaudible] انه اليوم شو سمعت الاعلام؟ ـ يعني ـ عندنا هيك العراقيين عندنا هيك. التلفزيون اليوم اعلنوا عنك وكذا وكذا ويقوم يخرطلك ويسمع الشيء اللي نحن ما رايدين ما يسمعه يعني بطريقة غير مقصودة.	But the most important thing is that they keep it to themselves and the persons he sees [inaudible] and we must be very careful that he is not killed in jail in one way or another or commit suicide. We must also not allow him to hear or read the papers and to hear from no one to [unintelligible] "what did you hear in the news today?" you know, how we the Iraqis are "hey the TV today announced news about you so and so" and then he goes off and tells him everything and then he [the suspects] hears unintentionally what we don't want him to hear.

Figure 77- 1993 WTC bombing conversation (5 of 7)

Tariq Aziz		صرح ناطق الرسمي [inaudible] توفرت لدى اجهزة المخابرات العراقية معلومات موثقة وخطيرة تتعلق بحادث تفجير المركز التجاري الدولي في نيويورك انه هذه المعلومات تثير شبهات عديدة حول الجهات اللي شاركت في الحادث او كانت ورائة. ان سلطات عراقية المختصة على استعداد للتعاون مع الجانب الاميركي للتعرف على الحقائق. بشرط ان تكون الجهة	[typing sounds] an official spokesperson stated [inaudible] that the Iraqi intelligence organizations have documented and serious information regarding the attack which occurred on the World Trade Center in New York. This information raises several questions regarding the entities that cooperated in this operation or who were behind it. The said Iraqi authorities are prepared to cooperate with the American people to identify the facts. On the condition that the American entity undertaking such
		الامريكية التي تتولى ذلك جهة نزية. ويفضل ان يتم ذلك بعلم الكنغرس الامريكي او اشرافه.	matter is an impartial [honest] one, and it is preferred that this is done with the knowledge of the American Congress or under its supervision.
Saddam		نعم انا ردت (مش واضح) نسويها قضية	Yes, I wanted to [unintelligible] to make it an issue.
Tariq Aziz		هي رح تبدي تغزل	It is going to start to make up stories.
Saddam		ايه تغزل ونحن في كل الاحوال على الاقل الهدف الاساءة اللنا بعد ما [inaudible] انتهى	Yes, make up stories and as for us in all cases the purpose of harming us after the [inaudible] is over.
Tariq Aziz		فجرنا القنبلة قبل ما	We pulled the trigger.
Saddam		فجرناها وخليناها عاشيه [inaudible] مو بالناس تغزل والعراقيين [inaudible] يبدوا – مفضلين مو على اساس مفضلين مفضلين	Yes, will be pulled and let it be [inaudible] but not allow them to make up stories about people and [inaudible] Iraqis – preferred but not on the basis of ….preferred…….preferred.
Tariq Aziz		نزل الدولار	The price of the dollar is down.
Tariq Aziz		احنا السلطات العراقية على استعداد تتعاون مع الجهات الرسمية للتعرف على الحقائق بشرط ان تكون الجهة الامريكية التي تتولى ذلك جهة رسمية	We, the Iraqi government, are willing to cooperate with the official entities to uncover the facts on the condition that the American party that undertakes the investigation is an official one.

Figure 78 - 1993 WTC bombing conversation (6 of 7)

MV:	تسمح سيادتك- يعني عائلة عبد الرحمن وجهنا للسكرتيرة نجيبهم ونحجزهم. انا ما أؤيد سيدي - هذول يعني مش رايد وعجوز و [inaudible] اذا نطلعهم اقله نشوف [inaudible] يعني من نخليه عندنا. [inaudible]	Sir, if you please, concerning Abed al Rahman family we issued directives to the secretary to bring them in and hold them. Sir, I don't support that Sir, he doesn't want to and he is an old man and [inaudible] if we let them go at least we can see [inaudible] when we keep them here [inaudible].
Saddam	يعني هي انثى [inaudible] هناك في امريكا وهي شافت [inaudible] من يروح ومن يجي والاخ هم يدري شكو مكو. لازم هذا اخ بالبيت يعني ما معقول تمر عليه والحكي بالتلفون [inaudible] القدر وهذا فجرنا وهذا ردنا نسويه وبالتلفونات واخ يسده وما يحكي. لازم عنده شيء يفيد — نستدعيه للتحقيق.	Well she is a female [inaudible] there in the US and she saw [inaudible] who comes and who goes and the brother also knows what is up and what is not. We must, he is a brother at home, impossible for something like this to pass by him, there was talk on the phone [inaudible] "ability and this was bombed and this we wanted to do" and on the phones, the brother could have just put the phone down and didn't say anything. He must have something useful- call him in for interrogation.
MV:	نحن حققنا سيدي — عفوا سيادتك — حققنا مرتين قبل اسبوع ولكن اليوم لاغراض الحجز لاغراض الاجراء الاحترازي	Sir, we questioned him Sir, pardon me Sir, we used to question him twice a week, but today for purposes of detaining him- for purposes of precautionary detention.
Saddam	ما انا اخاف ينهزمون	Well, I worry that they will flee.
Qusay?	ما ادري شنو درجة الانتباه اللي حطيط عليها	What level of alert have we placed on them.
Tariq Aziz	والله خيلهم اثنينهم محجوزين يعني بيها شيء مسيطر عليهم	Well, let them both stay in detention at least we can control them.
group	مش واضح	[unintelligible conversation]
Saddam	على الاقل اذا تجيب معلومات من هذا الاخ – [inaudible] ما تقول له اخوك اعترف قله نحن عندنا هيك معلومات فلان شيء فلان شيء فلان شيء- يبدي يفك عليها [inaudible] معلومات اكثر منه اساسا.	At least if you get information from this brother [inaudible] and you don't tell him that his brother has already confessed just tell him that we have such information that says this and this and this. Then he will start to tell you, [inaudible] more information than a basis.

Figure 79 – 1993 WTC bombing conversation (7 of 7)[309]

1.19 Al Qaida in Iraq

Saddam		والجلسة ال في هذه الجلسة حكينا عن ال الحرامية وحالة الضعف اللي الموجودة عند بعض النفوس الى الحد اللي تنزلق الى في التجاوز على اموال الدولة، شفت من المفيد لاغراض الموازنة النفسية ان تتطلعوا على جانب. يعني مو غريب هو قد يكون ولكن حتى اذا هو جانب الخيرين كيف يعملون، يعني همة الناس المومنين شلون يعملون.	And the session, in this session, we spoke about the, the thieves and the state of weakness that is present in certain souls to the extent of dipping their hands into the state's funds, I saw it is useful for the purpose of psychological balance that you take a look at one side. I mean this might not be odd, but it could be but even if it was the side of two options how they work, I mean the determination of believers and how they work.
Saddam		صارت فكرة انو عن التصنيع العسكري مع كل الامكانيات الاخرى تجند لتصليح المعدات اللي ممكن اصلاحها. يعني سواء كانت بالخدمة او خارج الخدمة. فنشأت فكرة استخدام امكانيات	The idea of military manufacturing began with the idea of utilizing all the other militarization capabilities to repair the equipment that was repairable. I

Figure 80 – Saddam discussing al Qaida (1 of 5)

Saddam	القوى الجوية وطيران الجيش والهندسة الآلية الكهربائية إلى جانب امكانيات التصنيع العسكري.	mean whether in service or not. The idea of using air power was born and air force and the engineering of electrical equipment along the military manufacturing capacities.
Saddam	فساروا حملة سموها نداء القائد لمدة شهرين، فبهذه الشهرين صلحوا معدات خارجة للاستخدام ما لها علاقة بمعدات الجيش اللي بيده الان.	They created a campaign they called it the call of the leader for two months, in the two months they repaired tools that were beyond usage which did not have to do with military tools that were in his hands now.
Saddam	فشنوا صلحوا، أصبحت جاهزة للعمل يعني وضعت في العمل بعد انتهاء المعرض بالمطار.	What did they repair, they were ready to be operated I mean it was put to work after the end exhibit at the airport
Saddam	250 ناقلة اشخاص مدرعة 40 دبابة 27 ناقلة 15 مدفع ذات الحركة 155 ملم 30 ناقلة من نوع آخر 9 دبابات شفتون 35 دبابة T-55 5 دبابات T-72 9 دبابات انقاذ 10 قاذفة انبوبية 90 عجلة مختلفة 9 مدفع 155 ملم 20 مدفع 155 ملم هذه أنواع، هذا نوع نمساوي هذا نوع ارجنتيني إلخ	250 Armored Personnel Carriers 40 Tanks 40 Transporters 15 Mobile Canons 155 millimeters 30 Transporters of a different kind 9 "Chifton" tanks 35 T-55 Tanks 5 T-72 Tanks 9 Rescue Tanks 10 improvised rocket launchers/tubes 90 Various vehicles/trucks 9 guns (155 mm) 20 guns (155 mm) These are kinds, this is an Austrian kind, this is an Argentinean kind, etc
Saddam	17 مدفع 152 ملم 1 مدفع 130 ملم 9 دبابات 55 ملم مركب عليها مدفع هاون 160 ملم 4 مدافع 120 ملم B-30 57 مدفع 105 ملم 2 مدفع 240 ملم 8 مدفع 120 ملم 151 مدفع هاون 82 ملم 305 مدفع هاون 60 ملم 30 ألف بندقية كلاشنكوف 1212 رشاشة RPK 852 رشاشة PKC 1912 قاذفة RPG-7 63 SPG-9 80 بندقية قنص 1 رشاشة أحادية	17 Canons (152 mm) 1 gun (150 mm) 9 Tanks (55 mm) attached with a 160 mm mortar 4 guns (120 mm) B-30 57 guns (105 mm) 2 guns (240mm) 8 guns (120mm) 151 mortars (83mm) 305 mortars (60mm) 30,000 Kalashnikov Rifles 1,212 RPK machine guns 852 PKC machine guns 1,912 RPG-7 bombers 63 SPG-9 80 Sniper Rifles 1 Single machine gun

Figure 81 - Saddam discussing al Qaida (2 of 5)

	1 مدفع 106 ملم	1 gun (106mm)
	50 مسدس مختلف	50 various guns
	10000 بندقية سمينوف	10,000 Simanov Rifles
	معدات صواريخ أرض أرض	Surface to surface missile equipment
	7 قاذفات صاروخ الرعد	7 Ar-Ra'd Missile Launchers
	22 ناقلة صاروخ الرعد	22 Ar-Ra'd Missile Transporters
	13 قاذفة صاروخ الطارق	13 At-Tareq Missile Launchers
	10 ناقلة صاروخ الطارق	10 At-Tareq Missile Transporters
	6 موقع قيادة للصاروخ	6 Missile Command Sites
	4 قاذفات صواريخ أبابيل	4 Ababil Missile launchers
	7 عجلات مساحة	7 Surveying wheels
	452 أجهزة لاسلكية مختلفة	452 Various Radio Tools
	659 معدة سلكية مختلفة	659 Field Phone Equipment
	125 محركات شحن توليد	125 generator engines
	1050 مضائد قاعدية	1,050 Anti-air bases
	50 رشاشة محورية (بكتا)؟	50 coaxial machine guns
	2 رشاشة ثنائية	2 bilateral machine guns
	7 قاذفة 30 ملم (قاذفة رمانات)	7 grenade Launchers (30mm)
	123 طائرة ؟ سمتية	123 helicopters Aircrafts
	18 طائرة مقاتلة ثابتة الجناح	18 Fixed Wing Fighter Plane
	11 طائرة تدريب	11 Training Planes
	هاي بشهرين، يعني أساسيات تقريبا؟	These in two months, I mean they are almost major ones.
MV	ممكن اقترح سيدي؟	Can I make a suggestion sir?
Saddam	نعم ؟	Yes?
MV	هذه الجهود الكبيرة ؟؟ بالنسبة للمجاهدين، انا اقترح انه يذكر اطلع مجلس الوزراء على هذه الجهود الكبيرة والخيّرة اللي قاموا بها هؤلاء المجاهدين وباسم المجلس يعني يُقدم لهم الشكر والتقدير العالي لهذه الجهود الخيّرة لخدمة العراق .	These big efforts [inaudible] regarding the Mujahideen, I suggest that [inaudible] the Council of ministers takes a look at these big and good efforts conducted by these Mujahideen in the name of the council I mean will present them with thanks and high appreciation for these good efforts in the service of Iraq.
Saddam	؟؟؟؟ ناس هدول شباب، يعني 123 طائرة سمتية، يعني هو كم دولة عندها بالمنطقة 123 طائرة سمتية؟ و 29 طائرة ثابتة الجناح.؟ هذه كلها خارج ال خارج الاستخدام يعني يروحون للمخازين ويفتشون ويلقون ويرغصون شيء على شيء ويروحون بالأسواق ويشترون ويجيبون و؟. يعني يشتغل كما لو كانت المعدة مالتو او اكثر. اكو فيه مستويات طبعا" اكو مستويات اخرى من النمط اللي اضطلعت عليه وهذه امر طبيعي	[inaudible] people These are young men, I mean 123 helicopters, I mean how many states have 123 helicopters, and 29 Fixed Wing planes? These are all outside the usage I mean they go to the arsenals, search, find, and are coerced with some things they go to the markets to buy and get and? I mean he would work as if the equipment is his own and even more. Of

Figure 82 – Saddam discussing al Qaida (3 of 5)

	يعني يكون في المجتمعات التي تعيش حالة غير اعتيادية في الصعوبة وفي الصعود يعني دائما تلقي بيها النقاء والصراحة. تلقي بيها ناس مثل ابو جهل وتلقي بيها ناس مثل ابو بكر الصديق او عمر او علي في الخندق الاخر المقابل؟؟ فرصيدنا الاساسي هم الناس الخيرين هم اللي بسببهم العراق صارت وهم بسببهم يصعد رغم كل هذه الصعوبات الاسطورية.	course there are levels there are other levels of pattern that I looked at and this is a normal matter I mean there are in societies that do not live a normal life in difficulty and improvement I mean you would find purity and blatancy. You would find people like Abu Jahl and you would find people like Abu Bakr or Omar or Ali on the opposite side of the trench [inaudible] So our essential capital are good people who, thanks to them, Iraq made it and thanks to the it is growing despite all these legendary difficulties.
	اكو مقترحات اخرى رفاق؟	Any other suggestions comrades?
	نعم ؟؟	Yes, [inaudible]
MV	اللي المقترح اللي تفضلوا فيه سيدي الرفيق محمد، احنا صلاحيات سيادتك الدستورية ما نقدر نقترحها ادبياً على سيادتك لكن في مرتين اتذكر سيادتك تطرقت الى اسامة الرافدين انه كان يمنح للناس اللي عندها خدمة طويلة بالدولة، يعني خدمة اعتيادية تقليدية وفي مثل هيك حالة واحدة يقارن بين الخدمة التقليدية اللي كان يمنح بيها اسامة الرافدين وبين الاعمال التاريخية المبدعة التي كلها طبعا بفضل سيادتك لكن هيك اعمال تاريخية	The suggestion that comrade Mohamed presented, your constitutional authority we cannot suggest it in a good manner to you but in two instances I remembered you tackled Osama Al-Rafedein that he was awarding people with long-time service to the state, I mean a normal and traditional service and in this case a comparison between traditional service that Osama Al-Rafedein was awarding and between historical creative works that of course happened because of you but these types of historical works.
Saddam	يعني بس على التوجيه. هو الخارجية اخرجتهم خارجية وهم كملوا	But I have to stress that the exterior made them outside and they continued
MV	سيدي كلها من سيادتك لاسباب يعرفها كل الحضور و الشعب العراقي يعرفها ماكو حاجة اشرح	Sir thanks to you for reasons that the audience and the Iraqi people know there is no need for me to explain
Saddam	الامور الاخرى هم هم الناس شلون تجاوبوا وشلون تفاعلوا مع الفكرة والا انا لا رحت عليهم ولا شفتهم شلون يشتغلون ولا دخلت بالتفاصيل ولا قلت لهم هاي معدة نقل من فلان هم ناس كلهم مستمرين وقائمون بواجباتهم	The other matters are the people how they react with the idea otherwise they will lose it I haven't seen how they do and I didn't get into the details and I haven't found any transportation equipment they are all professionals and effective in their duties

Figure 83 - Saddam discussing al Qaida (4 of 5)

MV	فيهيك ظرف سيدي صعب ويقدمون للعراق هذا التقديم الكبير أنا شوف يستاهلون كل التقدير والاحترام من عندنا والأمر متروك للقاعدة الله يحفظها. شكراً سيدي.	In this time it is difficult sir and they present Iraq with this big present I see they deserve all appreciation and respect from our part and the thing is left to al-Qaida God preserves it Thank you sir
Saddam	هم اقترحوا خارجية أنا ضاعفتهم المقترح مالهم فرحانين و مكيفين إنه أني مطلع على جهودهم إلى حد التفاصيل و كل ما يرفعون مطالعة نقول لهم سوا لفلان شي الخ يعني و هم يبادرون يعني ما	They suggested an exterior I doubled the proposal that's why they are happy that I am aware of their efforts to the details and every time they present a finding we tell them to do to this person this thing etc I mean and they take the initiative
MV4	شكراً سيدي سيدي الحقيقة ضمن الحملة اللي يعني مو بس من الارقام	Thank you sir, sir the truth is within the campaign that I mean not only from numbers
Saddam	هم خلصوكم من الاحراج الاسلحة ما طلعوها بالتلفزيون، خلوها مغطاء في مكان. العائدة لبعض الاطراف الاخرى نعم أخي خالد	The saved you the embarrassment they didn't show them on TV, they left them covered in a place, belonging to some other parties

Figure 84 – Saddam discussing al Qaida (5 of 5)[310]

Appendix

Coded Letter Form

From: Bakin Station
To: Director of the 4th Directorate

No.: 75
Date: 10 June 2001

Reference to your correspondence No. 49, dated on 09 June (.) the delegation left today 10 June, Shakir headed to Malaysia then to your region (.) whereas the other individuals were headed to Hong Kong (.) A letter for Tala was sent by Shakir (.) the letter sums up the following (.) it contains the details of sending your delegation to us, worth mentioning that the delegation resided in the Presidential housing of the Country (.) It is agreed with the so-called President adviser who met the delegation, and introduced himself as Tabkir Liyangh with Richard Wangh , who will receive the message of the afore-mentioned individual. He was told by them that Tabkir's father is the Secretary General of the Parliament (.) as they agreed on the following 1(.) directing invitation from the Embassy to the President Office, including invitation to the President to visit the region, as there is a personal envoy from Saqr Qurish will carry a letter regarding that issue 2(.) Include the Embassy memo, name of the personal envoy of Saqr Qurish as well as the accompanied delegation and the issues he wanted to discuss, during his meeting with the Chinese President, wherein, it is preferable to discuss the economic issues and the future of the economic relationships 3 (.) a letter should be sent today 15 June, in accordance with what is agreed upon…

(1-2)

Receiving Date:

Figure 85 – Shakir mentioned in IIS memo

Index

A

al-Abbas, Abu, 108, 135, 137, 138, 288, 289

Abouhalima, Mahmoud, 4, 150, 153, 154

Abu Sayyaf Group, 13

Afghanistan, 21-31, 33, 35-40, 88, 149, 151, 160, 175, 178, 179, 182, 183, 202-204, 222-223, 239, 240, 241, 243

Ajaj, Ahmad Mohammad, 4, 149, 151-154, 170

Ansar al-Islam, 203

Armed Islamic Group (Algeria), 12

Attash, Tawfiq Bin, 6, 178

Atta, Mohamed, 6, 179, 181, 182, 184-185, 187

Al Awja, 66, 67

Arab Cooperation Council (ACC), 92

Arab Socialist Resurrection Party, see Baath party

Arafat, Yasir,
  related to Amin al Husseini, 88
  met with Saddam Hussein, 96, 98, 99, 101, 107, 108, 110, 113, 115, 261

Arif, Abdul Rahman, 66, 67

Arif, Colonel Abd as Salaam, 57, 59, 61, 66

Ayyad, Nidal, 4, 5, 150, 153, 154

Aziz, Tariq, 75-77-81, 147, 155, 165, 166, 167, 183, 197

B

Baathist,
  Brezhnev supports, 24
  Saddam and Baathists overthrow Iraq government 45, 65-69

pan-Arab goal, 126
al Bakr, Ahmad Hasan, 61, 65-69, 149, 171
Banihammad, Fayez, 6, 185
Bara, Abu, 6, 178
Basit, Abdul, 5, 139, 140
Binalshibh, Ramzi, 6, 179-182, 185
Brezhnev, Leonid, 23, 24
Bush, George Herbert Walker, 94, 95,
   Planned assassination of 97
   Declared national emergency regarding Iraq, 101, 102
   Took action against Iraq, 103, 104
   Issued national security directive 110
   October 1, 1990 UN address, 112
   Unconditional withdrawal from Kuwait, 116, 118
   Convinced Israel not to retaliate, 120
   Declares a cease fire, 123, 149
   Addresses US Feb 26, 1991, 128,
   Saddam agrees to all UN Resolutions, 129
George W Bush, 11

C

Chemical, Ali, see Ali Hassan al-Majid
Clinton, William Jefferson,
   Confronting al Qaida, 159,
   Investigating 1993 WTC attack, 169, 170,
   Planned assassination of 176, 177,
   War on Terror, 208

E

Egyptian Islamic Jihad (EIJ), 4, 7, 12-16, 18, 19, 29, 30, 31, 36, 190, 235, 236 272, 273

F

Rev. Louis Farrakhan, 117

al-Faisal, Ghazi ibn, 54

al-Faisal II, Ghazi ibn, 54, 57

Fatwah, 13, 15, 30, 50, 148, 159, 227

Free Officers, 55, 57

G

Gamaa al Islamiya, see Islamic Group Organization

al Ghamdi, Ahmed, 6, 182, 183, 185

al Ghamdi, Hamza, 6, 183, 185

al Ghamdi, Saeed, 6, 182, 183, 186

H

al Hamzi, Nawaf, 6, 178, 179, 181, 186

Hanjour, Hani, 6, 181, 182, 184, 185

Harkut ul-Mujahidin (Kashmir), 13

al Hazmi, Salem, 6, 180, 182-184, 185, 186

al Haznawi, Ahmad, 6, 183, 186

Hitler, Adolph, 9, 83, 85, 86

al-Husayn I, Faisal Ibn, 49, 51, 55

Hussein, Saddam

  Classified documents of, 9-11

  Leader of the believer group of infidels, 15, 16

  Met with Umar Abed al Rahman 17

  Met with Zawahiri 18

  Disagreement with Mubarak, 35

With Baathists overthrow Iraq Government 45, 56, 63, 65-69, 71

Meets with Command Members over UN Inspections, 76

Threatens America, 89

Rebuilding Babylon, 90-92, 94

Threatens Israel, 96, 104, 117, 118

Support for State Terrorism, 133

1993 WTC attack, 139, 147, 148, 150, 155

9/11, 173, 178, 190, 193

Concealment of WMDs 195, 197

Islamic Propaganda, 202, 203,

Relationship with al Qaida 208, 209

Hussein, King of Jordan, 56, 57

al Husseini, Amin, 85-88

I

Iraq, 10-12, 14, 15, 17-21, 24, 32, 33, 35, 36

   History of, 45, 47, 48-57, 59-63, 65-67

   Iran-Iraq War, 70-84, 89-96

   Invasion of Kuwait, 97-131, 133-141, 143, 148, 149, 155-157, 159-167

   Support of State Terrorism, 171, 175, 178, 190, 191, 194, 195, 197, 198-209, 212-220, 245-260, 272, 274, 285-287, 290-293

Islamic Army of Aden, 13

Islamic Group Organization (IG), 12-15, 117, 134, 150, 171, 174, 175, 190, 204, 232, 234, 237, 238

Ismoil, Eyad, 154, 155

Islamic Army, see al Qaida

Islamic Movement of Uzbekistan, 13

Al-Itihaad al-Islamiya, 13

J

Jamaat e Jihal al Suri, 13

Jarrah, Ziad, 6, 179, 181, 182, 184, 186, 189, 190

Al Jihad, see Egyptian Islamic Jihad

L

Laden, Usama Bin, 4, 6, 10, 12-14, 21
  Soviet-Afghan War, 23, 27-35, 86
  Muslim Brotherhood, 88, 118
  1993 WTC attack, 148, 150, 152, 155, 159, 161, 170, 171
  9/11 attacks, 173, 177, 178, 181, 183, 185, 190
  Ties to Saddam, 202, 221
  Origins of al Qaida, 222, 224-228, 233, 235, 240, 241, 242, 244

Libyan Fighting Group, 13

M

Maktab al-Khidamat, see Services Office

al Majid, Hussein, 66

al-Majid, Ali Hassan, 66, 67, 82

al Mihdhar, Khalid, 7, 177-181, 183, 186

Mohamed, Ali, 4, 151

Mohammed, Khalid Sheikh (KSM), 6, 4, 138, 149, 174, 181, 183, 185

Moqed, Majed, 7, 182, 183, 186

Moussaoui, Zacarias, 7, 182, 184, 185

Mubarak, Hosni, 35, 92, 93, 95, 101, 116

Murad, Abdul Hakim, 176

al Musallat, Subha Tulfah, 66

N

al Nami, Ahmed, 7, 183, 186

NATO, 26, 55, 56,

Nazi, 83-88, 109, 170

National Revolutionary Command Council (NRCC), 61, 65,

O

al Omari, Abdul Aziz, 7, 183, 185, 187

Operation Iraqi Freedom, 9, 134, 208

P

Peshawar, 27, 30, 33, 152, 159

Q

Al Qaida, 4-7, 9-17,
- meets with Saddam, 18-27, 139, 178
- origins of al Qaida, 29-36, 101, 116-118, 127
- carries out orders with Saddam's Fedayeen, 135, 136, 138
- passport division, 139
- Salman Pak, 143
- operational ties to Saddam, 144
- 1993 WTC attack, 148-151, 157, 159-161, 164, 165, 171
- 9/11 attacks, 174, 175, 177-178, 181-183, 191
- in Iraq, 190, 193, 194, 199, 200, 202-209, 308-312
- origins of, 222, 232, 235

Qasim, Brigadier Abd al Karim, 57-61, 94

R

al Rahman, Umar Abed, 5
- acknowledged as spiritual leader of al Qaida, 13, 16, 36, 175
- issued fatwah for 1993 WTC attack, 15
- meeting with Saddam Hussein, 19
- Arab mujahideen, 28-32
- 1993 WTC attack, 150, 151, 153, 157-162, 168

oath to Bin Laden, 171, 233, 236-239

Rashid, Dr. Amir Muhammad, 76

Revolutionary Command Council (RCC), 65-69

S

Salafist Group for Call and Combat (Algeria), 13

Salameh, Mohammed, 4, 5, 138, 149, 150, 153, 154, 158, 171

Services Office, 23, 28, 29, 31, 150, 151

Shakir, Ahmed Hikmat, 7, 177, 313

Al Shehhi, Marwan, 7, 179, 181, 182, 184, 185

al Shehri, Mohand, 7, 183, 185

al Shehri, Waleed, 7, 183, 185

al Shehri, Wail, 7, 183, 185

Soviet-Afghanistan War, 21, 23, 24, 28, 29, 36

Strobel, Warren P., 9

Sufaat, Yazid, 177

al Suqami, Satam, 7, 183, 185, 187

T

Tikrit, 66, 67, 82, 84, 85, 155

U

United Nations, 20, 26, 49, 75, 76, 112, 115, 123, 129, 131, 141, 156, 194, 195, 199, 203, 207

W

Waldheim, Kurt, 109

Y

Yasin, Abdul Rahman Said, 5, 138, 149, 153-155, 157-162, 164-167, 171

Yousef, Ramzi, 5, 138-140, 149, 151-155, 169, 171, 174-177, 186

Z

al-Zawahiri, Ayman, 7, 13, 15, 18, 19, 29-30-34, 203, 223, 232, 237-239, 299, 300

al-Zarqawi, Abu Musab, 202, 203

Notes

Notes: Chapter 1

[1] Kevin M. Woods, and James Lacey, United States, Pentagon, Department of Defense, Iraqi Perspectives Project: Saddam and Terrorism: Emerging Insights From Captured Iraqi Documents, Alexandria, VA: Institute for Defense Analysis, 2008, Volume 1, Foreword.

[2] Warren P. Strobel, "Exhaustive Review Finds No Link Between Saddam and Al Qaida," McClatchy Newspapers 10 Mar. 2008, 8 June 2008 http://www.mcclatchydc.com/reports/intelligence/story/29959.htm.

[3] Ibid.

[4] Steve Schippert, "Cherry-Picking Intelligence: Saddam's Iraq and Terrorism," National Review Online (2008), 21 May 2008. Steven Hayes, "Saddam's Dangerous Friends," The Weekly Standard (2008), 27 May 2008.

[5] Woods, Kevin M., and James Lacey, Iraqi Perspectives Project: Saddam and Terrorism: Emerging Insights From Captured Iraqi Documents , Executive Summary ES-1.

[6] Steven Hayes, "Saddam's Dangerous Friends," The Weekly Standard (2008), 27 May 2008 <http://www.weeklystandard.com/Content/Public/Articles/000/000/014/889pvpxc.asp?pg=1>.

[7] United States of America vs. Osama bin Laden (United States District Court Southern District of New York),2/6/2001 (day two).

[8] Ibid.

[9] Rohan Gunaratna, Inside Al Qaeda : Global Network of Terror, New York: Berkley Trade, 2003, xviii, 88-89. United States of America vs. Osama bin Laden (United States District Court Southern District of New York), 2/6/2001 (day two)..

[10] Rohan Gunaratna, Inside Al Qaeda : Global Network of Terror, 33.

[11] United States, National Commission on Terrorist Attacks Upon the United States, The 9/11 Commission Final Report, 22 July 2004, 26 Apr. 2008 http://www.9-11commission.gov/report/911Report.pdf, 47.

[12] Rohan Gunaratna, Inside Al Qaeda : Global Network of Terror, xviii, 30-34. United States of America vs. Osama bin Laden (United States District Court Southern District of New York),2/6/2001 (day two), 294. Kohlmann, Evan F. Al-Qaida's Jihad in Europe : The Afghan-Bosnian Network. New York: Berg, 2004, 144.

[13] Kevin M. Woods, and James Lacey, Iraqi Perspectives Project: Saddam and Terrorism: Emerging Insights From Captured Iraqi Documents, Volume 3, 23 (pdf page 355).

[14] Rohan Gunaratna, Inside Al Qaeda : Global Network of Terror, New York: Berkley Trade, 2003, 48-49.

[15] Kevin M. Woods, and James Lacey, United, Iraqi Perspectives Project: Saddam and Terrorism: Emerging Insights From Captured Iraqi Documents, Volume 4, 48 (pdf 68).

[16] Powell, Colin. "U.S. Secretary of State Addresses the U.N. Security Council." 5 Feb. 2003.

Notes: Chapter 2

[17] Kenneth Katzman, United States, Congressional Research Service, The Library of Congress, Al Qaeda: Profile and Threat Assessment, 17 Aug. 2005, 25 Apr. 2008 http://www.fas.org/sgp/crs/terror/RL33038.pdf, 2.

[18] Watson, William E.,"The Collapse of Communism in the Soviet Union: The Brezhnev Doctrine and the Afghan War – Creating a Sphere of Influence", Historic Events ,Westport: Greenwood Group, 2001 Historic Events of the 20th Century, 20 Apr. 2008.

[19] Ibid.

[20] United States, Bureau of Public Affairs, U.S. Department of State, Background Notes: Afghanistan, July 1994. 22 Apr. 2008.

[21] Ibid.

[22] Ibid. Steve Coll, Ghost Wars : The Secret History of the CIA, Afghanistan, and Bin Laden, from the Soviet Invasion to September 10, 2001, New York: Penguin (Non-Classics), 2004.

[23] Maley, W. (2000, Feb 15). The Foreign Policy of the Taliban. Retrieved Apr 23, 2008 from http://www.cfr.org/content/publications/attachments/ForeignPolicy_Taliban_Paper.pdf

[24] Richard Labâeviáere, Dollars for Terror the United States and Islam, New York: Algora, 2000, 224.

[25] Kenneth Katzman, Al Qaeda: Profile and Threat Assessment, 1.

[26] Mary Crane, United States, Council on Foreign Relations, Does the Muslim Brotherhood Have Ties to Terrorism? 5 Apr. 2005, 28 Apr. 2008 <http://www.cfr.org/publication/9248/>.

[27] Richard Labâeviáere, Dollars for Terror the United States and Islam, New York: Algora, 2000, 222.

[28] Kenneth Katzman, Al Qaeda: Profile and Threat Assessment, 2.

[29] Kohlmann, Evan F. Al-Qaida's Jihad in Europe : The Afghan-Bosnian Network. New York: Berg, 2004, 39.

[30] Rohan Gunaratna, Inside Al Qaeda : Global Network of Terror, 30.

[31] United States of America vs. Osama bin Laden (United States District Court Southern District of New York),2/6/2001 (day two). United States of America vs. Salim Ahmed Hamdan (U.S. Dept of Defense Military Commissions December 5, 2007), 20206-216, 31.

[32] United States, National Commission on Terrorist Attacks Upon the United States, The 9/11 Commission Final Report, 22 July 2004, 26 Apr. 2008 http://www.9-11commission.gov/report/911Report.pdf, 47. Kenneth Katzman, Al Qaeda: Profile and Threat Assessment, 2. Andrew C. McCarthy, Willful Blindness a Memoir of the Jihad, 1st Ed. ed. New York: Encounter Books, 2008, 91.

[33] United States of America vs. Osama bin Laden (United States District Court Southern District of New York),2/6/2001 (day two).

[34] Rohan Gunaratna, Inside Al Qaeda : Global Network of Terror, 75.

[35] Ibid., 30.

[36] Ibid., 33.

[37] The 9/11 Commission Final Report, 56. Rohan Gunaratna, Inside Al Qaeda : Global Network of Terror, 30-34. Kohlmann, Evan F. Al-Qaida's Jihad in Europe : The Afghan-Bosnian Network. 33.

[38] Rohan Gunaratna, Inside Al Qaeda : Global Network of Terror, New York: Berkley Trade, 2003, 41.

[39] Ibid., 39, 42.

[40] United States of America vs. Enaam M. Arnaout, No. 02 CR 892 (United States District Court Southern District of Illinois).

[41] United States of America vs. Salim Ahmed Hamdan (U.S. Dept of Defense Military Commissions December 5, 2007) 3 (pdf 55).

[42] Rohan Gunaratna, Inside Al Qaeda: Global Network of Terror, 51-54.

[43] The 9/11 Commission Final Report, 170. United States of America vs. Enaam M. Arnaout, No. 02 CR 892 (United States District Court Southern District of Illinois).

[44] The 9/11 Commission Final Report, 170.

[45] Sharon Otterman, United States, Council on Foreign Relations, Islam: Governing Under Sharia, 14 Mar. 2005, 29 Apr. 2008 <http://www.cfr.org/publication/8034/#2>.

[46] Ibid.

[47] Nonie Darwish, Now They Call Me Infidel Why I Rejected the Jihad for America, Israel, and the War on Terror, New York, N.Y: Sentinel, 2006, 78.

Notes: Chapter 3

[48] Sharon Otterman, United States, Council on Foreign Relations, Islam: Governing Under Sharia, 14 Mar. 2005, 29 Apr. 2008 http://www.cfr.org/publication/8034/#2, 14.

[49] Nonie Darwish, Now They Call Me Infidel Why I Rejected the Jihad for America, Israel, and the War on Terror, 70, 82.

[50] United States, Cong. House, 9/11 Five Years Later: Gauging Islamist Terrorism, 109 Cong., 2nd sess., 7 Sept. 2006, 29 Apr. 2008, 14.

[51] Ibid.

[52] Ibid., 15.

[53] Bassam Tibi, The Challenge of Fundamentalism Political Islam and the New World Disorder, Berkeley: University of California P, 1998, 54, 56.

[54] Seyyid Qutb, Milestones, Kazi Pubns Inc, 1993, 7-10.

[55] Bassam Tibi, The Challenge of Fundamentalism Political Islam and the New World Disorder, 56. "Sayyid Qutb," Encyclopedia of World Biography, Farmington Hills: Gale Research, 1998, Biography Resource Center, 15 May 2008, keyword: Qutb.

[56] Seyyid Qutb, Milestones, Kazi Pubns Inc, 1993, 160.

[57] Gregory Starrett, Putting Islam to Work Education, Politics, and Religious Transformation in Egypt, Berkeley: University of California Press, 1998, 217, 222.

[58] "Sayyid Qutb," Encyclopedia of World Biography.

[59] Bassam Tibi, The Challenge of Fundamentalism Political Islam and the New World Disorder, 56.

[60] Seyyid Qutb, Milestones, 56.

[61] Seyyid Qutb, Milestones, 58, 88-89, 107, 129.

Notes: Chapter 4

[62] Mark Lewis, United States, Federal Research Division, Library of Congress, A Country Study: Iraq, The Ottoman Period, ed. Helen Chapin Metz, May 1988, 2 May 2008 <http://memory.loc.gov/frd/cs/iqtoc.html>.

[63] Ibid., Samira Haj, The Making of Iraq, 1900-1963 Capital, Power, and Ideology, Albany, NY: State University of New York P, 1997, 5, 19.

[64] Samira Haj, The Making of Iraq, 1900-1963 Capital, Power, and Ideology.

[65] Mark Lewis, United States, Federal Research Division, Library of Congress, A Country Study: Iraq, World War I and the British Mandate, ed. Helen Chapin Metz, May 1988, 2 May 2008 <http://memory.loc.gov/frd/cs/iqtoc.html>.

[66] Ibid.

[67] Mark Lewis, A Country Study: Iraq, ed. Helen Chapin Metz.

[68] Mark Lewis, A Country Study: Iraq, World War I and the British Mandate, ed. Helen Chapin Metz.

[69] "Husayn Ibn 'Ali," Britannica Online Encyclopedia Online. Samira Haj, The Making of Iraq, 1900-1963 Capital, Power, and Ideology. Mark Lewis, A Country Study: Iraq, World War I and the British Mandate, ed. Helen Chapin Metz.

[70] "Faysal I," Britannica Online Encyclopedia Online, 2008, 5 May 2008 <http://nclive.lib.ncsu.edu:2221/eb/article-9033866>.

[71] "Nations, League Of," Encyclopaedia Britannica, 2008, 19 May 2008 <http://nclive.lib.unc.edu:2153/eb/article-9055027>.

[72] Mark Lewis, A Country Study: Iraq, World War I and the British Mandate, ed. Helen Chapin Metz.

[73] The Avalon Project, 1996, Yale Law School, 27 Apr. 2008 <http://europeanhistory.about.com/gi/dynamic/offsite.htm?zi=1/XJ/Ya&sdn

=europeanhistory&cdn=education&tm=40&f=10&tt=14&bt=0&bts=1&zu= http%3A//www.yale.edu/lawweb/avalon/leagcov.htm>.

[74] Mark Lewis, A Country Study: Iraq, World War I and the British Mandate, ed. Helen Chapin Metz.

[75] Ibid.

[76] Ibid.

[77] Tareq Y. Ismael, Jacqueline S. Ismael, and Kamel Abu Jaber, Politics and Government in the Middle East and North Africa, Miami: Florida International UP, 1991, 154.

[78] Mark Lewis, A Country Study: Iraq, World War I and the British Mandate, ed. Helen Chapin Metz.

[79] Tareq Y. Ismael, Jacqueline S. Ismael, and Kamel Abu Jaber, Politics and Government in the Middle East and North Africa, 154.

[80] Mark Lewis, A Country Study: Iraq, World War I and the British Mandate, ed. Helen Chapin Metz.

[81] Ibid.

[82] Bassam Tibi, The Challenge of Fundamentalism Political Islam and the New World Disorder, Berkeley: University of California P, 1998, 192.

[83] Mark Lewis, A Country Study: Iraq, World War I and the British Mandate, ed. Helen Chapin Metz.

[84] Ibid.

[85] Tareq Y. Ismael, Jacqueline S. Ismael, and Kamel Abu Jaber, Politics and Government in the Middle East and North Africa, 155.

[86] Mark Lewis, A Country Study: Iraq, World War I and the British Mandate, ed. Helen Chapin Metz. Tareq Y Ismael, Jacqueline S. Ismael, and Kamel Abu Jaber, Politics and Government in the Middle East and North Africa, 155. "Nuri as-Said," Britannica Online Encyclopedia Online, 2008, 5 May 2008 <http://nclive.lib.ncsu.edu:2221/eb/article-9056525>.

[87] Mark Lewis, United States, Federal Research Division, Library of Congress, A Country Study: Iraq, Iraq as an Independent Monarchy, ed. Helen Chapin Metz, May 1988, 2 May 2008 <http://memory.loc.gov/frd/cs/iqtoc.html>.

[88] Ibid.

[89] "Nations, League Of," Encyclopaedia Britannica, 2008, 19 May 2008 <http://nclive.lib.unc.edu:2153/eb/article-9055027>.

[90] "Southeast Asia Treaty Organization," Encyclopedia Britannica, 2008, Encyclopedia Britannica Online, 20 May 2008 <http://nclive.lib.unc.edu:2153/eb/article-9068907>. Tareq Y. Ismael, Jacqueline S. Ismael, and Kamel Abu Jaber, Politics and Government in the Middle East and North Africa, 156. Samira Haj, The Making of Iraq, 1900-1963 Capital, Power, and Ideology, 108. Mark Lewis, A Country Study: Iraq, Iraq as an Independent Monarchy, ed. Helen Chapin Metz.

[91] Tareq Y. Ismael, Jacqueline S. Ismael, and Kamel Abu Jaber, Politics and Government in the Middle East and North Africa, Miami: Florida International UP, 1991, 156-157.

[92] "Neutralism," Encyclopaedia Britannica 2008, Encyclopaedia Britannica Online, Wake County, 11 May 2008, keyword: Nonalignment Movement. Mark Lewis, A Country Study: Iraq, Republican Iraq, ed. Helen Chapin Metz. Tareq Y. Ismael, Jacqueline S. Ismael, and Kamel Abu Jaber, Politics and Government in the Middle East and North Africa, 157.

[93] "The Sunni-Shi'Ite Division Within Islam," Britannica Book of the Year, 2008, Encyclopaedia Britannica Online, 17 May 2008 <http://nclive.lib.unc.edu:2153/eb/article-9439158>.

[94] Stephen Pelletiere, United States, The Library of Congress, Department of the Army, A Country Study: Iraq, The Society and Its Environment:Religious Life, May 1988, 17 May 2008.

[95] Tareq Y. Ismael, Jacqueline S. Ismael, and Kamel Abu Jaber, Politics and Government in the Middle East and North Africa, 158.

[96] Samira Haj, The Making of Iraq, 1900-1963 Capital, Power, and Ideology, 113.

[97] Tareq Y. Ismael, Jacqueline S. Ismael, and Kamel Abu Jaber, Politics and Government in the Middle East and North Africa,161.

[98] Ibid., 162-163.

[99] Ibid. Mark Lewis, A Country Study: Iraq, Coups, Coup Attempts, and Foreign Policy, ed. Helen Chapin Metz.

[100] "Ba'th Party," Encyclopedia Britannica, 2008, Encyclopedia Britannica Online, 17 May 2008 <http://nclive.lib.unc.edu:2153/eb/article-9013742>. "Michel 'Aflaq," Encyclopedia of World Biography, Farmington Hills, Mich: Gale Research, 1998, Biography Resource Center, 19 May 2008 <http://galenet.galegroup.com/servlet/BioRC>.

[101] Samira Haj, The Making of Iraq, 1900-1963 Capital, Power, and Ideology, 89.

[102] Ibid., 90.

[103] Ibid., 91.

[104] Ibid., 137.

Notes: Chapter 5

[105] Mark Lewis, United States, Federal Research Division, Library of Congress, A Country Study: Iraq: The Emergence of Saddam Husayn ed. Helen Chapin Metz, May 1988, 2 May 2008 <http://memory.loc.gov/frd/cs/iqtoc.html>. Saèid K. Aburish, Saddam Hussein the Politics of Revenge, 1st U.S. Ed. ed. New York, N.Y: Distributed to the Trade by St. Martin's P, 2000, 75. "Arab-Israeli Wars," Encyclopedia Britannica, Encyclopaedia Britannica Online, 2008, 4 June 2008 <http://nclive.lib.ncsu.edu:2221/eb/article-9008143>. Heather Lehr Wagner, Iraq, Philadelphia: Chelsea House, 2003, 78-80.

[106] "Saddam Hussein," Biography Resource Center, Farmington Hills, Mich: Biography Resource Center, 2008, 4 June 2008, keyword: Saddam Hussein. Heather Lehr Wagner, Iraq, Philadelphia: Chelsea House, 2003, 92.

[107] Saèid K. Aburish, Saddam Hussein the Politics of Revenge, 1st U.S. Ed. ed. New York, N.Y: Distributed to the Trade by St. Martin's P, 2000, 10-15.

[108] Mark Lewis, A Country Study: Iraq: The Emergence of Saddam Husayn ed. Helen Chapin Metz.

[109] Ibid. Saèid K. Aburish, Saddam Hussein the Politics of Revenge, 85.

[110] Heather Lehr Wagner, Iraq, 95.

[111] Mark Lewis, A Country Study: Iraq: The Emergence of Saddam Husayn.

[112] Ibid.

[113] Shaul Bakhash, United States, Federal Research Division, Library of Congress, A Country Study: Iran: The Coming of the Revolution, ed. Helen Chapin Metz, 8 Nov. 2005, 14 June 2008 <http://memory.loc.gov/frd/cs/irtoc.html>.

[114] Heather Lehr Wagner, Iraq, p. 94, "Ayatollah Ruhollah Khomeini," Biography Resource Center, Farmington Hills, Mich: Gale Group, 2001, Biography Resource Center, 17 June 2008, keyword: Khomeini.

[115] Heather Lehr Wagner, Iraq, p. 100. Mark Lewis, A Country Study: Iraq: The Iran-Iraq Conflict. Ayatollah Ruhollah Khomeini," Biography Resource Center.

[116] Joseph A. Kechichian, and Houman Sadri, United States, Federal Research Division, Library of Congress, A Country Study: Iran: The Original Iraqi Offensive, ed. Helen Chapin Metz, Dec. 1987, 21 June 2008 <http://lcweb2.loc.gov/frd/cs/irtoc.html#ir0031>. Heather Lehr Wagner, Iraq, p. 100. Shaul Bakhash, A Country Study: Iran: The Coming of the Revolution.

[117] Joseph A. Kechichian, United States, Congressional Research Service, Library of Congress, Country Study of Iraq: National Security, May 1988, 22 June 2008 <http://lcweb2.loc.gov/frd/cs/iqtoc.html>. Mark Lewis, A Country

Study: Iraq: The Iran-Iraq Conflict. Heather Lehr Wagner, Iraq, p. 100-101. Debra A. Miller, ed. Iraq, San Diego, CA: Greenhaven P, 2004. Joseph A. Kechichian, and Houman Sadri, A Country Study: Iran: The Original Iraqi Offensive. David Schaffer, The Iran-Iraq War, San Diego: Lucent Books/Thomson Gale, 2003, 38-43.

[118] David Schaffer, The Iran-Iraq War, 40.

[119] Joseph A. Kechichian, and Houman Sadri, Country Study: Iran: Ch 5 The Iranian Counteroffensive.

[120] Joseph A. Kechichian, Country Study of Iraq: National Security: Iraq Retreats, 1982-84.

[121] David Schaffer, The Iran-Iraq War, 52.

[122] Joseph A. Kechichian, Country Study of Iraq: The War of Attrition, 1984-87.

[123] Rolf Ekeus, "IRAQ," Washington Institute, The Washington Institute Luncheon with Rolf Ekeus, Executive Chair, U.N. Special Commission, The Washington Institute for Near East Policy, Washington, 29 Jan. 1997, 30 May 2008 <http://www.globalsecurity.org/wmd/library/news/iraq/1997/ekeus_970129.htm>.

[124] Ibid., 29 (pdf 49).

[125] Seth Faison, "Man in the News: Rolf Ekeus; Tracker of Iraqi Arms," The New York Times 28 July 1992, 30 May 2008 <http://query.nytimes.com/gst/fullpage.html?res=9E0CE3D91030F93BA15754C0A964958260>. Kevin M. Woods, and James Lacey, Iraqi Perspectives Project: Saddam and Terrorism: Emerging Insights From Captured Iraqi Documents, Volume 4 27 (pdf 47). (Appendix B, Figure 1, text boxes 1-3).

[126] Ibid., 28 (pdf 48).

[127] Ibid., 28-29 (pdf 48-49).

[128] Con Coughlin, Saddam His Rise and Fall, 1st Harper Perennial Ed., Fully Updated and Rev. ed. New York, NY: Harper Perennial, 2005, 127.

[129] Ibid., 128-129.

[130] Ibid., 30 (pdf 50).

[131] Joseph A. Kechichian, and Houman Sadri, Country Study: Iran: Ch 5 Iranian Mobilization and Resistance.

[132] Paul Kengor, "The Rise and Fall of a Murderous Dictator," Washington Times 10 Jan. 2007, 23 July 2008
<http://www.frontpagemag.com/Articles/Read.aspx?GUID=0F0945CE-A273-4865-B473-FCFB3337AE31>.

[133] Kevin M. Woods, and James Lacey, United States, Pentagon, Department of Defense, Iraqi Perspectives Project: Saddam and Terrorism: Emerging Insights From Captured Iraqi Documents, Alexandria, VA: Institute for Defense Analysis, 2008, Volume 4 30-31 (pdf 50-51).

[134] Ibid., Volume 4 31-32 (pdf 51-52).

[135] Ibid.,, Volume 4 32-34 (pdf 52-54).

[136] Genocide in Iraq:the Anfal Campaign Against the Kurds, Human Rights Watch, New York · Washington · Los Angeles · London: Human Rights Watch, 1993, 7 July 2008
<http://hrw.org/reports/1993/iraqanfal/index.htm#TopOfPage>.

[137] Khidhir Hamza, and Jeff Stein, Saddam's Bombmaker the Terrifying Inside Story of the Iraqi Nuclear and Biological Weapons Agenda, New York: Scribner, 2000, 200.

[138] Heather Lehr Wagner, Iraq, Philadelphia: Chelsea House, 2003, 106.

[139] Saèid K. Aburish, Saddam Hussein the Politics of Revenge, 1st U.S. Ed. ed. New York, N.Y: Distributed to the Trade by St. Martin's P, 2000, 248-249. Khidhir Hamza, and Jeff Stein, Saddam's Bombmaker the Terrifying Inside Story of the Iraqi Nuclear and Biological Weapons Agenda, 200-202.

[140] Con Coughlin, Saddam His Rise and Fall, 5, 6.

[141] Ibid., 19. Paul Kengor, "The Rise and Fall of a Murderous Dictator," Washington Times 10 Jan. 2007, 23 July 2008

<http://www.frontpagemag.com/Articles/Read.aspx?GUID=0F0945CE-A273-4865-B473-FCFB3337AE31>.

[142] Con Coughlin, Saddam His Rise and Fall, 13.

[143] Carl K. Savich, "The Holocaust in Bosnia-Hercegovina, 1941-1945," 8 July 2008 <http://www.serbianna.com/columns/savich/006.shtml>.

[144] Chuck Morse, The Nazi Connection to Islamic Terrorism, Lincoln,NE: IUniverse, Inc., 2003, 15.

[145] Carl K. Savich, "Islam Under the Swastika: the Grand Mufti and the Nazi Protectorate of Bosnia-Hercegovina, 1941-1945," (2001), 8 July 2008 <http://www.rastko.org.yu/rastko-bl/istorija/kcsavic/csavich-islam_e.html>.

[146] Chuck Morse, The Nazi Connection to Islamic Terrorism, Lincoln,NE: IUniverse, Inc., 2003, 66.

[147] Ibid., 67.

[148] Ibid., 93-94.

[149] Ibid., 94

[150] Ibid.

[151] World Leaders of the Twentieth Century, Pasadena, Calif: Salem P, 2000, 15.

Chapter 6 Notes:

[152] Saèid K. Aburish, Saddam Hussein the Politics of Revenge, 259.

[153] Duelfer, Charles. Comprehensive Report of the Special Advisor to the DCI on Iraq's WMD. United States. Central Intelligence Agency. Special Advisor to the Director of Central Intelligence. 2004, Volume 1, 4.

[154] Paul Lewis, "Babylon Journal; Ancient King's Instructions to Iraq: Fix My Palace," The New York Times 19 Apr. 1989.

[155] Ibid.

[156] Samira Haj, The Making of Iraq, 1900-1963 Capital, Power, and Ideology, 89.

[157] Efraim Karsh, and Inari Rautsi, Saddam Hussein : A Political Biography, New York: Free P, 1991, 204.

[158] Con Coughlin, Saddam his rise and fall, 247.

[159] Saèid K. Aburish, Saddam Hussein the Politics of Revenge, 272-273. Con Coughlin, Saddam his rise and fall, 247.

[160] Tareq Y. Ismael, Jacqueline S. Ismael, and Kamel Abu Jaber, Politics and Government in the Middle East and North Africa, 162-163.

[161] Ibid., 275.

[162] Ibid., 276-277.

[163] Con Coughlin, Saddam his rise and fall, 249. Dr. Eliot A. Cohen, Gulf War Air Power Survey Volume I Planning and Command Control, Department of Defense, Washington D.C., 1993, 83.

[164] Alan Cowell, "Iraq Chief, Boasting of Poison Gas, Warns of Disaster if Israelis Strike," New York Times 3 Apr. 1990. Efraim Karsh, and Inari Rautsi, Saddam Hussein : A Political Biography, New York: Free P, 1991, 216.

[165] Con Coughlin, Saddam his rise and fall, 253.

[166] Efraim Karsh, and Inari Rautsi, Saddam Hussein : A Political Biography, New York: Free P, 1991, 217-218. Gulf War Air Power Survey Volume I Planning and Command Control, 87.

[167] Ibid., 218. Saèid K. Aburish, Saddam Hussein the Politics of Revenge, 286-287.

[168] President George H. W. Bush, "Message to the Congress on the Declaration of a National Emergency With Respect to Iraq," Congress of the United States, 3 Aug. 1990.

[169] Ibid.

[170] Efraim Karsh, and Inari Rautsi, Saddam Hussein : A Political Biography, New York: Free P, 1991, 219.

[171] Dr. Eliot A. Cohen, Gulf War Air Power Survey Volume I Planning and Command Control, 88.

[172] Ibid., 94.

[173] President George H. W. Bush, "Address to the Nation Announcing the Deployment of United States Armed Forces to Saudi Arabia," 08 Aug. 1990.

[174] "Confrontation in the Gulf; Proposals by Iraqi President: Excerpts From His Address," New York Times by Associated Press 13 Aug. 1990.

[175] Woods, Kevin M., and James Lacey, Iraqi Perspectives Project: Saddam and Terrorism: Emerging Insights From Captured Iraqi Documents, Volume 1 p.27.

[176] "His Enemy Is the World," New York Times 17 Aug. 1990.

[177] Efraim Karsh, and Inari Rautsi, Saddam Hussein : A Political Biography, 233.

[178] "Confrontation in the Gulf; Proposals by Iraqi President: Excerpts From His Address," New York Times by Associated Press 13 Aug. 1990.

[179] "Confrontation in the Gulf; Waldheim to Travel to Iraq," New York Times 24 Aug. 1990.

[180] "Transcript of Iraqi Chief's Conversation With English-Speaking Captives," New York Times 24 Aug. 1990.

[181] Efraim Karsh, and Inari Rautsi, Saddam Hussein : A Political Biography, 234. John F. Burns, "Confrontation in the Gulf; Iraqi Leader says he Will Free foreign Women and Children," New York Times 29 Aug. 1990.

[182] National Security Directive No. 45, 3 C.F.R. 2 (August 20, 1990).

[183] Efraim Karsh, and Inari Rautsi, Saddam Hussein : A Political Biography, 234. John F. Burns, "Confrontation in the Gulf; Iraqi Leader says he Will Free foreign Women and Children," New York Times 29 Aug. 1990. Ibid., 229-230.

[184] Con Coughlin, Saddam his rise and fall, 258.

[185] Ibid., 258-259.

[186] President George H. W. Bush, "Address Before the 45th Session of the United Nations General Assembly in New York, New York," 1 Oct. 1990.

[187] Efraim Karsh, and Inari Rautsi, Saddam Hussein : A Political Biography, 230-231.

[188] Woods, Kevin M., and James Lacey, <u>Iraqi Perspectives Project: Saddam and Terrorism: Emerging Insights From Captured Iraqi Documents</u>, Volume 3 27.

[189] Dr. Eliot A. Cohen, <u>Gulf War Air Power Survey Volume I Planning and Command Control</u>, Volume 2, 83.

[190] Ibid., 238-239. Adam Clymer, "Confrontation in the Gulf; Bush asks Congress to Back use of force if Iraq defies deadline on Kuwait Pullout," <u>New York Times</u> 9 Jan. 1991.

[191] Patrick E. Tyler, "Confrontation in the Gulf; Hussein Tells Muslims Of Holy War in the Gulf," <u>New York Times</u> 12 Jan. 1991.

[192] Dr. Eliot A. Cohen, <u>Gulf War Air Power Survey Volume I Planning and Command Control</u>, Volume 2, 95.

[193] Ibid., 287-293.

[194] Ibid., 353-397. United States, Cong. Final Report to Congress, <u>Conduct of the Persian Gulf War</u>, 1992, 604.

[195] Ibid., 424-425.

[196] Dr. Eliot A. Cohen, <u>Gulf War Air Power Survey Volume I Planning and Command Control</u>, Volume 2, 410.

[197] Ibid., Volume 2, 407-413, Volume 1, 98.

[198] Ibid., Volume 2 419.

[199] Ibid., Volume 2, 427.

[200] Jim Nelson Black, <u>Saddam's Secrets : How an Iraqi General Defied and Survived Saddam Hussein</u>, Danbury: Thomas Nelson Incorporated, 2006, 175.

[201] Ibid., Volume 2, 408, 418-419, 428-432. Mason Carpenter, "Joint Operations in the Gulf War: An Allison Analysis," thesis, 1.

[202] Dr. Eliot A. Cohen, <u>Gulf War Air Power Survey Volume I Planning and Command Control</u>, Volume 2, 457. Andrew Rosenthal, "War in the Gulf:

The President; Bush Halts Offensive Combat; Kuwait Freed, Iraqis Crushed," The New York Times 28 Feb. 1991. Dilip Hiro, Iraq : In the Eye of the Storm, New York: Nation Books, 2002, 38.

[203] Patrick E. Tyler, "Confrontation in the Gulf; Hussein Tells Muslims Of Holy War in the Gulf," New York Times 12 Jan. 1991. Dr. Eliot A. Cohen, Gulf War Air Power Survey Volume I Planning and Command Control, Department of Defense, Washington D.C., 1993, Volume 2, 551.

[204] Ibid. Resolutions 660-661, United Nations, Official Records of the Security Council, 1990. George H. Bush, "Address to the Nation on the Iraqi Statement on Withdrawal From Kuwait," 26 Feb. 1991. United States, Cong. Final Report to Congress, Conduct of the Persian Gulf War, 1992, 145. Patrick E. Tyler, "Confrontation in the Gulf; Hussein Tells Muslims Of Holy War in the Gulf," New York Times 12 Jan. 1991.

[205] George H. Bush, "Address to the Nation on the Suspension of Allied Offensive Combat Operations in the Persian Gulf."

[206] United States, Cong. Final Report to Congress, Conduct of the Persian Gulf War, 1992, 709. Dr. Eliot A. Cohen, Gulf War Air Power Survey Volume I Planning and Command Control, Department of Defense, Washington D.C., 1993, Volume 2, 549-550.

[207] R.W. Apple Jr. "After the War: The Overview; U.S. Says Iraqi Generals Agree to Demands 'On All Matters'; Early P.O.W. Release Expected," The New York Times 4 Mar. 1991.

[208] Alan Cowell, "After the War; Baghdad Formally Agrees To 'Unjust' U.N. Conditions for Permanent Cese-fire," The New York Times 7 Apr. 1991.

[209] John Kifner, "AFTER THE WAR; Iraqi Refugees Tell U.S. Soldiers Of Brutal Repression of Rebellion," The New York Times 28 Mar. 1991.

Notes: Chapter 7

[210] Resolution 687, United Nations, Official Records of the Security Council, April, 3, 1991.

[211] Ibid., Volume 1, 45.

[212] Kevin M. Woods, and James Lacey, Iraqi Perspectives Project: Saddam and Terrorism: Emerging Insights From Captured Iraqi Documents, Volume 3 p.41 (pdf 373). Duelfer, Charles. Comprehensive Report of the Special Advisor to the DCI on Iraq's WMD, Volume 1, 74.

[213] Ibid., p.16.

[214] Kevin M. Woods, and James Lacey, Iraqi Perspectives Project: Saddam and Terrorism: Emerging Insights From Captured Iraqi Documents, Volume 1 p.15.

[215] Ibid., p.1.

[216] Ibid., p.19.

[217] Ibid., p.27.

[218] Ibid., Volume 3, (pdf 336).

[219] Ibid., 158.

[220] Laurie Mylroie, Study of Revenge Saddam Hussein's Unfinished War Against America, Washington, D.C: AEI P, 2000. 40.

[221] Ibid.,50, 55.

[222] Associated Press, "Uranium from Iraq reaches Canada," Los Angelos Time 6 July 2008.

[223] "Saddam's Nukes," Investor's Business Daily 7 July 2008.

[224] Rolf Ekeus, "The Washington Post," The Washington Post 29 June 2003.

[225] Powell, Colin. "U.S. Secretary of State Addresses the U.N. Security Council." 5 Feb. 2003. John Deutch, Information on Iraq's Biological Warfare Program, United States, Armed Forces, Medical Intelligence, Filename:008me.93d, 1993.

Notes: Chapter 8

[226] United States of America vs. Salim Ahmed Hamdan (U.S. Dept of Defense Military Commissions December 5, 2007).

[227] United States of America vs. Enaam M. Arnaout, No. 02 CR 892 (United States District Court Southern District of Illinois).

[228] Athan G. Theoharis, The FBI a Comprehensive Reference Guide, Phoenix, Ariz: Oryx P, 1999, 94.

[229] Laurie Mylroie, "The World Trade Center Bomb: Who is Ramzi Yousef? and Why It Matters," The National Interest (1995), 8 June 2008 <http://www.fas.org/irp/world/iraq/956-tni.htm>.

[230] Laurie Mylroie, The War Against America : Saddam Hussein and the World Trade Center Attacks: A Study of Revenge, New York: ReganBooks, 2001, 28-30.

[231] The 9/11 Commission Final Report, 72. Kenneth Katzman, 3. Richard Labâeviáere, Dollars for Terror the United States and Islam, New York: Algora, 2000, 222.

[232] United States of America vs. Osama bin Laden (United States District Court Southern District of New York), (Day Two).

[233] United States of America vs. Umar Ahmad Ali Abdel Rahman (United States Court of Appeals for the Second August 16, 1999), 8-9.

[234] Benjamin Weiser, "U.S. Ex-Sergeant Linked to Bin Laden Conspiracy," New York Times 30 Oct. 1998, 18 July 2008. Kenneth Katzman, 3.

[235] The 9/11 Commission Final Report, 177.

[236] United States, Cong. Senate, Hearing on "Foreign Terrorists in America: Five Years After the World Trade Center", 105 Cong., 1st sess., 24 Feb. 1998, 16

May 2008 <http://www.fas.org/irp/congress/1998_hr/s980224w.htm>.
William Glaberson, "Detainee Denies Membership in Al Qaeda," New York Times 17 Apr. 2007, 18 May 2008 <http://www.nytimes.com/2007/04/17/us/17gitmo.html>. The 9/11 Commission Report, 175.

[237] Hearing on "Foreign Terrorists in America: Five Years After the World Trade Center"..

[238] U.S. V. Salameh, no. Nos. 94-1312 to 94-1315, 107-108.

[239] Ibid.

[240] Ibid., 153-154, 137-138. Rohan Gunaratna, Inside Al Qaeda : Global Network of Terror, New York: Berkley Trade, 2003, p. 47.

[241] Ibid., 154-155.

[242] Ibid., 107-108. Peter Lance, 1000 Years for Revenge International Terrorism and the FBI--the Untold Story, 111.

[243] Ibid., 108.

[244] Ibid., U.S. V. Ramzi Ahmed Yousef, no. 98-1041 L, United States Court of Appeals for the Second Circuit, 4 Apr. 2003, 9. United States, Cong., Report of the Joint Inquiry Into the Terrorist Attacks of September 11, 2001, 2nd, 107 Cong., 2nd sess., 20 Dec. 2002, 17 July 2008 <http://www.globalsecurity.org/intell/library/congress/2003_rpt/intell-911-report-072403.pdf>.

[245] Anthony H. Cordesman, Saddam's Last Circle: the Core Forces Likely to Protect Saddam in the "Battle for Baghdad" Center for Strategic and International Studies, 2003, 10. "Tariq Mikhayl Aziz," Biography Resource Center Online, Gale Group, 2002, Biography Resource Center, 01 June 2008, keyword: Tariq Aziz.

[246] Andrew C. McCarthy, Willful Blindness a Memoir of the Jihad, 196-197.

[247] Kevin M. Woods, and James Lacey, Iraqi Perspectives Project: Saddam and Terrorism: Emerging Insights From Captured Iraqi Documents, Volume 4, 63 (pdf 85).

[248] Ibid., Volume 4, 65-66 (pdf 85).

[249] Ibid., Volume 4, 66 (pdf 85).

[250] Ibid., Volume 4, 66 (pdf 85).

[251] Laurie Mylroie, "The World Trade Center Bomb: Who is Ramzi Yousef? And Why It Matters," The National Interest (1995), 8 June 2008 <http://www.fas.org/irp/world/iraq/956-tni.htm>.

[252] Bill Turque, and Christopher Dickey, "The Trail to `the Jihad Office.'" Newsweek 21 Mar. 1993, sec. International: 38, Academic Search Premier, EBSCO, 30 Apr. 2008, keyword: Alkifah Refugee Center. Alison Mitchell, "After Blast, New Interest in Holy-War Recruits in Brooklyn," New York Times 11 Apr. 1993, 17 July 2008 <http://query.nytimes.com/gst/fullpage.html?res=9F0CE2DE1E3AF932A25757C0A965958260#>.

[253] Kevin M. Woods, and James Lacey, Iraqi Perspectives Project: Saddam and Terrorism: Emerging Insights From Captured Iraqi Documents, Volume 4, 66 (pdf 85).

[254] U.S. V. Salameh, no. Nos. 94-1312 to 94-1315, United States Court of Appeals, Second Circuit., 4 Aug. 1998, 13 May 2008 http://www.uniset.ca/islamicland/152F3d88.html, 108-109. U.S. V. Ramzi Ahmed Yousef, no. 98-1041 L, United States Court of Appeals for the Second Circuit, 4 Apr. 2003, 132. Andrew C. McCarthy, Willful Blindness a Memoir of the Jihad, 196-91. U.S. V. Ramzi Ahmed Yousef, no. 98-1041 L, United States Court of Appeals for the Second Circuit, 4 Apr. 2003, 231-232.

[255] Kevin M. Woods, and James Lacey, Iraqi Perspectives Project: Saddam and Terrorism: Emerging Insights From Captured Iraqi Documents, Volume 4, 66 (pdf 85).

[256] Laurie Mylroie, Study of Revenge Saddam Hussein's Unfinished War Against America, 2000. 40.

[257] Kevin M. Woods, and James Lacey, Iraqi Perspectives Project: Saddam and Terrorism: Emerging Insights From Captured Iraqi Documents, Volume 4, 67.

[258] Ibid., 71-72.

[259] U.S. V. Salameh, no. Nos. 94-1312 to 94-1315, United States Court of Appeals, Second Circuit., 4 Aug. 1998, 13 May 2008 http://www.uniset.ca/islamicland/152F3d88.html, 108-109. Laurie Mylroie, "The World Trade Center Bomb: Who is Ramzi Yousef? and Why It Matters," The National Interest (1995), 8 June 2008 <http://www.fas.org/irp/world/iraq/956-tni.htm>. U.S. V. Ramzi Ahmed Yousef, no. 98-1041 L, United States Court of Appeals for the Second Circuit, 4 Apr. 2003, 132. Andrew C. McCarthy, Willful Blindness a Memoir of the Jihad, 196-91.

[260] Kevin M. Woods, and James Lacey, Iraqi Perspectives Project: Saddam and Terrorism: Emerging Insights From Captured Iraqi Documents, Volume 4, 74-75.

[261] Ibid., Volume 4, 81-82.

[262] Con Coughlin, Saddam his rise and fall, 167-168.

[263] The 9/11 Commission Final Report, 72.

[264] U.S. V. Salameh, no. Nos. 94-1312 to 94-1315, United States Court of Appeals, Second Circuit., 4 Aug. 1998, 13 May 2008 http://www.uniset.ca/islamicland/152F3d88.html, 154-155.

[265] John Yoo, "Terrorist Tort Travesty," Wall Street Journal 19 Jan. 2008, 3 June 2008 <http://online.wsj.com/article/SB120070333580301911.html>.

[266] Laurie Mylroie, The War Against America : Saddam Hussein and the World Trade Center Attacks: A Study of Revenge, New York: ReganBooks, 2001, 28-30.

Notes: Chapter 9

[267] The 9/11 Commission Final Report, 72, 147, 153, 157.

[268] Marc Sageman, Understanding Terror Networks, New York: University of Pennsylvania P, 2004, 42.

[269] The 9/11 Commission Final Report), 72, 147, 153, 157. Lawrence Wright, The looming tower Al-Qaeda and the road to 9/11, Waterville, Me: Thorndike P, 2007, 178. Simon Reeve, The new jackals Ramzi Yousef, Usama Bin Laden and the future of terrorism, Boston: Northeastern UP, 1999, 87-89. U.S. v. Ramzi Ahmed Yousef, No. 98-1041 L (United States Court of Appeals for the Second Circuit April 4, 2003), 87-89. Rohan Gunaratna, Inside Al Qaeda : Global Network of Terror, 52.

[270] Stephen F. Hayes, The Connection : How Al-Qaeda's Collaboration with Saddam Hussein Has Endangered America, New York: HarperCollins, 2004, 1-7.

[271] The 9/11 Commission Final Report, 154.

[272] Ibid., 158.

[273] Ibid., 216.

[274] Ibid., 223-224, 246.

[275] Ibid., 225.

[276] Ibid., 231.

[277] Ibid., 234.

[278] Ibid., 235.

[279] Ibid., 236.

[280] Ibid., 242.

[281] Ibid., 248-249.

[282] Ibid., 5-6.

[283] Ibid., 10-12.

[284] Ibid., 13-14.

[285] Ibid., 14.

Notes: Chapter 10

[286] Powell, Colin. "U.S. Secretary of State Addresses the U.N. Security Council." 5 Feb. 2003.

[287] Kevin M. Woods, and James Lacey, Iraqi Perspectives Project: Saddam and Terrorism: Emerging Insights From Captured Iraqi Documents, Volume 5, 79.

[288] Rolf Ekeus, "The Washington Post," The Washington Post 29 June 2003.

[289] Ibid.

[290] Kevin M. Woods, and James Lacey, Iraqi Perspectives Project: Saddam and Terrorism: Emerging Insights From Captured Iraqi Documents, Volume 3, 24 (pdf 356).

[291] Ibid., Volume 3, 77 (pdf 412).

[292] Kevin M. Woods, and James Lacey, Iraqi Perspectives Project: Saddam and Terrorism: Emerging Insights From Captured Iraqi Documents, Volume 4 27-42 (pdf 47-62).

[293] Ibid., Volume 4 21-24 (pdf 41-44).

[294] Ibid., Volume 3 157-160.

[295] Ibid., Volume 3 137-138.

[296] Ibid., Volume 3 39 (pdf 371).

[297] Ibid., Volume 3 39 (pdf 371).

[298] Ibid., Volume 4 13 (pdf 23).

[299] Ibid., Volume 5, 79 (pdf 99).

[300] Ibid., Volume 3, 135-137.

[301] Ibid., 316-317 (pdf 336-337).

[302] Ibid., Volume 5, 268-270.

[303] Ibid., Volume 5, 268-270.

[304] Ibid., Volume 5, 79.

[305] Ibid., Volume 3, 184.

[306] Ibid., Volume 2, 507.

[307] Ibid., Volume 3, 265.

[308] Ibid.,, Volume 3, 12 (pdf 344).

[309] Ibid., Volume 4, 63-83.

[310] Ibid., Volume 4, 44-48.

www.ingramcontent.com/pod-product-compliance
Lightning Source LLC
Chambersburg PA
CBHW020736160426
43192CB00006B/216